Methods of Architectural Programming

COMMUNITY DEVELOPMENT SERIES

Series Editor: Richard P. Dober, AIP

CDS/29

Methods of Architectural Programming

Dowden, Hutchinson & Ross, Inc.
STROUDSBURG, PENNSYLVANIA

Henry Sanoff

NORTH CAROLINA STATE UNIVERSITY
AT RALEIGH

LIBRARY OF CONGRESS CATALOGING IN PUBLICATION DATA
Sanoff, Henry.
    Methods of architectural programming.
    (Community development series ; 29)
    Includes bibliographical references and index.
    1. Architectural   design—Computer   programs. 2. Architectural—Research.
I. Title.
NA2728.S26   720'.28'542   76-13231
ISBN 0-87933-253-0

To Joan

Series Editor's Foreword

We share the belief that *programming* brings maturity to the architectural arts. There are many reasons why this is so; not the least is the strongly felt conviction that programming is a necessary activity in any design process that claims to be responsive to user needs. And how many buildings do not fit that category?

Obviously physical environments that are highly specialized, machine dominant, and intricate in operation should be based on technical criteria, performance standards, and spatial relationships that are client determined. Planners and designers may develop expertise in special areas—for example, surgery suites and power plants—but even then such expertise is no substitute for the hands-on knowledge that the user possesses. In these instances, programming clearly is a way of systematically defining, ordering, and specifying goals, objectives, design intentions.

Not so clear, perhaps, are the reasons why *programming* is so important these days when dealing with building types for which the architect has laid claim to expert knowledge: housing, schools, playgrounds, commercial buildings.

What does the user know about construction costs; about building codes and regulations; about creating symbolic and functional forms; about applying building technologies and selecting environmental controls; about site conditions; about letting contracts and supervising construction? Where does common sense and knowledge about listing the important matters begin and end? How does one intelligently arrange for client, user and owner to determine what choices are available, and more importantly, how to choose among alternatives of which there are plenty even in the simplest building type.

Henry Sanoff's pioneering book *Methods of Architectural Programming* addresses these issues conceptually and in a very practical way shows how programming can proceed effectively, economically, efficiently. We are thus pleased to include his reference manual in the Community Development Series that has the purpose of facilitating the exchange of information, expert advice, and experience among professionals concerned with the built environment.

CDS publications include state-of-the-art books, handbooks, and manuals. They are offered to planners, architects, landscape architects, and others who would benefit from having such knowledge in a readily convenient format. Philosophically, the books are not bounded by traditional theory nor do they presume to establish a philosophic framework for all professional practice. There are themes that identify the series, however, and those who read this foreword should note the conceptual framework within which Sanoff's book fits. CDS books are concerned with active user and client involvement in problem defining and problem solving; systematic searching out of patterns, relationships, and behavioral settings as a prelude to design; a high regard for physical interdependence of communities; ecological ethics; an interest in not just finding appropriate solutions, but also in establishing ways and means for having those solutions implemented.

The visual qualities of the built environment are of equal interest. In that regard, there is another reason why programming seems basically important. The eminent critic, Ada Louise Huxtable, notes society's "growing delight in a more complex and eclectic expression." Beyond aesthetic caprice lies, we think, function-based designs. The more intricate we program, perhaps, the more intricate the design response. Architecture, the mirror of society, can reflect a more delightful, varied, and workable world if thus rooted in place and time through programming.

Richard P. Dober, AIP

Preface

This volume was prepared as a source book for designers; consequently it has neither a beginning nor an end. I have attempted to specify the ingredients necessary to develop a design program, but I have not provided a model program. The reason may appear to be obvious: there does not appear to be any consensus from researchers in the field about the availability or desirability of the best type of program. There is also some doubt about the adaptive nature of a standardized program considering the variability of designed artifacts and the diversity in size and type of organizations producing those artifacts.

The contents of this volume can be compared with a set of navigational aids, whereby the traveler decides upon his destination while the course is plotted with technical aids. The designer, too, must decide upon the final destination, as well as the amount of time available to reach that terminal point. The technical aids presented in this book will guide the designer to that destination as well as illustrate charted courses that other designers have taken. The manner by which the navigational aids are assembled is described as a "strategy," and the systematic recording of the events along the selected course is called the "program."

This book is designed to fill a void in the existing literature. There is very little in the way of literature in programming, although there are numerous statements commonly referred to as programs that bear slight resemblance to the material in this book.

I have attempted to integrate many of the pioneering contributions of others in order to identify the substance of programming for designers. Although this work is embryonic, it represents a culling of the strategies and techniques from the social, behavioral, and management sciences in order to build upon the developing efforts of other disciplines. The selection and assemblage of the contents represents a decade of personal exploration, testing, and evaluation—sometimes systematic, often random and exploratory.

The final organization of this book was arrived at as a result of Dick Dober's role as the devil's advocate, for which I am certainly grateful. I also wish to express my appreciation to Ron Wells for his editorial scrutiny and to Greg Centeno for his assistance in the review of literature.

Henry Sanoff

Contents

Methods of
Architectural
Programming

1

Preconditions to Programming

THE ROOTS OF PROGRAMMING

The architect's concern about the built environment is primarily for the accommodation of people: the people who use it, build it, design it, pay for it, and are directly affected by it. Clearly, when we discuss the people, their behavior, and their purposes as they relate to the built environment, we are bound to engage in conflicts, which is the very stuff of design decisions. The successful resolution of conflicts is based on a clear understanding of people's objectives and the methods of establishing priorities for making decisions; thus the recognition and understanding of people's needs and people's behavior is a prerequisite to the formulation of goals for a building program (and, moreover, a recognition that people are goal oriented and are trying to achieve some end). The architect, then, is the facilitator of the means by which the environment can flex and change to accommodate people's desires. All people, too, are architects to some degree, since they are always involved in manipulating their own environment. This constant alteration and modification, sometimes referred to as homeostasis, is the continual and growing need for a balance between people and their environment. This is an iterative process, in that people alter their environment and are in turn influenced by the environmental change. The difficulty occurs when there is a state of disequilibrium between people and their surrounding environment. The consequences are usually dissatisfaction and corresponding malfunction.

It is a long-standing tradition that initial client contacts and program formulation, however defined, are the domain of the seasoned architect. This heritage is rooted in the need for collective bargaining techniques, including those characteristics of firmness and judgment, the principle ingredients of long-term experience. Although it is not within the province of this book to argue against tradition, it is fair game to question the effectiveness of "playing it by ear" methods in favor of goal-oriented, client–user–architect interactions. It has also been the experience of numerous professional designers that the initial phase of the design process is the key link to profit or loss, the area in which most of the ambiguity and contradiction in the profession lies. This part of the process has been veiled in mystery, unobservable, yet inextricably linked to success.

The last decade has been a period of marked awareness of the potential contributions from the management and social sciences to the design professions. If those relevant tools and techniques become part of the designer's mode of operation, substantial changes in professional practice will be imminent. "It may well be that what we have hitherto understood as architecture, and what we are beginning to understand of technology, are incompatible disciplines. The architect who proposes to run with technology knows that he is in fast company, and that in order to keep up he may have to discard his whole cultural load, including the professional garments by which he is recognized as an architect. If, on the other hand, he decides not to do this, he may find that a technological culture has decided to go on without him."[1] Technology is best defined by Donald Schon as "any tool or technique, any product or process, any physical equipment or method of doing or making, by which human capability is extended."[2] The substance of this book, in part, is devoted to expanding the technological resources of the design profession.

This book is also about good sense—since that is the one endowment abundantly provided and assumed to be equitably divided. Good sense or reason is argued to be the same in all people, yet differences in opinion are not due to differences in intelligence but to the fact that we use different approaches and consider different things. René Descartes, a seventeenth-century philosopher, has stated that "those who walk slowly can, if they follow the right path, go much further than those who run rapidly in the wrong direction."[3]

It is generally agreed that René Descartes is considered the first, most important philosopher of our times. If we add to this the common belief that philosophy points to the way to development in other fields, it is evident that we ascribe an importance to Descartes that is comparable to the beginnings of intellectual culture in ancient Greece. Descartes was not an advocate of reform in general but only reform of his own ideas. In fact, he often stated that his decision to abandon all his preconceived notions was not an example for all to follow. Descartes did, however, believe in a set of precepts, of which he argued, logic is composed. They can best be described as the rules of method and are as follows:

> The first rule was never to accept anything as true unless I recognize it to be evidently such: that is, carefully to avoid precipitation and prejudgment, and to include nothing in my conclusions unless it presents itself so clearly and distinctly to my mind that there is no reason to doubt it.

> The second was to divide each of the difficulties which I encountered into as many parts as possible, and as might be required for an easier solution.

> The third was to think in an orderly fashion, beginning with the things which were simplest and easiest to understand, and gradually, and by degrees, reaching towards more complex knowledge, even treating as though ordered, materials which are not necessarily so.

> The last was always to make enumerations so complete and reviews so general that I would be certain that nothing was omitted.[4]

Descartes believed that the conscious awareness of those few precepts premitted him to solve many problems that he had previously considered difficult. Those precepts were individual, yet direction-giving commitments, dealing with important issues. Whether we describe Descartes' precepts as the roots of systems theory or systematic thinking, he clearly articulated, some 250 years ago, a decision-making process amenable to design thinking. When we attempt to integrate a more self-conscious approach to problem solving amid contemporary design concerns, we require a new technology to permit us to achieve an acceptable level of competence.

In the world of design today, there are increasingly more complex operations to be performed and a large body of information to be gathered. In order for the design professions to cope with new and unprecidented change, many modifications will be required in the nature and performance of design tasks. A self-evaluation is necessary with a resulting change in the "view of design."

Our increasing recognition of the relatedness of architecture to its contextual environment, of the need to incorporate the user as a vital ingredient toward change, and of the multidisciplinary and multieffect of the built environment is the beginning of a rationale for more order in the organization and more organization in the process. Quite simply, we need to program—and that is a matter of good sense.

THE PROGRAM

The concept of programming can fit into the complex net of designing, with its myriad of inextricably linked processes. The program is the first sequence of phases, the results of which ultimately effect some type of physical change in the environment. This change can take the form of an addition to a new or recycled building, a plan for the use of interior or exterior space, or other environmental modifications that require systematic forethought prior to proceeding with action.

The sequence of phases of a design project, beginning with a program, includes preliminary design, production, construction, and postcompletion evaluation (see Figure 1). This morphology outlines the phases that a design project usually goes through and is initiated when there is agreement to take action on a problem. Although there may be many interpretations, elaborations, and variations, it is generally thought of as a sequence of phases, and sometimes it is referred to as the design process.

It is necessary to distinguish this phased sequence of activities from those discussed in this book. The basic ingredient for sorting conflicts and decision making is the problem-solving process, which has its roots in stimulating the development of a program. Obviously the hints suggested for successful problem solving are useful for other stages in project development, as well as the wide range of complex decisions people make daily; however, the discussion of problem solving as described in the following section is in relation to the effective development of the design program.

The flow diagram in Figure 1 clearly reveals the inextricable connection between the program and postcompletion evaluation as the two important phases that complete the project design cycle. Since the program phase is the primary source of input into the subsequent design phases, it can be hypoth-

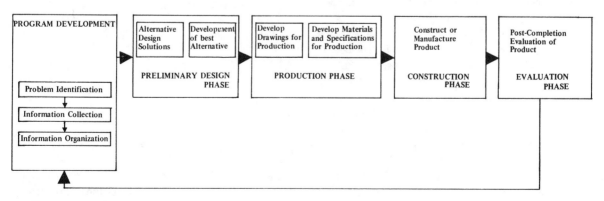

Figure 1
Phases of a design project.

esized that the quality of the program has a direct impact on the quality of the designed product.

Since the best interests of the design world evolve around quality to improve the condition of people, then knowledge about the development of the program can have a marked effect on the quality of the designed product.

A program is a communicable statement of intent. It is a prescription for a desired set of events influenced by local constraints, and it states a set of desired conditions and the methods for achieving those conditions.

The program is also a formal communication between designer and client in order to determine that the client's needs and values are clearly stated and understood. It provides a method for decision making and a rationale for future decisions. It encourages greater client participation, as well as user feedback. The program also serves as a log, a memory, and a set of conditions that are amenable to postconstruction evaluation.

The program conveys current information on the progress of the project and its various stages of development. Frequently it is perceived as an organizing procedure for codifying and classifying numerous bits of project information, sometimes misused, often forgotten. In sum, it is an operating procedure for systematizing the design process. It provides an organizational structure for the design team and a clear, communicable set of conditions for review by those affected by its implementation.

The program is not new to the world of architecture. Actually, evidence indicates that is has been used for more than a century, since an architectural competition was held for building new courts of justice in London. Prior to that, courts were built and found to be inadequate from the start. As judicial business increased and the establishment of a professional organization, the legal society, occurred, a strong campaign was mounted for centralization of courts of law. With the establishment of a Commission of Works, plans were underway for the development

of a book of instructions for competing architects as early as 1862. Although competitions for public buildings were presented as far back as 1819 (for a new general post office), submissions were deemed inadequate, and the work was given to an architect in the Office of Works. Generally, the outcome of competitions had proven to be unsatisfactory. With this vast background of competion results, clear precautions had to be taken to prevent the recurrence of such fiascos. The first step was the commissioners' elaborate inquiry into what was needed. In 1865, instructions for competing architects were published. They provided for the following:

> The existing courts were also made available for inspection. They [architects] were warned that "the arrangement of the Courts and Offices is of vital moment; on it mainly depends the success of failure of the concentration, and its importance cannot be overestimated". Light and quiet were major considerations and were to be indicated for each room on a three-point scale. Speaking tubes, telegraphic communications throughout the building, shoots for papers and lifts "for large models to be produced in Court, and for infirm persons" were to be provided. Refreshment rooms for judges, officers of the courts, clerks, the Bar and attorneys should be entirely separate from those jurors and witnesses, and first and second class must be provided. Bridges were required on the site of Temple Bar and over Carey Street to Lincoln's Inn—the latter preferably low, to discourage traffic. The chief points constantly to be kept in view, "to be treated as superseding so far as they may conflict, all considerations of architectural effect, are the accommodation to be provided and the arrangements to be adopted so as in the greatest degree to facilitate the dispatch and the accurate transaction of the law business of the country".[5]

DESIGN PROBLEM SOLVING

The approach to design programming that is implicit in this book might appear to be negative in that many of the strategies proposed are error correcting. While the intention of the suggestions for dealing with complex problems is a liberating one, the premise is clearly based on a history of problems and blockages faced by many designers in executing their daily problem-solving activities.

Many reasons for the difficulties that designers often confront stem from the multiplicity of processes necessary to work through a problem. The comprehension of these processes and the strategies appropriate for minimizing errors, then, is the province of this book.

The natural inclination in problem solving is to select the first solution generated for further development. Clearly, the disadvantage of this approach is that the first solution forecloses other possibilites, and it may not be the best solution after all. The strategy for maximizing the performance of each individual's abilities is to select the best alternative solution from a wide range of conceptual possibilities. There are often obstacles that prevent the designer from seeing the problem itself or the information necessary to solve the problem.

Before identifying and evaluating programming strategies, it is necessary to first establish certain preconditions, which are based purely on common sense. Mathematician G. Polya describes these preconditions succinctly in his book *How To Solve It.*[6] There are many appropriate questions that can be posed to find something unknown and similarly certain strategies that will generally be useful in solving a problem. These strategies suggest a certain conduct, a style of problem solving that, Polya argues, comes naturally to anyone who is seriously concerned with the problem and is endowed with common sense. Recognizing that this behavior is often subconscious and infrequently articulated, we will attempt to describe those internal processes that have aided successful problem solvers.

Many attempts at describing the activity of problem solving, however, are too often ambiguous. We are all familiar with this activity and discuss problem solving frequently, but because it is so unsystematic, there are no technical terms to describe it. The closest we can come to description are the broad categories of "analysis," wherein lies the problem; "synthesis" of possible solutions; and "evaluation," of which solution is most acceptable for implementation.

Problem solving can be described in terms of a set of strategies, which can increase an individual's ability to solve problems.

A problem is perceived as a state of conflict that needs to be resolved. Problem-solving literature has been stated in both positive and negative terms. The positive method is often referred to as *creative thinking*, while the negative approach is called removing *conceptual blocks*. Both viewpoints, however, lead toward the development of methods and strategies for solving problems. There are numerous strategies for eliminating conceptual blocks and thinking creatively. They are conscious methods that can influence the problem-solving process. First it is necessary to outline the stages that frequently occur in the problem-solving process.[7] Each stage in itself is a process, which is diagrammed in Figure 2.

Perception is a selection process that is learned and developed. It is also an ability to see and become aware. In order to begin consciously to be aware and develop a better understanding of sensory patterns, follow the key strategies developed in the matrix.

Definition is to state what is known about a problem in a precise way. Clearly, in order to make a statement of some accuracy already requires insight and understanding of the problem. The definition of the problem requires the establishment of boundaries or limits beyond which no solution is acceptable. This solution space, then, is the arene of possibilities within which the solution must lie. Defining a problem requires the recognition of constraints, descriptions, and assumptions, as well as values describing the limits of acceptability.

Analysis is the way in which the problem is disaggregated into manageable parts. For problems of unusual complexity, specific techniques or methods are appropriate for breaking the problem down into

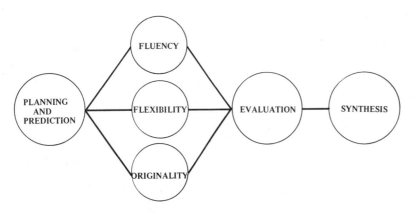

Figure 2

tractable parts. These analytic tools permit the management of complex and dynamic problems.

Planning and prediction are linked activities that require advanced thinking about the problem and the consequences of certain courses of action.

Alternative generation is also basic to the problem-solving process. In seeking the most creative solutions to problems, three basic ingredients provide the foundation for alternative generation. The first is *fluency*, which is the ability to produce ideas from one class of information. The second is *fexibility*, the ability to move between different points of view in the search for ideas. The third is *originality*, which is the ability to make basic transformations on information once it has been recalled.

Evaluation, critical judgement based on a set of values or criteria, is a critical link in the problem-solving cycle. Although it is advisble to defer judgment as long as possible, it is necessary to make explicit the values and standards that form the basis of an evaluation.

Synthesis is the integrative phase where all the parts come together to shape a solution. In most instances the assembly of the parts of the solution brings these parts into conflict with each other, requiring the synthesis phase to be one of constant balancing.

It is quite normal for individuals to experience obstacles or mental blocks during each of the stages of the problem-solving process. A simple yet effective strategy for removing those blocks is the use of manipulative verbs. A series of polar opposite verbs were selected for their applicability to facilitate mind stretching or block busting. The matrix in Figure 3 lists the verb pairs as well as their appropriate fit with the stages of the problem-solving process. When the flow of ideas ceases, it may be advisable to review these verbal strategies and select for exploration those concepts that may aid in removing the obstacles.

COLLECTIVE DECISIONS: GROUP PROCESSES

In the previous section we examined methods that an individual can incorporate into a personal repertoire for removing mental blocks and stimulating the development of creative ideas. As designers confront situations requiring groups of people to identify problems and make decisions, it is only logical that similar aids can be utilized to facilitate group activities. The composition and purpose of groups can vary from a multidisciplinary problem-solving focus to a client-designer review to a designer-user information-seeking purpose.

The nature of this expansion from the individual problem solver to the group is an outgrowth of the need for wider fields or reference with distinct areas of expertise that can be directed to solve those problems that do not respect traditional academic or professional boundaries. Group processes contain the unique advantage of facilitating learning through the transfer of expertise between participants. It is this experiential change that is the very dynamic of learning.

Collective decision making is a set of operations in which actions of some individuals have consequences for others because their actions are interdependent. Research into group behavior and creative problem solving has helped to develop principles of social interaction that subsequently have been incorporated into various types of group problem-solving situations. Many of the group behavior principles center around the development of group loyalty, the cohesion of groups as a function of outside threats, and the impact of shared responsibility for a decision on the kind of decision that will be made.[8]

A social system of any size or complexity can be understood if the small face-to-face group is considered a major component of it. Similarly, the small group is analogous to a complex social system, enabling us to learn more by placing the small group in an environment similar to the social system to be studied with similar resources and tasks.

Since our rational decision making occurs in social groups or organizations, Herbert Simon states, "Organizations are the least natural and most rationally contrived units of human association. It is only because individual human beings are limited in knowledge, foresight, skill, and time that organizations are useful instruments for the achievement of human purpose; and it is only because organized groups of human beings are limited in ability to agree on goals, to communicate, and to cooperate that organizing becomes for them a problem."[9]

BEST APPLICATION OF STRATEGIES	PERCEPTION	DEFINITION & ANALYSIS	PLANNING & PREDICTION	FLUENCY	FLEXIBILITY	ORIGINALITY	EVALUATION	SYNTHESIS
ABSTRACT-CONCRETIZE	■	■	■	■	■			■
ADAPT-SUBSTITUTE			■			■		■
ADD-SUBTRACT	■					■		■
ANALOGY-BRAINSTORM		■		■	■	■		■
ANALYZE-SYNTHESIZE		■			■	■	■	■
ASSUME-QUESTION	■	■	■		■	■	■	■
CHANGE-VARY	■	■	■		■	■	■	■
COMBINE-SEPARATE		■	■			■		■
COMPARE-RELATE	■	■	■	■		■	■	
CONCENTRATE-DISPERSE	■	■		■	■		■	■
CONSCIOUS-UNCONSCIOUS	■	■	■		■		■	■
CYCLE-REPEAT	■	■	■			■	■	■
DEFINE-SYMBOLIZE		■	■		■		■	■
DIAGRAM-CHART		■	■			■	■	■
DISPLAY-ORGANIZE	■	■	■				■	■
DIVIDE-MULTIPLY		■				■		■
DREAM-IMAGINE	■	■	■				■	■
EVALUATE-DEFER			■	■		■	■	■
EXPERIENCE-RECALL	■	■	■	■	■		■	■
FORCE-RELAX		■	■	■		■	■	■
INCREASE-DECREASE			■	■	■	■	■	■
INCUBATE-PURGE		■		■				
INTUIT-RATIONALIZE	■	■	■			■	■	■
INVOLVE-DETACH	■	■	■	■			■	■
LEARN-TEACH	■	■	■				■	■
LIST-CHECK	■	■	■	■			■	■
MOTIVATE-PRACTICE	■	■	■	■			■	■
OPTIMIZE-MINIMIZE			■			■	■	■
PLAN-PREDICT		■	■				■	■
RECORD-RETRIEVE	■	■	■	■	■		■	■
SEARCH-SELECT	■	■	■	■			■	■
SIMULATE-TEST		■	■			■	■	■
START-STOP		■	■	■			■	■
SYSTEMIZE-RANDOMIZE		■	■	■	■	■	■	■
TRANSFORM-MANIPULATE	■					■		■
VERBALIZE-VISUALIZE	■	■	■	■	■		■	■
WORK FORWARDS-WORK BACKWARDS	■	■				■	■	■
WORK IN-WORK OUT	■	■		■	■	■	■	■

Figure 3
Best application of strategies.

A SHORT GLOSSARY OF STRATEGIES

ABSTRACT: To remove from the context of a specific reality, to reduce to basic principles, to put in the most general terms, to express as simply as possible, to widen the scope of the problem. Abstraction encourages an overview of the problem by thinking in terms of principles, processes, and general directions. Abstracting allows one to try new combinations of ideas without being tied down to particulars.

CONCRETIZE: To make specific, to state in real terms, to illustrate by a particular set of conditions. Concretization is a good way to push ideas to their limit, to test them by specifying all their parts or by demonstrating their feasibility through reference to existing situations.

ADAPT: To modify, to make fit the situation; to make a slight change for a new purpose. Adaptation is a principal strategy for generating a new solution by making relatively small changes in an existing idea or object to serve in a new situation.

SUBSTITUTE: To put in place of another, to exchange, to replace, to find something else that could do the job. Substitution resolves the problem by locating critical elements and replacing them with new processes or parts often drawn from other fields.

ADD: To join or unite, to build up, to grow by induction. Addition is the process of growth and development of a solution by expansion incrementally in terms of individual elements or subsolutions. Additive growth is a common strategy for updating old solutions.

SUBTRACT: To take away by deducting, to reduce by elimination, to deduct, to simplify. Subtraction is a way of arriving at a solution by beginning with more than you need of material, processes, or ideas, and then progressively getting rid of what is not essential, as in carving out a sculpture or editing a manuscript.

ANALOGY: Resemblance in some particulars between things otherwise unlike, correspondence in function between anatomical parts of different structure and origin, an example from a different field. To look for an analogous problem and to examine its solutions for relevance is a good way to seek new ideas and to break away from fixations. In the synectics procedure three types of analogy are defined (direct, personal, and symbolic), and they are used to make an "excursion" away from the problem in order to come back at it from a new context through the process of "force-fitting."

BRAINSTORM: Brainstorming is a process that can be used individually or in groups to come up with a quantity of alternatives by spontaneously generating ideas and by deferring judgment on them. All ideas should be recorded.

ANALYZE: To study or determine the nature and relationship of the parts, to separate into component parts, to break down and study in smaller problems. Analysis can be considered an essential phase in problem solving and, as such, employs many of the other strategies.

SYNTHESIZE: To compose or combine parts or elements so as to form a whole, to resolve diverse conceptions into a coherent whole, to integrate. Synthesis is the process of building back up to a solution after the problem has been analyzed and alternatives generated. It is a phase of problem solving that incorporates many of the other strategies.

ASSUME: To take for granted or true, to suppose, to accept conditionally in order to proceed to another step. Assuming is a strategy for testing a potential solution to a problem by leaping over immediate uncertainties by ignoring them or fixing their values in order to investigate the consequences—an essential process in prediction and evaluation.

QUESTION: To doubt, to dispute, to inquire, to challenge concerning validity. Questioning all aspects of a problem, including your own solutions, is an essential strategy in problem solving. Self-questioning helps sustain an internal dialogue that can keep you thinking flexibly.

CHANGE: To make different in some particular, to give a different position, course or direction to, to move to another, to replace with another. Changing is a strategy for using other strategies. Changing approach or media is a way of reacting to developments in problem solving by shifting attack to become more effective; it involves awareness and flexibility in thinking.

VARY: To make a partial change in, to make different in some attribute or characteristic, to change a part in order to test its influence on the whole. Variation can be algorithmic, heuristic, or random. Variation induces change in order to investigate the relationship of factors in a problem (for example, systematically changing the dial on a lock to find the combination).

COMBINE: To bring into close relationship, to unite, to act together, to form a solution from several different parts. Combining and recombining are processes of simplification and synthesis: several different elements come together to produce totally new entities, as in chemistry.

SEPARATE: To make a distinction between, to divide, to sort, to break up into elements, to keep different things apart. Separating is a process of breaking apart a problem and dealing with different issues at different times. This clarifies the situation and concentrates energy on a limited field. Separating can be used to remove elements from context in order to study them more closely.

COMPARE: To represent as similar, to examine the character or qualities of, to discover resemblances or differences, to put side by side. Comparing is a strategy for examining two or more things aspect by aspect, checking for similarities and differences in terms of attributes or functions. Comparison is used generally to make a selection or to analyze through contrast.

RELATE: To show or establish logical or causal connection between, to develop a mathematic or symbolic equation that expresses how two or more elements affect each other, to make relationships. To relate is to find the force or theory that governs how two elements or variables behave with respect to each other. It is a critical strategy for understanding a problem and for developing a hypothesis or solution.

CONCENTRATE: To bring or direct toward a common center or objective, to gather into one body, mass, or force, to focus one's powers, efforts, or attentions. Concentrating in problem solving is a process of collecting and directing energy, your own personal psychic energy and attention, on one aspect of the problem in order to make as much headway as possible.

DISPERSE: To cause to break up and go in different ways, to distribute more or less evenly throughout a medium, to scatter. In problem solving dispersion is the process of letting your mind wander over the problem, not focusing on one aspect, stopping only to probe but not to become entangled. Dispersion is a quick way to explore a problem and to balance periods of concentration.

CONSCIOUS: Perceiving, apprehending, or noticing with a degree of controlled thought or observation, marked by thought, design, or perception; to be aware. To be conscious of mental processes in problem solving is an important ability to develop for any degree of mental self-control.

UNCONSCIOUS: Not knowing or perceiving, not aware, not consciously held or deliberately planned or carried out. Unconscious or subconscious thought processing is a complement to conscious thought and can, in fact, to some extent be purposefully directed. Strategies continue to operate subconsciously in spontaneous recall.

CYCLE: To pass through an interval of time during which a sequence of a recurring succession of events or phenomena is completed, to jump back and forth between several different strategies or points of view. Cycling is a process by which simultaneity or totality of view can be approximated by alternating between many different strategies. Thus problem solving can be seen as a heuristic or feedback process (concept formation, implementation, and evaluation).

REPEAT: To make do, or perform again, to try again, to keep attacking a problem from the same point of view. Repetition is important strategy for minimizing error and is basic to the process of learning in skill development. Many processes can be successful only after several repetitions.

DEFINE: To fix or mark the limits of, to determine the essential qualities or precise meaning of, to clearly express the problem. Defining is one of the most critical processes in problem solving and can be considered a definite phase, incorporating many other strategies. As the definition sets certain limits to the range of possible solutions, redefining as a reiterative process can be used to widen or narrow the scope of the problem.

SYMBOLIZE: To represent, express, or identify by a symbol (something that stands for or suggests something else by reason of relationship, association, convention, or accidental resemblance). Symbolizing alows you to represent or define an element of a problem as abstractly as possible and then to manipulate it with respect to other elements, concentrating only on relationships.

DIAGRAM: To explain in simple graphic language, to describe relationships in terms of graphic symbols, to abstract graphically. Diagramming is the most fundamental way of recording ideas visually in two or three dimensions. It uses a symbolic and nonrepresentational language to graphically express concepts in terms of relationships, sequences, and simplified features.

CHART: To represent the relationships between pieces of alphanumeric information graphically, to present sequences of events in time diagrammatically. Charting is really a special case of diagramming, specifically as a method for planning and scheduling sequences of events and activities by describing their relationships in graphic terms and then making projections concerning estimated real time, costs, and so on.

DISPLAY: To spread before the view, to make visible, to present graphically. Displaying is one of the most powerful conceptual strategies related to perception and problem solving. Graphic display relieves the short-term memory function of the human brain and allows information to be "remembered" simply by visually scanning. Its information density can be high because it does not need to be read in a particular sequence.

ORGANIZE: To arrange or form into a coherent unity or functioning whole, to make a pattern, to arrange elements into a whole of interdependent parts, to structure, to order. Organizing is the process of reducing large quantities of complex information into structures, often hierarchical in nature, that can be handled or remembered. To display and then to organize visually is one of the most powerful strategies in problem solving.

DIVIDE: To separate into two or more parts, areas, or groups, to distribute, apportion, or allocate, to divide mathematically. Dividing in problem solving is the process of allocating some precious resource—like time, energy, or space—in some proportion to some scale of values. It is an important strategy in planning and scheduling.

MULTIPLY: To increase in number greatly or in multiples, to augment, to propagate, to multiply mathematically. In problem solving multiplying is the process of augmenting whatever you have in the way of product or process by increasing its effectiveness through making it larger or more powerful. Man's power is augmented or multiplied through his technological artifacts.

DREAM: To have vivid thoughts, images, or emotions during sleep, to observe subconscious mentation during periods of lack of conscious intervention. Dreams can provide valuable understanding of how a problem is being treated subconsciously and what your feelings and motivations are toward it, for it is only during sleep that your consciousness is turned off. Dream thought can be a source of rich images, and the period of dreaming just before complete sleep, or hypogogic dreaming, can actually be induced and can provide great insights into aspects of a problem.

IMAGINE: To form a mental picture of (something not present), to form mental images, to visualize mentally. Imagining is a powerful way of projecting yourself into hypothetical situations and mentally experiencing them. A developed imagination can be a source of creative visions. Imagery can be used as a mental simulation of an experience or situation, involving all the senses.

EVALUATE: To determine or fix the value of, to examine and judge, to estimate. Evaluation, like analysis and synthesis, is really a metaheuristic and a phase of problem solving. Evaluating primarily involves testing against some standard of values and comparing, making a selection. Evaluation is a critical step in the feedback loop in heuristic behavior.

DEFER: To put off, to postpone, to delay (in reference to evaluation or judgment). Deferring judgment or evaluation is an important strategy during periods of alternative generation; it permits you to concentrate on "thinking up" ideas and not worrying about their ultimate quality. Deferred judgment encourages a positive environment and attitude and prevents budding ideas from being thrown out too soon.

EXPERIENCE: To consciously perceive or apprehend reality or an external, bodily, or psychic event, to directly participate, to have or make an experience. Experiencing in this context means to become as intimately and directly involved with the problem and the problem-solving process in order to have a rich source of information from which to draw. The more intense the experience and the more senses it involves, the more likely you are to remember it and derive useful information from it at a later date.

RECALL: To call back, to bring back to mind, to remember. Recalling or remembering is the basic process by which we can learn and retrieve information from previous experiences and may in fact be similar to the original act of perception.

Many of these strategies can be used to aid recall, and the development of our powers of memory can be an invaluable help in problem solving.

FORCE: To attain or to effect against resistance or inertia, to hasten the rate of progress or growth of, to make a great effort to. Forcing as a strategy refers to pushing an issue in a problem as far as it can go in order to investigate its validity. "Force fitting" is the process of trying to relate a seemingly unrelated idea to the problem in searching for new points of view (see *analogy* and *synectics*). Forcing also refers to forcing oneself to continue to follow a given procedure, especially in alternative generation, as we often give up too soon.

RELAX: To make less tense or rigid, to become lax, weak, or loose, to seek rest or recreation. Relaxing is the process of releasing mental and physical tension and is often essential for free and innovative thinking. Because of the strong relationship of mind to body, knowing how to physically relax is important, and you should seek a balance between tenseness and total collapse and lack of attention.

INCREASE: To make greater, to enlarge, to exaggerate. Increasing refers here to exaggerating and making more definite as in a feature of a design in order to make a stronger statement and to more easily detect and examine the effect of a particular variable. It is the process of moving away from the neutral to the upper limit.

DECREASE: To cause to grow less, to reduce, to lessen, to diminish. Decreasing refers in this context to lessening the effect of a particular variable in the problem, reducing it toward total elimination. *Increase* and *decrease* refer to the process of leveling and sharpening as described in cybernetics.

INCUBATE: To maintain under conditions favorable for hatching, development, or reaction, to cause to develop, to mull over, to "sleep on it." Incubation has been recognized as a common phase in problem solving, and there is evidence that strategies and plans continue to operate on the problem subconsciously during these periods, sometimes resulting in insight or a sudden transformation.

PURGE: To get rid of, to eliminate, to get out of your system. Purging is the process of getting rid of immediate ideas and preconceptions by expressing them and writing them down. Purging seems to result in a definite psychic release from the strain of having to consider and remember something. You then feel free to explore other alternatives before evaluation.

INTUIT: To immediately apprehend, to directly know or decide without rational thought and inference, to feel. Intuition is a valuable process in problem solving as it is a spontaneous result of all your past experiences and may well include factors that you have not consciously considered. Intuitive solutions are immediate responses to the problem and should be listened to but not accepted unconditionally.

RATIONALIZE: To make conformable to rational principles, to substitute a natural for a supernatural explanation, to be explicit and to try to understand, to justify. In problem solving rationalizing is the process of trying to explain as rationally and explicitly as possible all ideas and actions. To do so you must try to become aware and self-conscious of what you are doing in order to communicate your reasons behind decisions to others.

INVOLVE: To enfold or envelop so as to encumber, to draw in as a participant, to occupy absorbingly. Total involvement with a problem means to eat, sleep, and dream about it, in effect to become the problem. Periods of this kind of total absorption and empathy can be very productive because everything you experience becomes related to the problem, and chance happenings can lead to new insights. Involvement can be initiated by simply leaping in and getting "your feet wet".

DETACH: To separate from a larger mass, to disentangle, to withdraw. Detachment from a problem is a useful way to get away from it and see it in perspective. Detachment enhances incubation and also removes you from overweighted priorities and considerations.

LEARN: To gain knowledge or understanding of or skill in by study, instruction, or experience, to come to realize, to discover. Learning in problem solving means to be aware of strategies and to constantly look for new ones. To learn a strategy, you must perceive it, understand it conceptually, and then apply it in many different problem contexts. Over-learning is the process of practicing something so many times it becomes a skill.

TEACH: To cause to know, to instruct by precept, example, or experience, to educate. Teaching problem-solving abilities to yourself or to others is a strategy for improvement and should involve a conceptual understanding of the nature of problem solving, a knowledge of the individual strategies, and experience of using these heuristics successfully in many different kinds of problems.

LIST: To put down, to enumerate, to record in abbreviated form. Listing is the simplest strategy for recording ideas, numbers, and other items of information, writing them down one after another. Once pieces of information have been recorded in a list, they can later be recalled, organized, or evaluated. A list is the easiest form of graphic display to search.

CHECK: To compare with a source, original, or authority, to verify, to review. Checking in problem solving refers especially to the process of making and using checklists, reminders of operations to perform, issues to consider, and spontaneous ideas to include. Checking involves comparing what has been done with some statement of what should be done, and some systematic procedures can avoid great errors and lost time in dealing with complicated problems.

MOTIVATE: To offer incentive, to induce, to entice, to encourage to do something. Motivation and desire to solve in problem solving are critical factors, and it is good to develop ways of enticing yourself and other to plow through the more laborious phases of problem solving. You must *want* to solve a problem. You can overcome the initial fear of the unknown and possible failure often by simply leaping in and getting started.

PRACTICE: To perform or work at repeatedly so as to become proficient, to train by repeated exercise, to perform often, customarily, or habitually. Practice is a principal strategy for learning a process or skill through repeatedly performing it, ideally in a variety of situations, and thus developing a generalized cognitive structure, pattern of behavior, or conditioned response.

OPTIMIZE: To make as perfect, effective, or functional as possible (given some criteria). Optimization is the process of adjusting a set of variables so that the result is the best according to some scale of values. Where these variables can be mathematically defined, a simulation model can be developed, and in these cases there are some well-defined systematic tachniques for finding the optimum. The question to ask is whether the optimization of this particular set of variables leads to the optimum solution of the total problem.

MINIMIZE: To reduce to the least quantity assignable, admissible, or possible. Minimization is the opposite of optimization and is a strategy for dealing with variables that cannot be eliminated but can be reduced in a problem. With interdependent variables, the minimum value of one variable may not represent the minimum of the function of all the variables. The same set of systems techniques is available as for optimization.

PLAN: To devise or project the realization or achievement of, to develop a procedure for doing something. Planning in problem solving is the process of putting together these strategies into a program for attacking a problem. Planning involves thinking ahead, and plans may be no more than a set of intentions. The structure of plans has been discovered to be generally hierarchical.

PREDICT: To declare in advance, to foretell on the basis of observation, experience, or scientific reason, to anticipate, to think in the future. Predicting is a critical strategy in evaluating the effects of an alternative and involves understanding the problem situation enough to foresee the effects of possible changes. The ability to anticipate and project is distinctly different from being able to react to an immediate problem. Simulation techniques are often useful.

RECORD: To set down in writing, to register permanently, to copy in a retrievable form. Recording is the equivalent process in the external world to experiencing and memorizing in the human mind. A record is a permanent copy or image that can be recalled by searching and does not have the same limitations and susceptibility to change as information in the brain. There is theoretically no limit to the amount of information that can be recorded.

RETRIEVE: To discover and bring back, to locate and return, to access. Information retrieval is the equivalent to remembering and involves mainly search strategies. The great problem in information retrieval is the method of labeling and accessing, which ideally should have the same characteristics of cross-referencing and association as the human mind.

SEARCH: To look into or over carefully or thoroughly in an effort to find or discover something, to look for, to try to locate. Searching may well be the common denominator of all strategies. Problem solving may be defined generally as searching for a solution, and there are algorithmic, heuristic, and random methods.

SELECT: To take by preference from a number or group, to pick out, to choose. Selecting involves inspecting a number of alternatives, evaluating, and then actually choosing one (or possibly several). But it is the act of closure and selection, even if arbitrary, that is essential in order to proceed with dependent operations. It is the issue of commitment that makes selecting a difficult but important process to master.

SIMULATE: To give the appearance or effect of, to develop a model, to translate into other terms or media. Simulation is the process of developing a model of the problem situation on which you can test alternative solutions and prdict outcomes. Models can range from simple cardboard models of a building (iconic) to sophisticated computer models of transportation networks (symbolic). In a sense a model is an image or representation of reality and should behave analogously, in some way like its real counterpart. At least a crude kind of representation may be necessary in most problem solving.

TEST: To try, to experiment, to verify, to compare. Testing is basically the process of performing an operation on something and then comparing the results against some standard of expectation. The test phase can be considered the comparison stage before evaluation and forms a critical link in the feedback loop in heuristic behavior.

START: To perform the first stages or actions of, to cause to move, act, or operate, to begin. Starting in problem solving is the act of initiating a process. While it may seem to be a simple concept, the sense of when to start and what to start and the courage to actually start is a constantly troublesome issue.

STOP: To discontinue, to cease, to desist. Stopping in problem solving is the strategy of constantly checking to see if you should stop a particular approach and start another. The sense of when to give stop orders is another necessary issue in problem solving; to stop too soon may mean failure, but not to stop may mean futile waste of time.

SYSTEMIZE: To develop an organized procedure, to arrange methodologically, to make into a system. A systematic strategy in problem solving is a procedure that follows a given set of steps and can guarantee to completely search a set of alternatives. It is generally algorithmic in nature, rigid, and often lengthy to implement, but it does not involve much risk.

RANDOMIZE: To arrange tests, samples, and other factors so as to simulate a chance distribution, to proceed without a plan and by chance. Radomization is a strategy to reduce systematic errors in a procedure. In this sense it can be used to overcome fixation by randomly selecting a piece of information and trying to "force fit" it into relevance to the problem, or what has been called lateral thinking. Randomness induces chance, and chance has played a large role in the history of invention.

TRANSFORM: To change in composition or structure, to change in character or condition, to make go from one state into another. Transformations are operations or rules governing change from one state or position into another. In a sense, all strategies can be considered transformations on the problem state. Transformations can convert information into new or original forms.

MANIPULATE: To treat or operate with the hands or by mechanical means, to move around, to change position. Manipulation in problem solving is a particular set of transformations that pertain to the changing of physical position or relationship of entities, especially symbols. Manipulating can become a heuristic strategy when followed by an evaluation after each change, and, as such, accounts for a large percentage of trial-and-error procedures in literary and graphic composition.

VERBALIZE: To express in words, to describe verbally. Verbalizing is the process of explaining something in words, and in doing so can be considered a strategy for forcing yourself to be explicit. Verbal communication is the most common medium in a highly literate society.

VISUALIZE: To make visual, to see or form a mental image, to describe graphically. Visualization is a process of seeing or describing things in terms of perceptual images and is a very powerful, dense, and often underdeveloped ability. Where physical relationships and aspects of design are to be studied or communicated, visualizing is a necessity.

WORK FORWARDS: To proceed conceptually from where you are to where you are going, from the problem to the solution, to work inductively. Working forwards seems so obvious at first that we forget that there are other basic strategies. Induction is basic to the scientific method and is required to build a logically watertight argument.

WORK BACKWARDS: To . . ., go from the solution state back to the problem state conceptually, to work deductively.

Working backwards is a powerful strategy when you know roughly what the solution should be but do not know how to get there. Working backwards can be used in conjunction with working forwards to narrow the difference between the problem state and the solution state until the gap is conceptually bridged.

WORK IN: To close in from outside, to narrow the scope, to limit. Working in is the strategy behind linear programming or the limiting of solution space by examining constraints. Often you know more about what is *not* the solution than what is and thus can dramatically limit the range of possibilities by considering first what you know cannot solve the problem.
WORK OUT: To develop incrementally, to grow, to proceed form a core and move out. Working out as a strategy in problem solving involves starting with what you know must exist and slowly building on that. It is extremely useful in complex situations and can provide a first foothold on the problem.

In spite of what seems a logical and apparent observation that decision making occurs most frequently in groups, most models of decision making assume the decision maker to be operating as a single individual. In order to effect practical application, however, methods must concern themselves with several individuals having conflicting interests. This section will describe five group decison-making strategies: role playing, brainstorming, synectics, buzz sessions, and discussion groups.

Role Playing

Role playing is a powerful group participation strategy that can be used by designers to simulate client or user group situations for training or informational purposes. It is a method for creating responses to particular situations to provide the designer with better insights into the behavior of a selected population. It can be used as an in-house method for increasing the designer's awareness and sensitivity to other members of the organization. It is also effective when time and financial constraints permit only a brief but intensive exposure to a user population.

Role playing is an enactment of a situation, either fictional or real, where one or more people assume designated roles in relation to a particular problem in a specific situation. It is an unrehearsed drama that forces the actors or participants to project into that situation and consider all the factors that influ-

ence the situation. A role includes not only a formal job description but also the informal understandings, agreements, expectations and arrangements with others that influence interpersonal relationships. The outcome for the participants includes the stimulation of new attitudes about the situation, themselves, and other people and the ability to illustrate and discuss specific behaviors that influence the situation under observation.

The first step in the role-playing process is role negotiation to clarify each participant's role assignment, his relationship to each other, and his expectation from other members. Participants should feel comfortable with their role assignments and must adhere to those roles.

It is desirable to have the role-playing situation observed and the results reported back to the group for further discussion. This follow-up is necessary to aid the participants in their interpretation and application of the outcome.

Brainstorming

Brainstorming is a group facilitation session used to develop an inventory of ideas. It is desirable that the participants have some expertise pertaining to the problem situation. Participants can be designers seeking a fresh way at looking at their problem or a group of individuals with some expertise in the domain of the problem under observation.

Brainstorming is an idea-generating group activity

that involves oral expression with particular constraints on discussion, analysis, or criticism. The underlying rationale for brainstorming is that each individual taking part in the discussion receives ideas and can originate them. Ideas are encouraged to flow without formality to minimize the resistance of the individuals to participating in order to provide a favorable atmosphere for the synthesis of ideas.

Unavoidably, when individuals feel free to respond, or their negative resistance is lowered, a great deal of commonplace and possibly irrelevant and useless information will be communicated. Any attempts to discriminate impose censorship on the group, resulting in individuals personally testing their ideas before transmitting them, which impedes spontaneity and innovativeness. Participants should be encouraged to fantisize, which also minimizes judgments. The quantity of ideas, too, is important in that there is a greater likelihood of quality with increased quantity. This rapid-fire system of idea generating stimulates group enthusiasm and releases inhibitions.

A group leader is important to encourage and stimulate the participants while avoiding directiveness. All ideas should be recorded and presented to the group in a feedback session to let the participants know how productive they have been. They also expect some action to result from their ideas.

Synectics

Synectics is an operational theory designed to increase the probability of success in problem-stating and problem-solving situations.[10] The method is a way of increasing the level of consciousness directed toward creativity, while the focus of all activity is to arrive at a novel solution.

Synectics attempts to study creative processes in motion while they are occurring, through nonrational, free-associative concepts. Based on the assumption that creative processes in humans are describable and ultimately useful in effecting the creative output of individuals, synectics theory applies to the integration of diverse individuals into a problem-solving group.

The premise underlying synectics theory is that creative efficiency in people can be markedly increased if they understand the psychological processes by which they operate. Since the major effective components of creative processes are subconscious, creative solutions to problems traditionally contain a high incidence of accident. It is difficult to purposely repeat a process that is only subconsciously perceived. Synectics attempts to make explicitly conscious some subconscious mechanisms so that they can be evoked when the need arises.

In order to look at specific synectic operations, it is helpful to understand that the process basically involves making the strange familiar and making the familiar strange. When confronting a problem-oriented situation, the primary responsibility of the problem solvers or participants in the process is to understand the problem. This is basically an analytic step in which the participants become aware of the consequences and ramifications of a problem while placing it into a context of known relationships and acceptable patterns.

If only the analytical step is taken, the synectics argument is that a novel solution would not be possible. Novelty demands a fresh viewpoint. A new way of looking at the problem increases the potential for a new solution.

To make the familiar strange is to distort, invert, or transpose the everyday ways of looking and responding, which render the world a secure and familiar place. It is a conscious attempt to achieve a new look at the same old world, people, ideas, feelings, and things. The following specific synectics mechanisms, which are metaphorical in character, will help make the familiar strange.

1. Personal analogy is the identification with the elements of a problem by means of empathy as well as first-person identification of facts and emotions.
2. Direct analogy is a single comparison of two

concepts. In "A crab walks sideways like a sneaky burgler," the subject of the analogy is the first part of the comparison ("the crab"). The analogue of the analogy is the thing to which the subject is compared ("a burgler").

3. Symbolic analogy is an outgrowth of an emphasis on the rational or scientific method while the rest of the possible contributions of man tend to be disregarded.

4. Fantasy analogy is where one assumes the best possible of all solutions.

Synectics holds that without the presence of these mechanisms, no problem-stating or problem-solving attempt will be successful. The mechanisms are reproducible mental processes: tools to initiate the motion of the creative process and to sustain and renew the motion. In the use of the mechanisms a willingness to operate on a nonrational basis is the basic requirement to successful functioning of a synectics group. The ultimate solution to any given problem will inadvertently be rational, but the process is not.

Buzz Sessions

For multidisciplinary or user groups to reach consensus, identify distinct points of view, or stimulate interest in a project, the buzz session is an appropriate group activity. Groups are temporarily formed for the purpose of discussing a specific topic. The primary interest of this type of group interaction session is the expression and critical analysis of ideas related to the topic. The formation of the group is to promote an understanding of all viewpoints held by the participants, yet arrive at consensus on certain points.

When an issue has been identified by the group, smaller subgroups of about five people can be formed to discuss and analyze specific topics. These buzz-groups should be given a time limit and location to develop their ideas. A discussion leader is usually appointed to facilitate interaction, along with a

recorder to keep brief notes for reporting and further analysis.

Discussion Groups

A discussion group is a small-group activity designed for sharing knowledge among participants, stimulating the development of new attitudes, and arriving at well-considered decisions. The group size can vary from seven to fifteen people who consent to meet over a prolonged period of time. It is desirable for the participants to have some diversity in knowledge and attitudes.

The group leader is a pivotal individual who requires training in techniques for leading discussions. It should not be assumed that informed, personable individuals can effectively lead a group; highly informed individuals may well inhibit group discussions.

All participants in the group should be informed of the purpose and proposed outcome of their activities. Similarly, participants should be encouraged to be open-minded in their assessment of ideas discussed and seek consensus on all major issues. Voting should be avoided since it usually reflects the group's unpreparedness to reach consensus. Similarly, tendencies that seek everyone participating should be avoided. The discussion leader should exercise control by limiting his or her own remarks and by creating an atmosphere conducive to free interaction.

A discussion group should not be organized to support a previously arrived at decision. Participants are generally aware of manipulative attempts by group leaders and tend to function inefficiently.

The Auction

The conscious process of disclosing values about environmental concerns points to many decision conflicts that require resolution. Value-based information generally guides the direction and emphasis of the design program. Any type of group decision-making process inadvertently raises value-based issues while conflict-resolving strategies frequently attempt to expose and clarify the participants' values. This clarification concept can be most frequently implemented during the goal-setting process as well as any program stage that seeks to identify and sort out a group's priorities.

There are numerous game strategies designed to examine values, ideals, and goals. Any attempts at involving user groups in decision making must actively make users aware of their own feelings, their own ideas, and their own beliefs so that their choices and decisions are conscious, deliberate, and based on personal value systems.

One such game strategy is based on the principles and procedures of an auction. This is a highly theatrical approach to group value clarification, particularly since it relies upon a lively auctioneer to stimulate the bidding process and encourage competitive bidding.

The procedure has four distinct stages: setting priorities; weighting priorities; bidding at auction; and discusssing results. The props should include an introductory statement, a deck of option cards, and a priority ranking and weighting schedule. Opening statements can be very general, such as, ''What do you want most for your community?'' or they can be specific statements pertaining to a building or a space planning problem. The option cards should identify a wide range of possible choices, from the most practical to the most utopian options. The schedule is a recording sheet to note the choices and priorities each participant makes.

After the introductory statement has been read, each participant reviews the deck of option cards and selects those he or she considers personally important. From this set, the participant selects the ten most important cards and lists them in order of their importance. Each participant is given 100 units of value to distribute among the ten options. The units or weights are then assigned individually and recorded on the schedule. Once this preparatory assignment of

priorities and values is completed, the group is ready to compete for items of value. The entire deck of cards is to be auctioned off, each to the highest bidder. Only those items actually purchased by each participant are considered to fulfill the requirements of the purpose statement. The goal is to get as many high priorities on the value list as possible. Each participant is evaluated on the number of weighted cards from the initial list of ten that is bought at auction and by the weighted value originally assigned to them.

Participants may bid only for those cards identified on their priority list. For each item won, participants are credited with the number of priority points originally set for the item irrespective of what is actually paid at auction to win the bid.

A review of individual scores, items selected, and intensity of competition is an important measure of the worth of the items to each participant. This strategy for clarifying personal values is particularly effective when played with a heterogeneous population such as those found in health facilities projects where administrators, physicians, nurses, staff, and patients have different and conflicting needs that must be satisfied by one facility.

It is important to be aware that a considerable amount of preparation time is necessary to develop these materials, as well as to organize the appropriate participants. Game props, including the issues, should be generated and even pretested prior to the formal application of the auction.

While the auction has had limited past application to design programming, it is sufficiently flexible and engaging and requires only imagination for an appropriate application.

MANAGEMENT BY OBJECTIVES

As designers expand the scope of their activities to include programming, their organizational methods of management must change to accommodate these new activities. Management by objectives (MBO) is

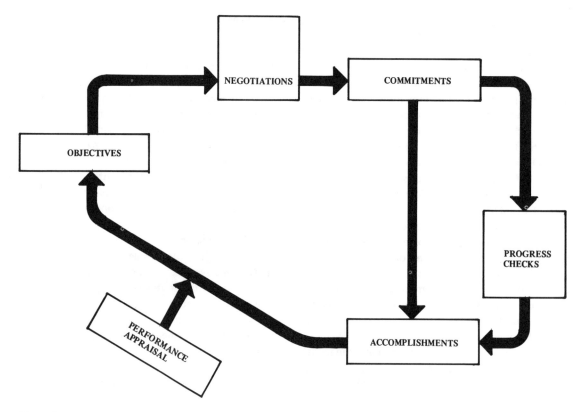

Figure 5
The process of management by objectives.

1. The subordinate establishes short-term performance goals and some longer-range personal development goals.
2. The superior and the subordinate discuss the requirements necessary to fulfill these goals and adjust them for consistency with organization goals, capability of the individual, and so on.
3. At mid-year there should be a meeting between superior and subordinate to evaluate how successfully goals were met, to discuss what should be done to increase the probability of success, and to set new goals for the next six-month period.

The Result

The MBO organizational orientation is result oriented since responsibilities are classified, and jobs are organized and evaluated. The superior–subordinate role relationship is improved and changed to the extent that the subordinate plays a more active career role, which is future oriented. The emphasis on performance, however, may be at the expense of developing human relations. Trivial items may assume undue importance because they are measurable. This may also encourage the setting of easily reached goals.

Goals need to be stated in terms of end results,

results that are achieveable within a defined time frame. The goals must be described in terms of a definite accomplishment and related to an importance for the job. Goals should require the individual to grow and improve effectiveness through the process of accomplishing them. Workable goals are never ambiguous, idealistic, or theoretical.

Guidelines for Writing Goals and Objectives

The following points can help the designer develop goals and objectives. Sometimes a given goal or objective may not lend itself to all of these criteria; nevertheless it should be checked against each of them anyway.

1. It should start with the word *to* followed by an action verb. This is a critical step because a goal or objective is the statement of an overt behavior act, or result that will occur.

2. It should specify a single key result to be accomplished. Avoid combining goals and objectives because you may achieve one and not the other. You would then be weakening your chance for accurate evaluation and measurement.

3. It should specify a target completion date. Set a realistic time span that is focused on a specific date or time for completion. This target date should help in using the time available most efficiently.

4. It should be as specific as possible. This will enable all concerned to fairly measure the extent to which the goal or objective is accomplished.

5. It should relate to your role and missions—a simple but often forgotten point. Keep goals and objectives within your own fields of responsibility. Make them ones you have the power and resources to accomplish.

6. It should not be limited to the resources on hand. Consider all possible resources required to develop the goals and objectives needed for the plan. You may have to develop some of the resources your-

self or seek them out in the community to carry out your plan.

7. It should be communicated in face-to-face discussion as well as in writing, and full agreement should be reached before you construct a program to accomplish it. This is an excellent way to minimize misunderstandings as well as to obtain top-level and subordinate commitment to achieving the goals and objectives, thereby increasing the motivation of all involved.

THE STRUCTURE OF A PROGRAM

If something as amorphous and dynamic as a program can ever by discussed rationally, it is necessary to describe its structural characteristics and partition them into stages. The structure of a program is similar to an industrial process that converts raw materials into useful energy. The program converts raw information into useful design information with the aid of a vast array of catalysts.

The prerequisites to developing a program incude recognition and identification of the problem. The stages of a program can generally be described as expansion, classification, and evaluation. All of the techniques discussed earlier in this chapter can be utilized in at least one stage, and often more frequently.

The initial phase of expansion is the opportunity to inject new information into what is already known. (In order to encourage a synthesis of this information, the ideational stage logically follows where the seeds of conversion begin to occur.) Techniques that stimulate the fluency of ideas nurture the expansion process to yield a new by-product that requires classification. This stage is primarily rooted in organization whereby the classifying methods permit the reduction of the problem into manageable parts suitable for designing. Evaluation is the final stage of the programming sequence where all the alternatives within a category are reassessed on the basis of the

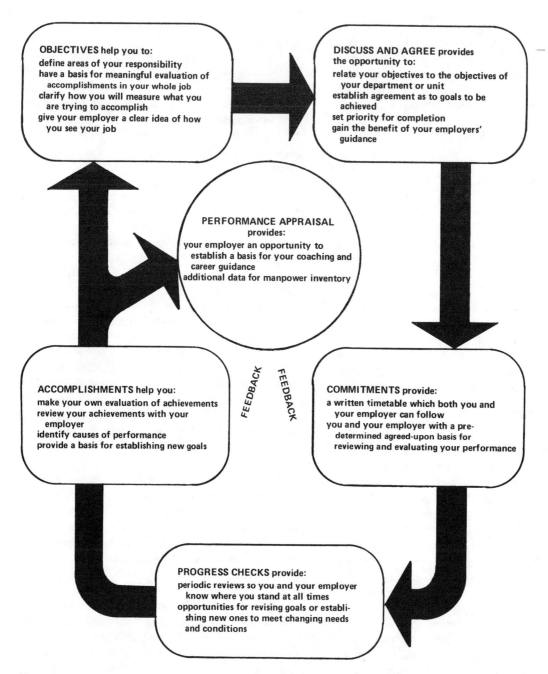

OBJECTIVES help you to:
define areas of your responsibility
have a basis for meaningful evaluation of
accomplishments in your whole job
clarify how you will measure what you
are trying to accomplish
give your employer a clear idea of how
you see your job

DISCUSS AND AGREE provides
the opportunity to:
relate your objectives to the objectives of
your department or unit
establish agreement as to goals to be
achieved
set priority for completion
gain the benefit of your employers'
guidance

PERFORMANCE APPRAISAL
provides:
your employer an opportunity to
establish a basis for your coaching and
career guidance
additional data for manpower inventory

ACCOMPLISHMENTS help you:
make your own evaluation of achievements
review your achievements with your
employer
identify causes of performance
provide a basis for establishing new goals

COMMITMENTS provide:
a written timetable which both you and
your employer can follow
you and your employer with a predetermined agreed-upon basis for
reviewing and evaluating your performance

FEEDBACK   FEEDBACK

PROGRESS CHECKS provide:
periodic reviews so you and your employer
know where you stand at all times
opportunities for revising goals or establishing new ones to meet changing needs
and conditions

Figure 6
Management by objectives: why you do it.

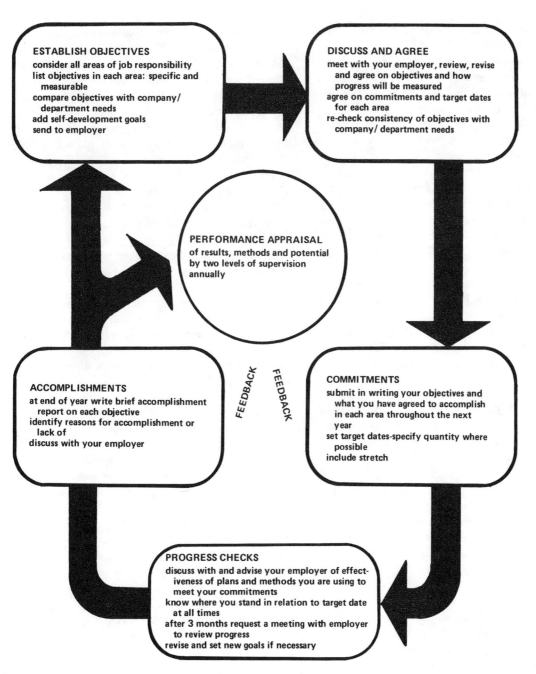

ESTABLISH OBJECTIVES
consider all areas of job responsibility
list objectives in each area: specific and
    measurable
compare objectives with company/
    department needs
add self-development goals
send to employer

DISCUSS AND AGREE
meet with your employer, review, revise
    and agree on objectives and how
    progress will be measured
agree on commitments and target dates
    for each area
re-check consistency of objectives with
    company/ department needs

PERFORMANCE APPRAISAL
of results, methods and potential
by two levels of supervision
annually

ACCOMPLISHMENTS
at end of year write brief accomplishment
    report on each objective
identify reasons for accomplishment or
    lack of
discuss with your employer

FEEDBACK   FEEDBACK

COMMITMENTS
submit in writing your objectives and
    what you have agreed to accomplish
    in each area throughout the next
    year
set target dates-specify quantity where
    possible
include stretch

PROGRESS CHECKS
discuss with and advise your employer of effect-
    iveness of plans and methods you are using to
    meet your commitments
know where you stand in relation to target date
    at all times
after 3 months request a meeting with employer
    to review progress
revise and set new goals if necessary

Figure 7
Management by objectives: how you do it.

original guiding criteria in order to diaggregate the best of the alternatives.

The development of the program, then, obviously leads to implementation of the solution. Upon completion of the solution, evaluation assesses performance of the completed solution.

The Process of Designing

An expanded view of the design process is described in six sequential stages that follow:

Recognition The primary introduction to the process is based on the establishment of the existence of a problem and the decision to do something about it.

Indentification and exploration It is then necessary to make a determination about the nature of the problem. Often the problem requires restating into more useful terms for the designer. Certain operating assumptions need to be established to clarify any restrictions or constraints on the area of study.

Search and expansion All the information pertinent to the problem should be collected. Data that are known should be gathered for the investigation as well as the relevant techniques for analysis of the data. Usually when large amounts of information are available, it is useful to break down or categorize this information for a detailed study. This is the time when the information can be evaluated to determine which variables are essential and which can be eliminated. When a short list of significant variables is identified, each should be examined to assess the type and extent of relationships they exhibit.

Classification and analysis The data should then be assembled into a tentative configuration that is suggested by the analysis. The problem should be examined for any recognizable form or structure. The problem structure should be studied to see whether it suggests analogous problem solutions in other areas.

Evaluation Alternative solutions are then generated in compliance with the information available. The evaluation phase entails the selection of a solution. This is accomplished by comparing the possible solutions according to the value system established in the identification phase. Decisions should be made in accordance with the priorities previously established, and the solution accepted should acknowledge the available information.

Implementation The solution must now be acted upon through presentation, public hearing, or other marketplace mechanisms. It is also necessary to develop a plan for implementation and effectuation of the solution.

Postcompletion The information gained about the user's satisfaction with the solution will be used for future problems.

Though the stages appear to be ordered into a sequential pattern, it is clear that the design process is iterative and constantly cyclic in nature. In order to describe the process, as well as understand its components, it is necessary to take a static view of a dynamic process.

The Product Development Program

Bruce Archer, an industrial designer, has stated that "the great majority of design tasks are carried out by designers on behalf of employers or clients, rather than on their own behalfs."[11] Similarly, many of the tasks commissioned are regarded, by the client, as investments calculated to offer a given probability of yielding a prescribed return by way of income or capital gain. The clients, sometimes referred to as developers, are those people who control the development of financial resources in a project. When the developer is responsible for raising capital for the conduct of a project, he should be able to show evidence of the degree of risk attached to and the extent of return expected from the venture. The design act, Archer argues, must therefore be seen within the context of a more extensive process, which includes the realization of design proposals as well as the formulation of them. This overall process is referred to as a product development program.

The intensity of a problem is a function of the certainty required in the solution relative to the certainty exhibited by the input variables. Clearly it is much more difficult to produce a highly predictable result on uncertain data than to produce a very approximate result on reliable data. It is possible, nevertheless, to develop a design that is relatively insensitive to inaccuracies in the data or to reduce uncertainty by a carefully graduated development and test program.

Taking the model plan of work published by the Royal Institute of British Architects as a basis, a prototype program for a building would be as follows:

Stage 1: Inception.
Set up client organization for briefing.
Consider requirements.
Appoint architect.

Stage 2: Feasibility.
Carry out study of user requirements.
Carry out study of site conditions.
Examine planning, design, and cost feasibility.

Stage 3: Outline proposals.
Develop brief further.
Complete study of user requirements.
Carry out study of technical problems.
Carry out study of planning, design, and cost problems.

Stage 4: Scheme design.
Finalize brief.
Full design of project by architect.
Preliminary design by engineer.
Prepare cost plan.
Prepare full explanatory report.
Submit proposal for all approvals.

Stage 5: Detail design.
Complete designs for every part and component of building.

Complete cost checking of designs.

Stage 6: Production information.
Prepare final production drawings.
Prepare schedules.
Prepare specifications.

Stage 7: Bills of quantities.
Prepare bills of quantities.
Prepare tender documents.

Stage 8: Tender action.
Dispatch tender documents.
Examine tenders and select tenderers.
Let contracts.
Notify unsuccessful tenderers.

Stage 9: Project planning.
Arrange effective communications system.
Agree on project program.

Stage 10: Operations on site.
Provide design and construction information.
Implement construction program.
Install and effect budgetary control.
Install and effect quality control.

Stage 11: Completion.
Inspect completed construction.
Specify rectification of defects.
Rectify defects.
Complete contracts and settle accounts.
Relinquish possession to owner.

Stage 12: Feedback.
Analyze job records.
Inspect completed building.
Study building in use.

As work proceeds on a phased program basis, it is relatively easy to monitor the activities. So that the certainty of result improves. This entire process, whether a building or a product development program, can be characterized as an attempt to achieve greater certainty yet maintain a proper balance between the increasing cost of allowing greater certainty and the diminishing return from that investment.

A design project is almost a sequence of design problems. As new information is added and synthesized, new design problems arise and must be solved. In this approach Archer advances the notion that the design program indicates the sequence of decision-making activities. The effectiveness of the design program, then, is increased as each step in the sequence of project stages is anticipated with the appropriate time allowance made available.

NOTES AND REFERENCES

1. Reyner Banham, *Theory and Design in the First Machine Age*, 2d ed. (New York: Praeger Publishers, 1967).
2. Donald Schon, *Technology and Change* (New York: Delacorte Press, 1967), p. 1.
3. René Descartes, *Discourse on Medthods and Meditations*, trans. Lawrence J. Lafleur (Indianapolis: Liberal Arts Press, 1960).
4. Ibid.
5. M. H. Port, "The New Law Courts Competition, 1866/67," *Architectural History* 2 (1968).
6. G. Polya, *How to Solve It* (New York: Doubleday, Anchor Books, 1957).
7. The organizational framework and manipulative verbs have been adapted from the unpublished work of D. A. Straus and S. Van der Ryn, *Problem Solving Notebook*, University of California at Berkeley, 1969.
8. John R. Raser, *Simulation and Society* (Boston: Allyn and Bacon, 1969), p. 46.
9. Herbert Simon, *Models of Man* (New York: John Wiley & Sons, 1957), p. 199.
10. William J. J. Gordon, *Synectics* (New York: Collier Books, 1961).
11. Bruce Archer, "The Structure of the Design Process," unpublished manuscript, 1968.

2

Information Retrieval Methods

The object to be designed has to fulfill as many of its set of purposes as possible. This means that design decisions have to be made in order to attain these objectives. The designer is required to know which design decisions will eventually lead to an object that has the desired properties.

The essential problem is that of predicting future events from a limited set of past observations—with the additional difficulty that one's own decisions will influence those future events. The difficulty increases with new and unprecedented design decisions whose consequences are more difficult to predict in advance. Nonetheless, this prediction is required in most cases because few clients are willing to invest their means without a reasonable expectation of some desirable outcome.

Every design task is approached under the risk of failure because there is no way of obtaining certainty for the prediction of future events. Thus, the act of designing becomes probabilistic. The process from data collection to forecasting can be called a *prediction system*.

There are various ways of making reasonable guesses about the future behavior of the environment to be designed. The methods are outlined as follows:

Casuistics is a search for previous cases where an almost identical problem has occurred. The designer can then replicate those cases where the problem has been solved in a satisfactory manner. This method is hazardous, however, since problem contexts may invalidate logical transference of a solution from one setting to another. Casuistics nevertheless can be an effective way to evaluate similarities and differences between apparently similar problems.

Analogy establishes a correspondence between two sets of events.[1] One of the sets of events is simple and understandable enough so that predictions can be made for this set of events. The relationship in the first set of events is then transferred to the other set of events, and outcomes can be predicted.

The assumption in analogy is that both sets of events are similar enough to operate alike.[2]

Experimentation requires that a subsystem under consideration be isolated and built as realistically as necessary. The subsystem is then subjected to the conditions expected, and its performance is observed. Modifications are made until a solution is found that will perform satisfactorily. For example, American Society of Testing Materials isolates and tests manufactured products and building components by experimentation.

Simulation requires the building of a mock-up, or scale-model, of the component under consideration with as much resemblance to the actual system as necessary where the design parameters can be varied until a satisfactory solution is found. Simulation is an abstraction of real conditions.

Introspection is to imagine what the effect of a particular design decision might be by logically scanning the possibilities. The designer develops a prototype for future users by utilizing his knowledge and experiences as judge.

Taking the risk is to do anything you have a good reason to do, although its performance is totally unpredictable.

Hindsight can be a method used to avoid prediction of the future behavior of the environment by resolving conflicts and repairing faults only after they are manifest. Hindsight is most frequently the method used in vernacular building. (You have to build one house, try it out, then remodel it or build another house before you get what you want.)

All of these ways of meeting the difficulties of estimating the consequences of design decisions for performance are actually used. In architecture, the most frequent practice is that of casuistics, even though inventiveness is limited by that strategy. The great breakthroughs were based on taking the risk of failure. Experimentation is generally expensive and more complex because of its uniqueness. In brief, there are no general principles that would prescribe when any of the practices described should be applied.

Clearly, then, decision making is predictive. The

TABLE 1
Prediction Systems

	Deterministic	*Probabilistic*	*Capricious*
Problem Types	Functional Mechanical Structural	Production Marketing	Motivational Aesthetic

outcome depends on the course of action taken. A systematic designer must trace the consequences of each of the alternative lines of action.[3]

In a problem-solving situation, when predictions about the outcome of a decison can be made under conditions of certainty, the system is described as deterministic; a situation in which no predictions can be made is termed a capricious system.[4] The problems that fit into this classification system are described in Table 1. As our present state of knowledge progresses, more systems that have been regarded as capricious become probabilistic, and as the degree of control over the quality of materials and processes increases, previously probabilistic systems become deterministic.

HOW TO CONDUCT SURVEY RESEARCH

Among the nonscientific population the most common methods for establishing facts are through intuition, something you believe to be true; or by authority, where an expert says it is so; or by logic, where certain things are deduced because they follow specific rules.

The scientific community has contributed to these methods a process of systematic observation, carefully and reliably recording behavior. This section will present a way of looking at cause-and-effect relations between facts.

Define the Research Problem

There is a variety of sources for research ideas. These sources incude individual experiences, hunches, books, journals, personal conversation, and research findings. One possible source for a research problem is the architect's values. For example, if an individual believes that an open office plan is best, he may test that hypothesis that work productivity and satisfaction will be higher in open office situations than with other alternatives.

Testing ideas based on personal values is legitimate as long as biases are controlled in conducting the research project. Once idea that can be tested or researched is developed, whatever its source, the investigator should familiarize himself with past and current thought and research in the area.

Research Design

A research design communicates the plan by which individuals are compared and analyzed. While it is evident that no design may result in absolute certainty, its purpose is to limit the number of alternative interpretations of its results.

Various research designs are available based on the purpose of the study.

The case study The case study involves the systematic observation of one population at one point in time. The major purpose of the case study is to describe a unit. For example, the case study may involve user satisfaction with a public housing project.

Survey designs The two most often used are called the correlational study and the panel design. The correlational study compares two or more units at one point in time. To illustrate, two housing projects with a different number of floors may be compared to resident satisfaction. The panel design studies a sequence of events over time or a social process. It yields a large body of information about respondents. A panel design may be defined as repeated observations of the same sample over a period of time. To observe children's play behavior in a residential setting, a panel is necessary to measure play variation and setting variation over time.

Similarly, people's attitudes to per- and post-environmental changes over time can be measured to assess the effectiveness of the change.

Experimental design Suppose, now, that a control group is used. This group has and will not be undergoing any type of change. If we are interested in the measurable effects of change, then an experimental group would be introduced into the design. Their responses would be compared with those of the control group in order to identify the factors influencing any change.

The various forms of research design range from highly controlled to loosely structured participant observation or case study. Most research involves a segment of the population and is usually associated with the observational techniques of the questionnaire and interview. Each approach has its strengths and weaknesses; for example, experimental design usually requires small groups in a highly controlled setting yielding a low degree of representativeness. Surveys, as compared with experiments, are characterized by a high degree of representativeness but a low degree of control. Compared with experiments, a case study is low on control, and compared with surveys it is low on represntativeness. It does, however, provide descriptive examples from an intensive study.

Sample Selection

A population refers to all or any specified group of objects, methods, responses, geographic areas, or persons residing within the area under study.

A sample may be defined as a limited number of elements selected from a population to be representative of that population, an effort which means the elements chosen to be included in the study have been drawn in a random, unbiased manner. It should be noted here, however, that a representative sample refers to the process of selection and not necessarily to the extent to which samples approximate population characteristics, which are often unknown.

Rarely are we concerned only with the data obtained from a sample except insofar as these statistics (such as sample means or standard deviations) can be used to estimate the corresponding values or parameters in the population. Sampling involves defining the population, selecting the sample, and estimating the population's parameters from the knowledge obtained from the sample statistic.

Generalizing from known characteristics of a sample to unknown characteristics of a population or universe is known as *statistical inference*. The statistical inference provides an estimate of the parameter and the amount of error that can be expected.

The problems involved in selecting samples include a biased estimate of a population. Biased statistics are overestimates or underestimates of parameters. With unbiased samples, as we increase the number of cases, statistics tend to equal the corresponding value of the parameter. Some methods of selecting cases in an unbiased manner are simple random sampling, stratified random sampling, systematic sampling, and area (cluster) sampling.

Simple random sampling A sample is selected randomly when every member of the population has an equal chance of being included in the sample; no population element has been either deliberately or inadvertently omitted or excluded from the sample except by chance. The selection of cases at random is most simply accomplished by using a table of random numbers. The researcher assigns a number to each member of the population, enters a table of random numbers at any point, and, moving in any predetermined direction, reads the numbers of the individuals to be included in the sample.

Stratified random sampling Stratified random sampling makes use of random sampling procedures as part of its design. Stratification is the process of dividing a population into a number of strata, or subpopulations, so that the variability of elements selected within each stratum is more homogeneous than is the variability of elements between strata. Samples are then drawn independently and randomly from each stratum, and an estimate of the parameter is computed over all strata.

Stratification allows us to take advantage of whatever information we might possess concerning the characteristics of the population. Second, since sampling errors occur only within strata, and not between, if we can reduce the variability within each stratum, the estimate of the parameter will be more accurate than if we had to sample randomly throughout an entire population without benefit of stratification. Then too, stratified sampling allows us to select cases within each stratum in different ways and in different proportions.

Systematic sampling Selecting a sample by counting every fifth, tenth, or hundredth person until the desired sample size is obtained is called systematic sampling, the first element being chosen at random. This method is usually easier from the standpoint that wherever population elements are listed, we can avoid using a table of random numbers and simply select every nth case. Systematic sampling gives us some assurance that we are sampling broadly throughout the population.

Area or cluster sampling Where lists of individuals are unavailable or the characteristics of the population are not well known, it is possible for the researcher to sample areas or clusters of elements first, and then to sample individuals or elements within the clusters.

Generally, cluster or area sampling costs less than a simple random sample of the same size, but there is usually a corresponding decrease in the accuracy of predicting parameters. Any given cluster is likely to be relatively homogeneous, and differences between clusters are likely to be quite large.

This method is most efficient when dealing with a geographic area. Several methods can be employed in the selection of specific elements to be included in the sample. This can be accomplished with census tract maps, with aerial photos, or by field survey.

Sample size Among the elements determining the size of a sample is the extent to which the population is homogeneous. Homogeneity here is defined as the degree to which people are alike with respect to the particular characteristics of the community being studied, such as their political attitudes. The kind of sampling procedure being used in a survey also affects sample size. Stratified samples require the least number of cases in general, the simple random samples somewhat more, and cluster samples as many or more than the simple random sample—for the same level of precision.

Sampling error Because we are interviewing just a sample of the population, any measure we get enables us only to estimate a characteristic of the population. Sampling implies some discrepancy between the actual and the estimated value of a characteristic. The discrepancy between the sample estimate and the number (value) that would have been found under identical conditions by a census of all residents is called sampling error. The amount of sampling error for which we must allow affects the precision (reliability) of the sample estimate.

Developing a Questionnaire

Content of questions to be asked is the focal point around which a questionnaire can be developed, determining to a large extent the kind of questions that will be needed. Essentially, there are four basic types of questions, related to a large extent to each other: questions of fact; opinion and attitude; information; and self-perception.

Fact questions The question of fact asks the respondent to provide information about himself—his social and personal characteristics. These "demographic" questions seek to paint a picture of the respondent in terms of his age, sex, income, education, marital status, occupation, religion, ethnic group, home ownership, household composition, political party affiliation, race residence, voter registration, past voting behavior, union membership, group affiliations, and so on. These respondent characteristics are required in order to check the representativeness of the sample against census data

for those same characteristics in the population. The data also are used to compare responses by different demographic classes—men against women, young against old, high income against low income. A common assumption is that within such classes people tend to show similarities in behavior and that this behavior differs from people in other population classes. These similarities need to be checked with survey data.

Opinion and attitude questions These questions focus on emotional perceptions, for they deal with feelings, beliefs, ideals, and misconceptions, hence providing a basis for understanding the respondents' reactions, both behavioral and attitudinal.

Opinion questions seek to determine thoughts or feelings at a particular point in time about a particular subject. Those thoughts or feelings at any given time are the fruits of an underlying deeply ingrained attitude structure. Questions designed to tap attitudes, then, seek understanding about people's basic personality orientation acquired over many years of experience and learning.

Distinguishing between opinion and attitude is no simple task; it requires probing into the reasons behind answers and the intensity with which they are held.

Information questions Information questions are used to find out what people know, how much they know, and how they happen to know. The knowledge a person has of any subject is related to his attitudes toward it. This is the principle of selective perception (that is, we see things the way we want to see them). However, information can be measured even when attitudes are contrary or vague.

Self-perception questions Here the individual is asked to evaluate something about his own behavior in relation to that of others. Such self-designation involves the person's reporting of "facts" he knows about himself and others as colored by his attitudes. Examples of self-perception questions are those asked about the number of social visits he makes in a week.

The form of question used depends on the kind of information desired. Although form may differ in a variety of ways, questions are one of two basic types—open-ended and structured. The more structured the questions, the greater the chance for uniformity.

Open-ended and unstructured questions In an open-ended question the respondent is encouraged to talk freely and at length about the subject at hand. Unstructured questions are used when trying to discover the reasons people have for liking/disliking as they do.

This type of question is especially useful (1) where the researcher has limited knowledge as to the kind of answers a particular question is likely to provoke, (2) where he anticipates a great range of responses, (3) where he is interested in what the respondent will volunteer on a subject before specific prompting, or (4) where he wants to go deeper into the respondent's motivations.

On the other hand, open-ended questions are unwieldy. The interviewer has to record all answers verbatim, consuming much interviewing time and limiting the number of questions that can be asked before the respondent wearies of the mental burden imposed upon him. They also require considerable questionnaire space; and to interpret verbatim comments, it is necessary to devise a category system to group responses for meaningful analysis. Categorizing, however, means sacrificing subtle meanings of the data.

Structured Questions The second major type of question used in interviewing presents the respondent with fixed-response alternatives; that is, the respondent can answer only in terms of two or more alternatives.

Structured questions are easy to administer in the field because they are precoded. They are also easy to work with in the analysis because they can be punched directly onto computer cards, if that is the desired means for analysis.

With structured questions, however, the researcher sacrifices much of the intensity and color of the respondents' feelings in order to determine prior to data collection which analysis will be meaningful in

terms of specific data to be collected. This system does, however, force the people to decide how they stand in light of the researcher's criteria, and they are allowed to classify themselves.

One kind of structured question offers a dichotomous choice, attempting to elicit only yes-no answers (true–false, wrong–right, good–bad). The multiple choice item compels the respondent to choose one of several fixed alternatives.

A prime disadvantage of structured questions is the difficulty in interpreting the degree of intensity with which the correspondent holds his opinion. This problem can be partially overcome by using scaled responses with different psychological weights, that is, having weighted measures of the psychological distance between each response alternative. Weighted scale responses add more exactness to measures of public opinion on a given topic because they yield information about how much difference there is among structured responses.

Example: How serious a problem is air pollution in Raleigh at this time? . . . Would you say very serious, somewhat serious, not very serious, or not a problem?

1) very serious
2) somewhat serious
3) not very serious
4) not a problem

Rating scales present the respondent with a word, phrase, or a statement and ask him to indicate the extent to which the word, phrase, or statement is descriptive of his feelings.

The semantic differential is one of the best-known techniques of this sort, expecially useful to designers in understanding attitudinal reactions to an environmental setting. It offers the respondent a set of word pairs, each word the polar opposite of the other. Typically the respondent fills out the scale himself. In doing this, he is told to indicate the direction and intensity of his feelings by placing a single mark on one of the spaces along the continuum between the words.

Example: How would you describe this neighborhood?

Friendly _____ _____ _____ _____ _____ _____ _____ Unfriendly

Another rating scale, to discern the direction and intensity of agreement with phrases or statements, could be used to describe, say, an ideal neighborhood:

Example:

The ideal neighborhood: Agree	1	2	3	4	5	Disagree
Should be small	☐	☐	☐	☐	☐	☐
Must be well kept up . .	☐	☐	☐	☐	☐	☐

A third variation of structured questions involves the use of a series of statements, which themselves form a scale on which respondents can be ranked. Such attitude scales depict the degree to which different respondents are liberal/conservative in relation to others in the sample. They are typically agree/disagree statements.

Ranking is a technique that can be useful to designers in understanding the priorities of facilities as perceived by the users. If, for example, we are interested in learning which of the suggested facilities people in a neighborhood want, we would present a random listing of the facilities and ask respondents to rank each in descending order in desirability or need. An overall comparison of rankings then reveals the priorities of the community. Ranking can be made more visual with the aid of steps, or a ladder, and this concept can be applied as follows:

Example: Considering everything about Raleigh, how would you rate it as a place to live on the following steps, 1 being the best possible place to live and 9 being the worst possible place to live?

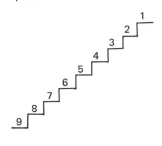

Another type of ranking uses the ladder.

Example:

Using the ladder representing happiness of life, choose the rung that best describes your life right now.

Best Possible Life

Worst Possible Life

Content of questions The job of the questionnaire is to build and maintain a certain amount of rapport with respondents so that emotionally charged issues—age, income, personal health—can be broached without enmity. In order to set the stage for a painless exchange of questions and answers, questions must be constructed with several considerations in mind:

Question wording problems Wording of an individual question can seriously affect the kind of response it triggers. Ambiguity, misperception, and loading sometimes creep in. Some general rules on wording follow.

1. Questions that are exact in their meaning are much easier to grasp and respond to.
2. Avoid imprecise or incomplete questions, such as not using exact places, time, and names or not making it clear what is being made reference to.
3. Consider the population you are addressing in terms of utilizing a vocabulary that has meaning to the respondent.
4. Somewhere between the extremes of complete inexperience and overfamiliarity, each question must be worded so that it has just one meaning for all respondents, regardless of how they differ by education, residence, occupation, and so on.

5. The atmosphere in which a question is asked must be natural. A question is loaded when something in the question suggests to the respondent that one particular response is more desirable than another.

6. Emotionally charged words detract from the intentions of the question and lead to distortion of meaning.

7. If embarassing questions are tactfully worded, they will elicit truer responses than if they are bluntly worded.

8. Limit the length of questions, and make them sound as simple as possible.

Our discussion thus far has pertained to descriptions of the primary stages involved in conducting survey research; an operational guide to setting up each stage is available. There is a suggested phasing for conducting an environmental assessment that is best described in the sequence proposed in Figure 8. The column on the right outlines an abbreviated version of the operations that should be conducted, reading from top to bottom. The left column suggests key words that define the purpose of each operation.

Sequence of questions Most questionnaires are designed in four parts: the introduction, warm-up questions, the body of the study, and the demographic questions.

The introduction must create a good impression of the interviewer and the questionnaire. Therefore, it must be short; it should identify the sponsor and the broad nature of the study without fuss. It should be easy to memorize and realistically worded to sound natural and nonthreatening while being pleasantly firm.

The warm-up questions are a set of specific, innocuous inquiries used to build respondent rapport. The ease with which the respondent can answer these questions prepares the ground for the more specific questions to follow.

The body of the study deals with the crux of the questionnaire. It is usually the most lengthy section,

and the content has been already established with the previous work.

The demographic characteristics are, for the most part, personal items common to most surveys. Questions about age, occupation, length of residency, type of tenure, and even name, address, and phone number should come easily and naturally by this stage of the questioning.

Data Analysis

The results of observational studies are large amounts of data that must be reduced into a form for making meaningful interpretations. The process of data reduction consists of grouping information into a few categories in order to describe adequately the characteristics of the sample population. Descriptive statistics are computed to determine the characteristics of the data generated from the study. They can be actual numbers, percentages, averages, or measures of relations. They describe available data. Inference statistics attempts to impute findings from sample population characteristics of the population from which the sample was drawn.

A frequency distribution is the grouping of items into a class and the number of individual items within each class. It is the basis for computation for many statistical tests and is an important descriptive tool. It is a summary technique of data reduction. For example, the hypothetical frequency distribution of house tenure in Table 2 shows that most people are renters; the most frequent category is apartment renters, and the least frequent is apartment owners.

TABLE 2
Hypothetical Frequency of House Tenure

Type of Tenure	Frequency (f)
House owners	5
House renters	8
Apartment renters	17
Apartment owner (cooperative)	3

identify sources attitudes personality behavior		Identify human characteristics
inventory		Review assessment methods
isolate key variables operationally define variables		Define variables
develop response format role play interviewer sample selection		Develop assessment media
develop questionnaire identify observational characteristics		Construct scales
pre-test		Respondent tasks
collect primary data interviewing observation verbal records	scale values response frequency	Collection methods
administer questionnaire		Test
refine instruments		Analyze
establish criteria confirm hunches develop new insights operate hypothesis	discover facts or principles describe phenomenon	Apply findings

Figure 8
Assessment sequencing phase.

In most instances we are interested in comparing several variables simultaneously. A table that may cross classify several variables in an arrangement of numberical data placed in rows and columns with specific labels identifying the data. Table 3 reveals that this particular group meets with friends and relations in their own home and spends free time in their own home; consequently they will have special housing requirements.

The average score of a particular variable is often referred to as a *central tendency*, which is the reduction of data to one value. The averages most commonly used in research are the median, the mode, and the arithmetic mean.

APPLICATIONS OF ANALYSIS AND EVALUATION METHODS

If it is accepted that common sense, intuition, and practiced experience alone are inadequate to struggle with the growing complexities of modern society, it follows that designers will require complexities of modern society, it follows that designers will require assistance in the decision-making processes when they seek to formulate principles that will guide society. Some of the techniques presented have been adapted from management science, operations research, and sociology. It is suggested that these techniques, despite their pitfalls, are necessary aids to the understanding of the complex and rapidly changing social and economic environment for which design development plans influence future behavior.

The models cannot replace the designer's own normative judgment. They can, however, relieve the designer of detailed analysis that statistics and computing machines are designed to handle. They can also provide a framework for design and planning systems of projection and mechanisms that measure the likely effects and implications of alternative decisions from which a choice may be made.

H. A. Simon in *Models of Man* states that "the capacity of the human mind for formulating and solving complex problems is very small compared with the size of the problems whose solution is required for objectively rationality," and he advances the thory of bounded rationality.[5]

We design and plan in a world of limited knowledge in which facts are probabilities and values are debatable. We can, however, argue that perfect rationality need not be attained so long as progress toward it continues and views architecture as a cybernetic process of moving toward control systems and feedback rather than a vison of an ideal state.

TABLE 3

Comparison between Locations Where People Allocate Social Time

Location	Meeting with Friends		Spend Free Time		Spend Time with Family	
Home	44	(42.3)	75	(72.0)	45	(43.3)
Church	18	(17.3)	6	(5.8)	6	(5.8)
Movies	1	(1.6)	3	(2.9)	2	(1.9)
Out of town	1	(1.0)	2	(1.9)	8	(7.7)
Miscellaneous	10	(9.6)	7	(6.8)	2	(1.9)
Not applicable	30	(28.8)	11	(10.6)	41	(39.4)
Total	104	(100%)	104	(100%)	104	(100%)

From "Social Perception of the Neighborhood" in *Integrating User Needs in Environmental Design* by Henry Sanoff (Springfield, Va.: National Technical Information Service, 1973).

There is general agreement that very little is known about the actual performance of designed environments in comparison to what the designer expects their performance to be. Although several testing procedures have been developed to assess the technical aspects of performance, there are no measures for judging and comparing the value of a physical artifact from the user's point of view.[6] The wide range of possible user input can be categorically stated by four questions. Responses to the questions will provide a user profile and more accurate definition of user needs.

1. How are spaces actually used compared with their intended use?
2. What is the subjective comfort level of the user?
3. What is the image of the arifact as it should be (which refers not only to the visual features but also to all other kinds of knowledge and expectations)?
4. How are artifacts identified?

The proceding questions are of significant importance, and all of them require explicit answers. The intent, therefore, is to develop techniques for identifying major factors that influence decisions.

Designers have long been operating with a stock of principles inherited from historic concerns of planning environments, and these principles predispose designers to make certain assumptions about what people want and ought to want. The user has been taken for granted, his characteristics merely assumed as undifferentiated constants. Though the architect today may be dissatisfied with the appropriateness of his solutions, he is still unable to predict accurately the consequences of his decisions.

Good design is an essential factor in the production of most artifacts. In the minds of users and developers, design is usually equated with style, but style has little to do with the essential livability of an environment. A measure of good design is overall efficiency and economic value combined with a high level of amenity and aesthetic quality. The design process by which this is achieved is based upon understanding the needs of the users of these designed environments.

There is also general consensus that the process of designing involves analysis of the situation and its problems, synthesis of possible solutions, and evaluation of which solution is most acceptable for implementation. Analysis leads to the program of a building. Synthesis helps determine the best way to support the desired behavior.

In architecture today, evaluation is the missing link in the design process. Evaluation, programming, and design are three linked activities drawing information from a systematic look at how people use existing environments. Analyzing existing environments leads to programming. It is time, therefore, for the architect to conduct his own surveys into how people use their environment, what they like and dislike about it, how well behavior patterns of users fit the way architects organized the spaces, and what kind of environment users would prefer.

Since we have not developed a facility for visualizing how a particular solution would fit a multidimensional situation, solutions have been given symbolic or verbal forms so that they can be manipulated by the rules of logic. This enables the testing of the solution in the abstract against the spectrum of requirements in the situation and thereby makes it easier for the designer to arrive at an evaluation. In doing so, both objective and subjective measures of performance are necessary. Having evaluations, decisions can be made for which solution to adopt.

These techniques for information retrieval are prerequisites for systematic learning and thus for improving the facility for better design.

ANALYTIC METHODS OF INFORMATION RETRIEVAL

There is some mysticism that meaning cannot be subjected to measurement. Many social scientists, however, agree that a person's behavior in a situation depends on what the situation means to him. This cognitive state of "meaning" is part of a process that includes that aspect of the environment which we are interested in with the human response condition.

Analytic techniques to measure meaning can be used to describe expressions of varied and subtle reactions to environmental phenomenon through descriptions of the images they evoke. Assessment criteria describing "feelings" about the environment, or their "connotative characteristics" are illustrated in such adjectives as *attractive, appeal, desirable, interest, impressive, elegant, cozy, warm, coherent, friendly*.

There is also a range of physical descriptors that can be incorporated into an environmental assessment scheme. They are frequently referred to as the denotative characteristics of the environment and include concepts of useful, private, safe, durable, each of movement, efficient, light, secure, convenient, noisy, cost effective, frequency of use, and maintenance.

There are numerous features about the built environment that are amenable to quantification. These characteristics are easily measurable because people can respond directly and immediately to them so that much of user insight is programmable. Some of these measurable characteristics include the following: exterior appearance of the environment, interior appearance of the environment, room layout (access, traffic patterns), spatial comfort (lighting, temperature, acoustics), spatial performance, spatial use patterns, spatial adequacy, and view from the environment.

This section includes a representative array of methods for eliciting user information that can substantially aid the designer in decision making. Each of the methods has been utilized by researchers in the field, and all are easily adaptable for a wide variety of decision-making situations. The methods are essentially used for genrating primary data or information where none is presently available or where the affected population is sufficiently heterogeneous that a quantified response would provide a good basis for decision making. A particular method

should be selected in accordance with the plan for conducting research as described in the previous section.

Since all the methods have been utilized by other fields for collecting information, they have been identified by their most commonly used titles. Although the methods are described by the language of their originating discipline, their approaches to data collection may be familiar to many designers. Generally architects use personal observation as a source of informational input and evaluation. Many evaluation techniques also rely on obervation, but they are based on group responses and are quantifiable. These data are useful for developing a fund of knowledge that may have general applicability to diverse situations.

There are specific techniques that can be used to answer evaluation questions.

1. Observation and behavioral mapping is a way to look at what people do in the designed environment.
2. The activity log is a way to view a person's behavior over a period of time in order to compare the actual use with the intended use of spaces.
3. Social mapping helps to explore and identify relationships between people in designed environments.

The following subsections will illustrate how each of the techniques is employed in an environmental setting.

BEHAVIORAL MAPPING

Observation can be used to better understand people's behavior in the environment.[7] Interaction between people and the environment may leave physical evidence. By observing this evidence, additional facts can be learned. Worn footpaths across grassy lawns indicate where most people walk. In a museum, the glass cases surrounding those exhibits

Exterior Appearance

Interior Appearance   View from the Environment

Figure 9
Visual appearance.

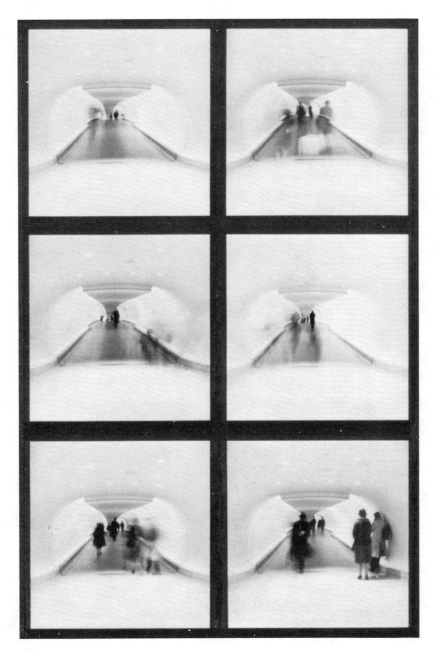

Figure 10
Spatial use patterns.

viewed by most people will bear a greater number of hand and nose prints. Psychologist Roger Barker observed children in a small town in Kansas to see how space affected them.[8] Without being observed, Barker and his assistants watched children at home, school, clubs, stores, and play areas. They found that different children behave in the same way when they are in the same environment. Barker concluded that in all types of environment, the nature of the space influences the behavior of the people in it. Clearly this is a cultural phenomenon where the space transmits cues about appropriate behavior.

Psychologists William Ittelson and Harold Proshansky observed and recorded the activities of patients in hospital rooms.[9] Comparing the sociability of patients in single room, double rooms, and wards, they found that when the number of patients in a room is smaller, social activity is greater. Psychologist Edwin Willems observed the location of patients' activities in a hospital and found that the area of a patient's activity is small in comparison with the total hospital size.[10] Willems also found that interaction between patients and nonpatients usually occurred in particular spaces.

Environmental psychologists Gary Winkel and Geoffrey Hayward observed people in subway stations in New York City to investigate causes of congestion.[11] They recorded where benches, stairs, vending machines, and columns were located and the places where people walked through or waited in the station. Their study resulted in a list of suggestions describing the placement of different elements, the best widths for stairs and aisles, and the size and shape of each area.

Research architects Henry Sanoff and Gary Coates studied children at play in a multifamily housing project for the project architects who wanted to see how children used the different types of outdoor play spaces. Observers noted the location, age group, sex, and activity of each child and recorded the number of children in a group, and the number and type of activities in each play area. Sanoff and Coates found that younger children were observed

most often, suggesting that the play areas were more conducive to their types of activities. The community open space had the highest frequency of all types of activities. Teenagers and adults were most often seen working on cars or conversing in the parking areas.

By observing unobtrusively, designers can learn what people do in the environment. It is a method of looking at action between people and their environments. The word *environment* might here include everything except the people themselves; the environment can be a complete building, a part of a building, or an outdoor area.

People may modify their actions if they realize they are being observed. To avoid this possibility, the observers can use a special booth with a one-way mirror or some other screening device so that the people cannot see them. In some environments, observers may take part in the activities rather than hide. In a hospital where the staff is large and patients are admitted and discharged daily, an observer walking in the hallway would not be noticed. Similarly, on a busy street, swiftly moving people may scarcely notice the observer. Observing unobtrusively allows the study of people's behavior without their realizing that their activities are important. It may prevent the distortion of people's behavior and therefore distortion of data about what people do in spaces.

Observations can be recorded by mechanical devices. A cine camera will record people's activities over a period of time, and a photograph will show what people are doing at a specific time. A tape recorder will record all the noises in a space, or an observer may use it to log quickly what he sees so that he can use the information later. Another device is the hodometer, a system of mats sensitive to pressure.[12] Each mat can be connected to a counter that records the number of footsteps on it. The floor of the art museum at the University of Kansas was covered with such mats, each a foot square, showing which paths most people took through the museum.

Valuable information can be obtained when behavior is systematically recorded. Casual observation may result in incomplete findings that show

GENERAL INFORMATION

Location of Observer _____

Time of Observation _____

Date _____

Weather Conditions _____

Activity Types _____

Objects Used _____

Physical Parts _____

PARTICIPANT INVENTORY

Participant	Black Male	Black Female	White Male	White Female
Infant				
Preschool				
Young Ch.				
Adolescent				
Teenager				
Adult				
Aged				

BEHAVIOR MECHANISM RATING

Mechanism	High	Medium	Low
Gross Motor			
Manipulat.			
Verbal			
Affective			
Thinking			
Mood	Active	Normal	Passive

Figure 11
Behavior settings data sheet. This can be used to organize and record information about the people. The participant inventory shows the kinds of people that use the space. The behavior mechanism rating and action pattern rating describe the group's activity according to several classifications.

only what seems to be obvious. Carefully planned observation will enable designers to accurately collect and use all the peices of information that describe human behavior. In order to observe systematically, four basic components should be considered.

1. What might one need to know about people? Important information could include the number of persons, the amount of time each is observed, the sex, age, and exact location of each person, and whether people are in groups. The behavior settings data sheet, shown in Figure 11,[13] provides room to record specific information on approximate age, race, sex, and the number of people in a group.

2. The observer can also record whether a person's behavior is active or passive. A subject can be considered active when his participation is necessary for an activity to continue, and passive if the activity would continue without his participation. For example, a person playing volleyball would be considered active, while a spectator of a volleyball game would be passive.

3. Activities will be the things people are doing—the defined, physical interaction between a person and an environmental cue. Having been designed to support specific activities, cues will tell people what activities should occur in a space. Different types of furniture and equipment will identify the activities each room was designed for. Activity sets are groups of activities that will occur together. These groups may be activities that serve the same purpose, or they may be made of one centrally important activity and those activities that support it. Figure 12 shows some of the activity sets Willems included in his hospital study: sleeping, hygiene, conversing, exercise, and nursing care. The activity set "exercise" includes such activities as walking, running, conversing, lifting weights, and special therapy. Some activities, such as "conversing," may occur in most of the activity sets.

4. What might one need to know about the setting? Cues should define settings, where the activity sets should occur. One may think of buildings as groups of rooms with physical boundaries: the ceiling, floor,

and walls. Each room may support one or more activity sets. A classroom may have such activity centers for science, math, reading, and art. A hospital foyer may have settings for visiting, admitting patients, discharging patients, giving out information. Since settings may not have physical boundaries such as walls, observers may need to divide each square into settings by dividing where each activity set occurs.

In order to evaluate timing each setting might be observed at specific time intervals, which will depend on how the activity schedule of the building affects people's behavior. Observations may not be relevant during special times such as holidays becuase behavior may change then. Observation should take place during a complete time cycle, a time period during which all activities occur. This cycle may be the five-day working week, or it may include the weekend if the building is in use seven days a week. It may even include several weeks or months. Weather may also be important, since it can affect human behavior.

In planning an observational study, decisions need to be made about the type of study desirable. Since buildings have been planned with spaces for activity sets, observations may help the investigator

ACTIVITY SETS

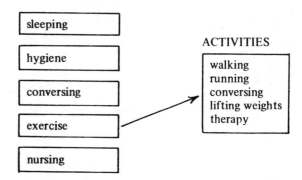

Figure 12

Activity–activity set relationship. Several activities may be a part of each activity set.

Time of Day _____

Date _____

Day of Week _____

Weather _____

MAIN FLOOR	Walking		Social Behavior		Other Activities		Total	
	E	O	E	O	E	O	E	O
Entrance lobby								
Major lounge								
Library								
Craft room								
Mailbox area								
Elevator area								
Total								

FLOOR	Open Doors	Laundry	Lounge		Hallway		Total	
			E	O	E	O	E	O
2								
3								
4								
5								
6								
7								
8								
9								
10								
11								
12								
13								
14								
Total								

Figure 13
Observation schedule. An observation schedule enables the careful recording of the different pieces of information. It can help the observer to organize what he sees, which simplifies the review and analysis of the data.

to find out wheteher the spaces are used for the planned activity sets. Comparisons of different types of spaces, planned for the same activity sets, can be made. (The Ittelson-Proshansky study mentioned earlier compared the social activities of hospital patients who stayed in single rooms, double rooms, and wards with several beds.) After it is decided what is to be looked for, decisions can be made about the parts of each of the four components needed to be observed and recorded.

A data form can be used to record each piece of information. (Figure 13 shows a sample data form.) There might be sections for the time of day, the date, day of the week, and the weather conditions. Or the form might have a place for each setting that will be observed. Figure 13 has spaces for various settings and places to record facts about people in each setting. It also has spaces to record the activity sets and the number of people in each setting, distinguishing between the elderly (E) and others (O). There can also be a space in which to record unexpected activities. Enough copies of the data sheet should be produced so that a new one can be used for each observation.

To discover how people use spaces, architects may wish to develop behavioral maps of the setting, which record people's locations and activities (see Figure 14). It may show people's behavior in each setting and indicate how cues (such as furniture and equipment) influence behavior. By noting people's locations and activities, designers can make determinations when conflicting activities occur in a particular setting. A behavioral map can be used to compare the number of people using a space with the number of people for which the space was designed. To make a behavioral map, a floor plan of the building or a site plan of an outdoor space should be drawn. People's locations can then be plotted on the plan and their behavior recorded. Each person should be located carefully in the plan so that groups can be identified.

Once the forms and plans have been prepared, the researcher can collect the data by observing each setting until all the settings have been observed the

desired number of times. The simple act of observation will suggest ways in which the data can be used. For behavioral maps, architects can transfer all the observations onto one plan to discover how people make use of each space. By looking at maps of different time periods, they can see how the spaces are used at different times.

To make use of the information on the data sheet, they can construct comparison charts to compare the number of people or activities in each space over a period of time (See Figure 16, which is based on the Figure 14 data sheet.) A chart such as that shown in Figure 16 may aid in a comparison of the number of people with different activities in each setting, and the number of activities that actually occur in the designed settings.

Observation and behavioral maps make a variety of studies possible. These techniques mentioned here can be used to describe people's behavior in part of a building, in a complete building, or in an outdoor space. They can be used for private, commercial, institutional, recreational, residential, and industrial environments. This discussion provides an overview of the way in which an observational study should be conducted. There cannot be simple, step-by-step instructions that cover all types of environments because of the variety of environmental settings that lend themselves to observation. The process will become more evident when a specific environment is approached with a plan to observe it. In the same way, it will be understood how the data can be used after conducting the observations. Observers should feel free to experiment with observational techniques and data, particularly since observational analyses contribute to one's intuition and subsequently to better design decisions.

Social Mapping and the Sociogram

Environmental analysis is a means of gaining insight into and evaluating certain connections between people and designed environments. It has been shown

Figure 14
Observation and behavioral mapping. A behavioral map shows the location of
people in an environment. The environment may be different parts of an out-
door area or different spaces in a building.

that the semantic rating scale aims at describing how people feel about qualities in an environment. How people feel is one kind of man-environment connection. Observation, behavioral mapping, and the activity log indicate what people do in particular spaces. A second man-environment connection is concerned with people's activities, the locations in which these activities occur, and, ultimately, how well these activities are accommodated. A third man-environment connection is the influence that the physical environment has on psychosocial behavior and the effects of this influence on relationships between people.

Social mapping enables the architect to explore

PEOPLE IN SETTINGS, ACCORDING TO TIME OF DAY													
Number of People in Each Space													
	Entrance		Lounge		Mailbox		Elevator		Library		Crafts		Total	
Time	E	O	E	O	E	O	E	O	E	O	E	O	E	O
8:00am														
9:00														
10:00														
11:00														
12:00														
1:00														
2:00														
3:00														
4:00														
5:00														
6:00														
7:00														
8:00														
9:00														
10:00														
Total														

Figure 15
Analysis charts. Analysis charts facilitate the comparison of different categories of information. For example, they may be used to compare such categories of information as the number of people, different types of people, the different spaces, or the time of day.

and identify the social interactions that exist between people in a particular environment. It is an approach that consists of preferences and rejections expressed by individuals in terms of how they perceive themselves in relation to other members of the group.

When architecture is considered in terms of its influence on social interactions, the spatial organization is one aspect commonly examined. Research psychologist B. W. P. Wells points out that spatial organization can be viewed in terms of both the physical and the functional distance between persons, groups, a nd activities.[14] In addition, Wells, architect W. Moleski, and others indicate that spatial organization can be looked upon as a communications network, an arrangement of parts that either helps or hinders social interaction and information flow.[15]

In a recent unpublished analysis of a North Carolina youth prison, an attempt was made to discover how various aspects of the environment were affecting the inmates.[16] Of particular importance was the

COMPARISON OF ACTIVITY SETS IN SPACES												
Activity	Entrance		Lounge		Library		Crafts		Elevator		Mail	
	E	O	E	O	E	O	E	O	E	O	E	O
Conversing												
Waiting												
Reading												
Singing												
Playing piano												
Walking												
Check out books												
Ceramics												
Handicrafts												
Total												

Figure 16
Analysis chart.

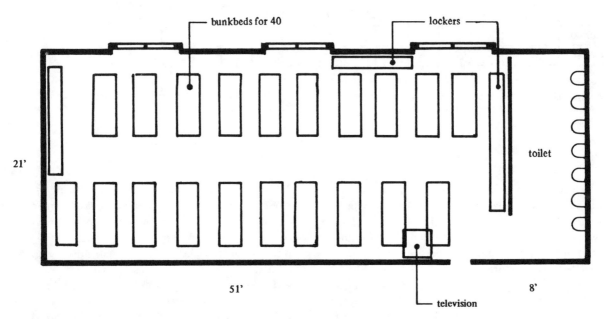

Figure 17
Original floor plan of bunkroom. This is the base map for the sociogram in

identification of sources of stress. Stress in the inmate was used as an indicator of points of discord between the inmates and the environment.

Evidence of environmentally induced stress was found. High density, lack of privacy, close proximity, uncontrollable noise, disagreements among adjacent bedmates about ventilation, smoking, and television watching were some of the factors cited as possible causes of stress. Since the inmates spent a great deal of time in the dormitory bunkroom (Figure 17), it was hypothesized that possible changes in this location might lower the stress levels of many of the inmates. Two potential sources for change existed. The first was to alter some elements of the spatial organization. A second was to alter the social organization.

By asking each inmate in one of the bunkrooms to list his three best friends, information was generated to identify who was friendly with whom. Figure 18 shows a friendship rank of the inmates. By giving a first choice three points, a second choice two points, and a third one point, it was possible to rank the choices by who was chosen the most, down to the inmate chosen the least. The ranking was a result of summing up the number of points scored by each inmate.

A scaled floor plan with beds identified was used as a base for mapping the friendship patterns. Figure 19 shows that since primary choices were not among adjacent bedmates, it was clear that proximity was not a strong determinant of friendship patterns that developed in prison bunkroom settings.

Figure 20 is a conceptual diagram showing a plot of the first two choices. Each inmate, represented by his bunk number, was connected to his first choice (solid arrow) and to his second choice (broken arrow). This composite friendship diagram shows clusters and links between them. These clusters became a potential guide for an alternative arrangement of the social organization of the inmates.

Recalling that density, privacy, proximity, and disagreements among adjacent bedmates were suggested as possible sources of environmentally induced

INMATE BED NUMBER	RANK	SCORE
15	1	26
37	2	20
38	3	14
8	4	13
39	5	12
1	6	10
26,23	7	8
	8	
34,19	9	7
	10	
13,2	11	6
	12	
17,16,14	13	5
3,35,22	14	
	15	
	16	
	17	
	18	
30,21,40	19	4
	20	
	21	
24	22	3
	23	
29,36	24	2
	25	
32,7,11	26	1
	27	
	28	
33,5,10,12	29	0
28,27,25	30	
	31	
	32	
	33	

Figure 18
Friendship rank of inmates. Each inmate is identified by his bed number. An inmate who is a first choice is given three points, a second choice two points, a third choice one point. The ranking is a result of summing up the number of points each inmate scored by being chosen.

stress, the question then was what spatial and/or social elements could be changed in order to reduce some of that stress.

One possible alternative was to encourage group solidarity and friendship. This goal suggested that perhaps proximity of friends in the bunkroom would be more meaningful than arranging nonfriends near

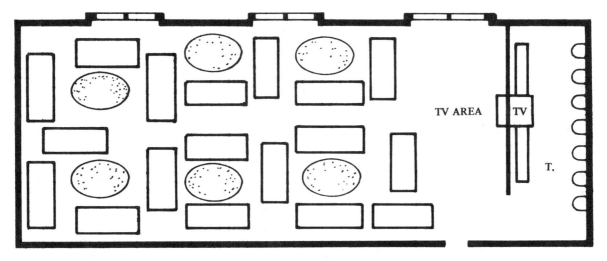

Figure 21
Suggested spatial reordering. This spatial and social reordering resulted from
the friendship choices. It is an example of a physical or spatial change in response
to social-interaction data.

There are two types of sociograms. the first, mutual choice, has a lateral quality and is concerned with social relations among peers (persons being connected by a liking or disliking relationship). The second, the all-choice or hierarchical sociogram, has a vertical, as well as a horizontal, quality.

Two patterns occur in sociograms—that of choosing and that of being chosen. The position of the circles and arrows is determined by the similarity in choosing and being chosen.

In terms of the direction of the data being plotted, there are two general tendencies: upward flow and downward flow. Upward flow tends to occur when describing the direction of questions and suggestions. Downward flow tends to occur when decisions, guidelines, and information flow are being plotted.

A final characteristic of the sociogram is that it may show both clusters—where an individual is chosen by several others—and isolates—where an individual is chosen by no one.

Wells's study of the formation of work groups in an office building demonstrates some possible effects of spatial arrangements on social interactions.[18] The degree of reciprocity in friendship choices was used as the existence of cohesive work groups. Wells questioned 295 office workers on one floor about whom they preferred to work next to. Of the total respondents, 214 worked in a large open area and eighty-one in one of three small enclosed areas. The results indicated that there were distinct differences between social interaction in the large and in the small work areas.

Choices were directly related to the distances between workers, with men and women preferring others who were already in close proximity. Workers in the small enclosed areas more frequently preferred office mates from their own section. There were more mutual choices in the small area groups. In addition, they formed more cohesive groups with fewer links to other groups. More isolates (individuals chosen by no one) were found in the small area groups. The open area group was characterized by

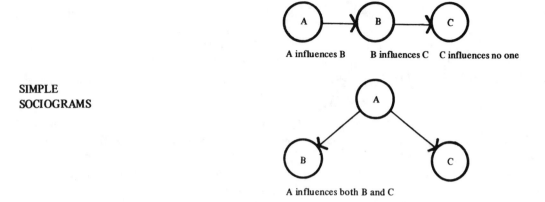

A influences B   B influences C   C influences no one

A influences both B and C

SIMPLE SOCIOGRAMS

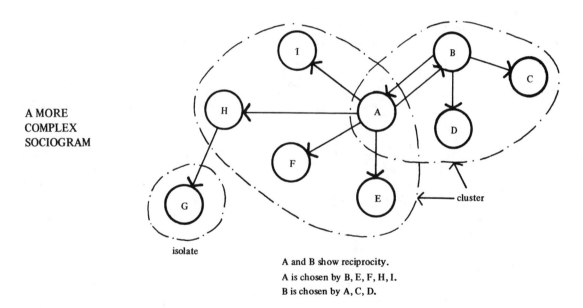

A MORE COMPLEX SOCIOGRAM

isolate   cluster

A and B show reciprocity.
A is chosen by B, E, F, H, I.
B is chosen by A, C, D.

Figure 22
Symbols for sociograms. The sociogram symbols are the circle, which represents
an individual, and the arrow, which represents the direction of influence.

having a lower proportion of reciprocity; there were fewer mutual choices, less cohesion, and better interconnections to other departments.

In addition to Wells, J. T. Gullahorn has shown that, in the office setting, the frequency of social interaction and friendship choice are closely related to spatial relationships.[19]

In a recent unpublished analysis of a problem-solving agency, the researchers attempted to evaluate the staff members as they performed activities in their physical setting and evaluate the performance of the physical setting in terms of how it accommodated social behavior along with the activities.[20]

Each respondent was asked to rank order in terms of importance who affected him the most in the following ways: (1) those authorized to pass on information, policy, and guidelines; (2) those from whom they received the information vital to their position; (3) those on the secretarial staff with whom they worked the most; (4) those on the professional staff with whom they worked the most; (5) those with whom they were most friendly; (6) those with whom they preferred to work; (7) those who were influenced most by one's activities; (8) those who influenced most one's own activities; (9) those who were key decision makers.

Sociograms were plotted for each ranking to each question. Figures 23 and 24 show two sociograms that resulted from the question, "From whom do you receive information necessary in the performance of your job?" Figure 23 is a hierarchical sociogram with a downward flow. The network itself forms a large cluster. There are no isolates. Figure 24, the second-choice sociogram, is also hierarchical and shows one large cluster, made up of three subgroups. Note the similarities in choosing and being chosen around Team Leader A (TL/A).

Analysis of the sociograms demonstrated that there were indeed differences between the formal organizational structure of the problem-solving agency and the actual functioning organization. The sociograms indicated that some of the staff members were influential beyond the scope of their defined positions. The change to accommodate this finding may have been nonphysical, that is, redefinition of the scope of each position. If the change were to have been physical, a spatial reordering to allow closer proximity of the source of influence and those who were influenced was possible.

Another finding from the sociograms was that the staff itself was operationally quite casual—yet it was defined to be formal in structure. This disparity was indicated by a strong preference for personal contact in the exchange of information. The spatial organization of the office setting might have reflected and encouraged the lack of formality.

There is a basic procedure for using the sociogram. First, decide upon the critical issues being tested and formulate the hypotheses. (In Wells's study[21] the issue was the actual influence of office size on social interaction.) Second, determine the questions to be asked. Be specific about what the choice means. For example, is the question about friendship, about perceived authority, or about information flow? Third, devise a reply sheet similar to that shown in Figure 25. Preferences are to be given in a ranked order. Fourth, determine what an adequate sample is. For a group with fewer than forty people, each individual should be a respondent. For a group with more than forty people, make certain that a distribution of the overall group is represented. Next, sort the data in terms of the critical issues being tested. Then plot a sociogram for each ranked choice. If one question calls for three choices, there should be a sociogram for each ranking. The analysis of the data, which can be carried out in two phases, is next in the process. The first is to determine the effect of personal variables (such as sex or age) and position on the choices made. The second phase is to determine the physical distance (measured on a scaled floor plan) between the person making the choice and the individuals being chosen. Finally, based on the findings, evaluate the existing setting and explore possible spatial and social reorganization that may encourage a more responsive connection between man and the particular environment.

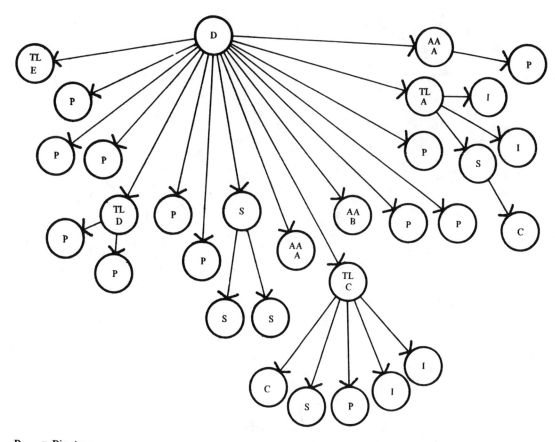

D = Director
P = Professional
TL = Team Leader
AA = Administrative
      Assistant
S = Secretary
I = Intern
C = Consultant

First Ranking Sociogram For:
"From whom do you receive
information necessary in the
performance of your job?"

Figure 23
Example of a sociogram. Note the large cluster around D and the smaller clusters around TLD, S, TLC, TLA.

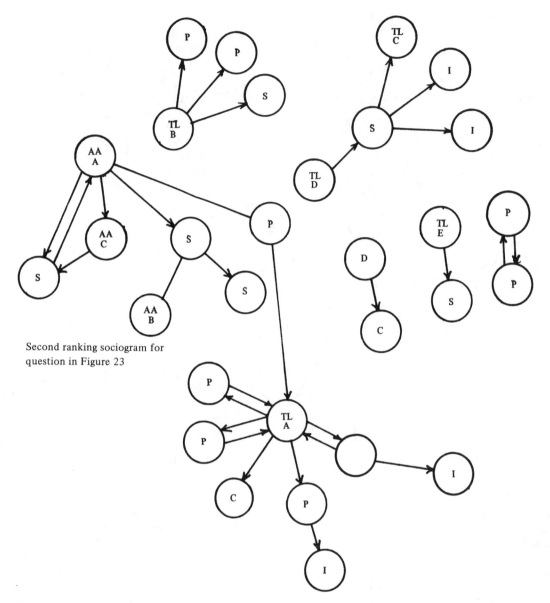

Second ranking sociogram for
question in Figure 23

Figure 24
**Example of a sociogram. Note clusters, reciprocity, isolates. See Figure 23 for
key to symbols.**

ALL REPLY SHEETS ARE CONFIDENTIAL

NAME_____ DATE_____

1. Who are the three persons you prefer to work with?
   Rank order the three choices:
   a)_____
   b)_____
   c)_____

2. Who are the three persons you confide in?
   Rank order the three choices:
   a)_____
   b)_____
   c)_____

Figure 25
Reply sheet. Each respondent is given a reply sheet. A time limit of thirty to sixty seconds is adequate for each question to be answered. Each group of answers to each question is plotted on a sociogram, or, as in Figure 24, a composite can be made.

NAME _____   DATE_____

TIME	ACTIVITY	PURPOSE	PARTICIPANTS	LOCATION	EQUIPMENT
8:00 to 8:15					
8:15 to 8:30					
8:30 to 8:45					
8:45 to 9:00					
9:00 to 9:15					

Figure 26
Activity log form. An activity log form can be filled out for a workday or for a twenty-four-hour period. The time increments will vary depending upon the type of setting being evaluated. This figure should serve only as an example, to be modified if necessary.

Social mapping and the sociogram offer the architect a chance to extend evaluation of a physical setting toward a point closer to understanding man, his activities, his goals, and his social interactions as they occur in a designed environment. These techniques, although quite simple to use, help in demonstrating somewhat complex pieces of information: how individuals in a group interrelate and what these relationships mean in terms of a spatial organization.

Activity Log

The activity log is a means by which an architect can discover how people use spaces over a period of time. It is essentially an observation tool. Rather than being oberved—as in unobtrusive observation—the subject is required to observe himself. Self-observation is like keeping a diary in which entries are made at regular, predetermined time increments over a specified number of days. Figure 26 shows a log form.

While it is generally recognized that most people usually follow a daily routine, the places in which these activities are carried out will often vary. Activity logs enable the architect to discover relationships between people, places, activities, and time durations. These relationships in turn provide insight into how accommodating a designed environment actually is.

In an analysis of high-rise dormitories at the University of California at Berkeley, research architects Van der Ryn and Silverstein used the activity log to help assess how effective the dormitories were in accommodating the students and their activities.[22] Since studying occupied more student time than any other single activity, it was assumed that the quality of a student's learning effort was, in part, related to the environment in which studying was undertaken. Eighty students volunteered to observe themselves by recording their activities at each hour over a four-day

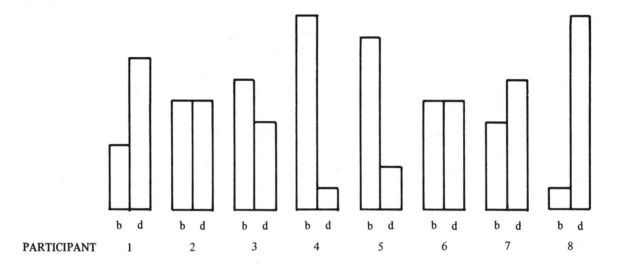

b = bed
d = desk

Figure 27

Data graph. Each participant's study time equals 100 percent. To demonstrate to which location the bed and the desk are actually moved, tabulate the percentage of 100 percent for the bed and the desk. Participant 4 spent 90 percent of his study time on the bed, and 10 percent at the desk.

period. On the log form the students recorded what they were doing (activity), where they were (location), what furniture or equipment they were using, and the number of interruptions that occurred.

Two kinds of information resulted from the completed activity logs. First, the data were organized to describe relations among activities, locations, furniture, and frequency of use. In other words, each item was compared with the others. These comparisons began to show relationships that were, to some extent, constant. For example, during study hours, roommates rarely occupied their room together. In addition, the results revealed whether a location (space) was being used for those activities it was intended to accommodate and whether the particular location was effective in supporting the activities

that actually occurred in it. It was found that the bed—not the desk—was the primary piece of study furniture. Reading and writing were commonly done on the bed while the desk was used for storage.

A second kind of information provided by the data focused on group or social activities: where and when the students met, what activities tended to occur simultaneously, which activities were sequential (that is, which ones tended to follow another), and where these activities occurred. The findings indicated that spontaneous social exchange occurring in corridors and the laundry room were dominant and that the lounges and large gorup spaces were not very supportive of social interaction.

Here again, it was possible to discover whether a space was actually accommodating the activities for which it was intended. Furthermore, by looking at group activities, it was possible to find out potential strategies for change in the spaces to better support the students' social activities.

The respondents for the activity logs in the Berkeley dormitory analysis constituted a homogenous group. All eighty respondents were students. It was not so vital to know who did what. The emphasis was on the activities, locations, equipment, and furniture. In another case study the activity log was used by a heterogeneous (diverse) group of respondents. The individuals in this group were members of a staff of an organization. In this instance, each staff member was definable by a range of tasks (activities) for which he was responsible. In this case, who performed an activity became an important piece of information.

In an attempt to evaluate the effectiveness of an educational problem-solving group as it functioned in its physical environment, the activity log was used to find out what the staff members did over the course of time. The items of the log that were recorded at fifteen-minute intervals over a two-day period were: the activity, the purpose of the activity, the staff participants, the nonstaff participants, the number of people involved, and the location.

The resulting information was analyzed in three ways. First, the various activities were described in terms of frequency of occurrence, the participants, and the supporting locations. Second, the locations were looked at in terms of frequency of use, the participants, and the activities performed therein. Third, the particular persons were described in turn by the activities, locations, and the time they spent involved in the various activities.

After the logs were completed, the relationships were achieved by arranging the information by the percentages of time involved in various activities in terms of types of persons involved. This approach began to delineate a range of activities of different groups, which, in part, defined the basis of the staff's structure.

To use an activity log first determine the hypotheses to be tested. Then devise a log form that provides spaces for entries to be made in terms of time, activity, location, furniture, and other items as needed. Try to get subjects to volunteer. If the group is small, say under thirty people, you will want everyone to observe himself. For groups with more than thirty people, the sample ought to be representative of the group. Determine an adequate time increment (fifteen minutes, thirty minutes, hourly) and the number of days for the subjects to observe themselves. As a general rule, those people—as the students—whose routine activities are likely to extend over an hour's time (classes, study, eating, socializing) may make entries at that increment. In the office example, activities are frequent, diverse, and quite often take only a few minutes. Therefore, a smaller increment is chosen. Once the logs have been completed, sort the data in terms of the different hypotheses being tested and group and record the data on graphs and charts. To analyze the data, set up correlations between three general items: (1) the activity with respect to frequency of types, participants,

	1. ACTIVITY	2. ACTIVITY	3. ACTIVITY	4. ACTIVITY	5. ACTIVITY	6. ACTIVITY	7. ACTIVITY
PARTICIPANT 1							
PARTICIPANT 2							
PARTICIPANT 3							
PARTICIPANT 4							
PARTICIPANT 5							

Figure 28
Percentage correlation chart for activity log data. This is an example of a chart used for recording individual participation in activities. The percentages are obtained by dividing the time interval for the individual by the total time intervals for that individual. The same chart format will serve to record other correlations such as activity location.

furniture and equipment, intensity, sequence, prox- imity, and extent; (2) each location with respect to total frequency of all types of activities, frequency of particualr activities, range of activities, similarities among locations, participant, number of participants, and density; and (3) the participants with respect to density, activities, locations, and equipment. When the data have been analyzed, explore what possible physical changes may be made to encourage the effectiveness of the physical environment as a place for people doing things.

There are several advantages to the activity log. It has a potential for analyzing designed environments whose participants have diverse goals and unlike backgrounds. The data generated from activity logs can be a useful method of obtaining information for evaluating people's verbally specified behavior, particularly in settings occupied by a few individuals where an observer would interfere with the various types of behavior he was monitoring. Finally, the activity log provides an impression of the dynamics of people, activities, and location over time.

COMPARISON METHODS

This section includes various methods for compar- ing statements or concepts to determine orders of preference and desirability. Ranking is an ordering concept most frequently used to compare design objectives, evaluation criteria, and alternative solu- tions to a problem. Each method is described and accompanied with an illustration of its most practical application.

Paired Comparisons Method

Purpose The paired comparisons method is a psychological scaling method that can be used to de- termine the attitudes of individuals toward a given psychological object. This technique was used to de- termine the attitudes of the North Carolina State Uni-

versity Architecture faculty with regard to the content of a new curriculum. In this study, nine factors were listed, and the faculty was requested to select the six possible pairs. The task was to rank order, in terms of importance, the components of a "desirable" architec- tural curriculum as expressed by the faculty. The data from this study are used as an example of the paired comparison method.[23]

Description The ordering of objects upon the basis of judgments is said to be on a psychological continu- um. The paired comparisons method is $n(n-1)/2$ pairs of statements that require comparative judgments as to which member of each pair is more favorable. The oridinal data will consist of frequencies corresponding to the number of times that each statement is judged more favorable than every other statement. Their rela- tive degree of favorableness is scaled along a psycho- logical continuum ranging from least to most favorable.

Figure 29 shows the list of factors given to the fac- ulty. Figure 30 gives the thirty-six paired comparison choices and instructions for making a selection. Figure 31 gives the F matrix, or the frequency with which each column statement was judged more favorable than the row statement. The diagonal entries involving a comparison of each statement with itself are as- sumed to be equal to $N/2$ (3.5). In the example pre- sented the total number of comparative judgments for each pair of statements is 7, the number of individuals making the judgments. The total number of judgments made by each individual is $n(n-1)/2$, or 36.

Figure 29.
List of factors.

1. Building materials.
2. Construction systems and production.
3. Perception and communication in the environment.
4. Design methods.
5. Man and environment.
6. Graphic communication.
7. History of the environment.
8. Social and cultural factors in architectural design.
9. Environmental control systems.

Figure 30
Paired comparison table. Place a circle around the statement in each pair judged to be most favorable

①	2	3	4	5	6	7	8
2	③	4	5	6	7	8	9
1	2	3	4	5	6	7	
③	4	5	6	7	8	9	
1	2	3	4	5	6		
4	5	6	7	8	9		
1	2	3	4	5			
5	6	7	8	9			
1	2	3	4				
6	7	8	9				
1	2	3					
7	8	9					
1	2						
8	9						
1							
9							

Statements	1	2	3	4	5	6	7	8	9
1		5	6	7	6	1	5	5	4
2	2		4	6	5	1	3	4	4
3	1	3		3	5	1	4	5	2
4	0	1	3		4	1	3	4	3
5	1	1	1	3		2	3	5	2
6	6	5	5	6	5		5	6	5
7	2	3	2	4	4	2		4	4
8	2	3	1	3	2	1	3		1
9	3	3	4	4	5	1	3	6	

Figure 31
F matrix for nine statements made by seven individuals. This matrix gives the frequency with which each column stimulus was judged more favorably than the row stimulus. Reciprocal of $N = 1/7$. Each cell in the F matrix is multiplied by 0.143 as shown by corresponding figures in the P matrix in Figure 32.

Figure 32 gives the *P* matrix corresponding to the *F* matrix of Figure 32. If we let *n* be the total number of individuals doing the judging, then, although comparative judgments are not obtained for each stimulus

State-ments	1	2	3	4	5	6	7	8	9
1	.5	.715	.858	1.001	.858	.143	.715	.715	.572
2	.286	.5	.572	.858	.715	.143	.429	.572	.572
3	.143	.429	.5	.429	.715	.143	.572	.715	.286
4	0	.143	.429	.5	.572	.143	.429	.572	.429
5	.143	.143	.143	.429	.5	.286	.429	.715	.286
6	.858	.715	.715	.858	.715	.5	.715	.858	.715
7	.286	.429	.286	.572	.572	.246	.5	.572	.572
8	.286	.429	.143	.429	.286	.143	.429	.5	.143
9	.429	.429	.572	.572	.715	.143	.429	.858	.5

Figure 32
P matrix corresponding to F matrix of Figure 31.

with itself, it may be assumed that if such judgments had been obtained, f_{ij} would be equal to $n/2$. (f_{ij} means the frequency with which the ith or column stimulus is judged more favorable than the jth or row stimulus.) If each of the cell entries of Figure 31 is divided by n, this will give p_{ij} entries shown in Figure 32. The cell entries in this table give the proportion of times that the column stimulus is judged more favorable than the row stimulus. These entries may be obtained most conveniently by multiplying the cell entries of Figure 31 by the reciprocal of n. $p_{ij} = (1/n)f_{ij}$.

Figure 33 gives the *Z* matrix corresponding to the *P* matrix of Figure 32[24] (by means of Table 1 in the Appendix of *Techniques of Attitude Scale Construction* by Edwards). Cell entries are from the Table of Normal Deviates *Z* corresponding to Proportions of a Dichotomized Unit Normal Distribution. The final rank order of the nine factors in this example is obtained from the *Z* matrix tabulation. This is shown in Figure 34.

Method of triads In this method each pair of stimuli is judged $n-2$ times, where *n* is the number of stimuli. Each pair of stimuli is a constituent of a triad with each of the remaining stimuli in turn, and when the individual says of the stimuli *A*, *B*, and *C* that he prefers *A* most and *C* least, he is placing them in a rank order of preference *A*, *B*, *C*. This rank order of preference is equivalent to three transitive paired compari-

Statement	1	2	3	4	5	6	7	8	9
	.000	.568	1.07	2.326	1.071	-1.067	.568	.568	.181
	-.565	.000	.181	1.071	.568	-1.067	-.179	.181	.181
	-1.054	-.179	.000	-.179	.568	-1.067	.181	.568	-.565
	-3.09	-1.067	-.179	.000	.181	-1.067	-.179	.181	-.179
	-1.067	-1.067	-1.067	-.179	.000	-.565	-.179	.568	-.565
	1.071	.568	.568	1.071	.568	.000	.568	1.071	.568
	-.565	-.179	.565	.181	.181	-.565	.000	.181	.181
	-.565	-.179	-1.067	-.179	-.565	-1.067	-.179	.000	-1.067
	-.179	-.179	.181	.181	.568	-1.067	-.179	1.071	.000
(1) Sums	-6.014	-3.325	-.878	+4.293	+3.140	-7.532	+.422	+4.389	-1.265
(2) Means	-.668	-.369	-.097	+.477	+.349	-.837	+.047	+.487	-.140
(3) Means + .760	.268	.687	1.433	2.007	1.879	.000	1.577	2.017	1.390

Figure 33
**Z matrix corresponding to P matrix of Figure 32. From Table 1 in the appendix to A.
Edwards, *Techniques of Attitude Scale Construction* (New York: Appleton-Century-Crofts,
1957). Cell entries are from the Table of Normal Deviates Z Corresponding to Proportions
P of a Dichotomized Unit Normal Distribution in Edwards, p. 246.**

Z Matrix Tabulation	Factor Number	Rank Order
2.017	8	1
2.017	4	2
1.879	5	3
1.577	7	4
1.433	3	5
1.390	9	6
.687	2	7
.268	1	8
.000	6	9

Figure 34

sons *AB*, *BC*, *AC*. It is important to note that this transitivity has been imposed by the method. Because each paired comparison judgment between a given pair of stimuli is made $n-2$ times, it is apparent that the method of triads permits the consistency of a paired comparison judgment to be tested in the context of a third stimulus.

Evaluation Inconsistency in judgments occurs whenever there is a "circular" triad present in the $n(n-1)/2$ judgments. For example, if statement *A* in a set of *n* statements judged on a continuum is judged more favorable than statement *B*, and statement *B* is judged more favorable than statement *C*, then to be consistent, the subject should judge statement *A* to be more favorable than statement *C*. If statement *C*, on the other hand, is judged more favorable than statement *A*, these three comparative judgments would constitute a circular triad. The greater the number of circular triads occurring in a set of comparative number of judgments of a given subject, the more inconsistent the subject may be said to be. Above a certain number of circular triads (10 percent) the scale may be invalid.

Ranking Chart

Purpose This chart is a device that enables a rank ordering to be stated when the alternatives are not easily differentiable or when the alternatives appear to be of equal value. The test reduces the decision-making process to a series of choices between pairs of alternatives.

As a tool, it is valuable to individuals and to groups.

It enables individuals to clearly see their decision-making process, and it allows groups to decide upon areas of emphasis and indicates the group attitudes concerning alternate courses of action.

Description The alternatives from which a ranking is desired are placed in a matrix (see Figure 35).[25] A binary notation is used to record individual preferences. If the vertical factor is preferred to the horizontal factor, a 1 is placed in the box. If, however, the horizontal factor is preferred to the vertical one, a 0 is placed in the intersecting box. This procedure is repeated until all horizontal factors have been compared to all vertical factors, excluding the neutral row where a factor is compared to itself. When the process has been completed, the 1s are totaled for each row, and the rank ordering of the items is revealed.

Suppose that it is desired to determine the importance to a particular social class of eight criteria for buying a house. The test would be administered to a random sample of the group. Each individual would produce his own rank ordering of the factors. The individual rankings are compiled in a table similar to Figure 36.

Evaluation The horizontal rows of Figure 36 are

	Judges (Group)												Total	Rank
Factors	A	B	C	D	E	F	G	H	I	J	K	L	Total	Rank
Cost	4	3	3	2	1	4	1						18	1
Neighborhood	8	2	6	5	5	2	2						30	4
Schools	6	6	2	3	4	5	3						29	3
Churches	1	1	5	6	2	1	4						19	2
Amenities	3	5	8	1	3	8	5						33	5
Friends	2	7	4	7	7	7	6						40	7
Ethnic Ties	5	4	7	4	8	3	7						38	6
Distance	7	8	1	8	6	6	8						44	8

Figure 36

totaled, and the Kendall coefficient of concordance test is applied to determine the extent of association among the several sets of rankings.[26] The test helps determine the agreement among the various individuals taking the test. A high or significant value of the degree of concordance may be interpreted as meaning that the judges or participants applied the same standards in ranking the factors under study. The pooled or social ordering that results from a significant value does not mean that the ordering is correct. It may easily be incorrect with respect to some external criteria. All the people may agree in ordering the factors because all may have applied the wrong criteria.

If a significant value of concordance is obtained, the best estimate of the "true" ranking of the factors is provided by the order of the various sums of the ranks. The most important or preferred factor is the one with the smallest sum of the individual rankings (cost, with a total of 18 in Figure 36).

The chart is useful because it systemizes and records the procedure by which an ordering is developed. Two significant difficulties should be noted, however, which hinder its usefulness. Perhaps the most serious problem is the fact that subjects taking the test are not forced to be transitive. In simpler terms, a subject may indicate a preference of factor *A* over factor *B* and factor *B* over factor *C*, and then indicate that *C* is preferred to *A*. There is no clear explanation for such an occurrence. It seems probable that one of two things

COST OF HOUSE
NEIGHBORHOOD
SCHOOLS
CHURCHES
CULTURAL AMENITIES
FRIENDS & RELATIVES
ETHNIC TIES
DISTANCE TO WORK

Figure 35

is happening: either there is little real preference between the three factors or the subject is being confused by the test. These two possibilities also apply to the second major difficulty.

The test compares each pair of factors twice. Subjects taking the test often reverse their preferences. The first time they indicate a preference for *A* over *B* and later they prefer factor *B* over *A*. Again it is not known whether indifference or complexity causes this phenomenon.

Preference Matrix

Purpose This test is a modification of the ranking chart. As such, the overall purposes are similar to the ranking chart: to systematically develop a rank ordering from a set of alternatives that are not easily differentiable.

Description The test simplifies and reduces the actions of the subjects taking the test. The ranking chart requires each factor to be compared twice. This can complicate and confuse the subjects, however, thereby reducing the usefulness and reliability of the test.

The factors of alternatives that are to be ordered, are placed in a chart similar to Figure 37, and each factor is given an identifying number. Each factor is compared to all other factors, and each time a priority is established. The number of the factor with the higher priority is written in the intersecting box. After all the items have been compared, the numbers are tabulated by counting the number of times each number appears. The number that appears most often represents the item of greatest importance. The factor that is represented the second greatest number of times is ranked second, and so on serially through all items.

Using the same problem as used in the ranking chart we may arrive at the same results, using the matrix in Figure 37. This particular example places distance to work as the most important consideration in the selec-

Rank*	Tabulation*	
2	6	1. Cost
4	4	2. Neighborhood
3	5	3. Schools
7	1	4. Churches
5	3	5. Cultural Amenities
6	2	6. Friends & Rel.
8	0	7. Ethnic Ties
1	7	8. Dist. to Work

*To be Completed By Investigator

Figure 37
Preference matrix.

tion of a house, and ethnic ties as the least important consideration.

Evaluation The evaluation of a group of modified preference tests is identical to the evaluation of the ranking chart. The problems of intransitivity still apply to all groups, and the test has proven too complicated for unsophisticated groups. The yielding of identical results with less time and effort on the part of the subjects is a distinct advantage however.

Ranking and Weighting Method

Purpose The procedure is predicated upon opinion in order to establish quantitative relationships among variables that cannot be obtained by theoretical considerations or by previous data resulting from past performance. These opinions are solicited either individually or collectively and indicate preferential merits of each variable as compared to the value of combinations of variables within the same system. The final decision is reached after continuous reevaluations of each variable and a relative ranking established on an arbitrary scale that is consistent with each of the decisions reported during the evaluation process.

Description The first step in the procedure is the tentative listing of variables in their order of importance. The variable at the head of the list is arbitrarily assigned a value of 100, and the remaining variables are assigned numerical values indicating their estimated importance relative to this variable. These values are qualitative in nature and serve only as a temporary ranking for subsequent readjustment.[27]

The individual, or group, is then requested to register an opinion as to the relative merit of the initial variable compared to the combined effect of the second and third variables in the listing. The three possible responses to the question are: (1) the initial variable is more important than variables two and three; (2) it is less important; (3) they are equal. In the case of the first response, the value assigned to the second and third variables, which were used for comparison. Conversely the latter total must exceed the first value if the second response is received. Obviously, they must be equal in the event of the third response. This procedure is repeated until the initial variable has been compared with all combinations of two variables within the previous listing.

In a similar manner, the second variable is compared with combinations of variables below it in the original listing. This process is continued until each variable has been evaluated and the numerical values adjusted to conform with the individual decisions.

The qualities of an environment as ranked in order of importance without assigning quantitative values.

O_1	Spaciousness
O_2	Beauty
O_3	A character that is good for children
O_4	Exclusiveness

A tentative value of 1.00 is assigned to O_1 (the most valued variable) and values that initially seem to reflect the relative values of the other variables (O_2 = 0.80, O_3 = 0.50, O_4 = 0.30). The table below represents the first estimates of the "true" values.

V_1	1.00	O_1
V_2	0.80	O_2
V_3	0.50	O_3
V_4	0.30	O_4

A comparison is then made of spaciousness (O_1) versus beauty (O_2), a character that is good for children (O_3), and exclusiveness (O_4). O_1 versus (O_2 and O_3 and O_4).

If spaciousness is preferable to the sum of the other variables, then the value of V_1 would be adjusted so that $V_1 > V_2 + V_3 + V_4$.

Retaining the values of O_2, O_3, O_4, assume that the new value for spaciousness (O_1) V_1 = 2.00. If it is also assumed that the second ranking objective, (O_2) beauty is not preferred to O3 + O4, then further adjustment is necessary (V2 H V3 + V4).

$$
\begin{aligned}
\text{Then} \quad V_1 &= 2.00 \\
V_2 &= 0.70 \\
V_3 &= 0.50 \\
V_4 &= \underline{0.30} \\
&\ \ \ 3.50
\end{aligned}
$$

The values are now consistent with the evaluations. To normalize the values divide each by 3.50.

$$
\begin{aligned}
V_1 &= 2.00/3.50 = 0.57 \\
V_2 &= 0.70/3.50 = 0.20 \\
V_3 &= 0.50/3.50 = 0.14 \\
V_4 &= 0.30/3.50 = \underline{0.09} \\
&\quad\quad\quad \text{Total} = 1.00
\end{aligned}
$$

Evaluation The method does not provide any estimate of the accuracy or bias of the judgments. This serious defect is shared by all existing techniques for estimating the measures of preferences. If two or more weighters were to list items in order of importance, and their results disagreed, there would be little basis for arbitration. Herein the specific points of agreement and disagreement are exposed, facilitating the attainment of ultimate agreement.

Ranking and Weighting a Large Number of Objectives

Purpose When faced with the task of establishing quantitative relationships among a large number of objectives, it may become necessary to adopt a procedural variation of the ranking and weighting method.[28]

Description 1. Rank the entire set of objectives in terms of preference without assigning quantitative values: $O_1, O_2, \ldots, O_{12}$.

2. By random assignment, subdivide the set of objectives into groups of equal size. Each objective should be included in one and only one group.

Group A	Group B	Group C
O_4	O_7	O_9
O_{12}	O_{11}	O_6
O_5	O_8	O_1
O_{10}	O_2	O_3

3. Select at random one objective from each group formed in step 2.

4. Using the method of weighting objectives, obtain unstandardized values for the objectives formed in the group (see the ranking and weighting method above):

$$O_3 = 1.00$$
$$O_4 = 0.60$$
$$O_8 = 0.30$$

5. Replace the objectives in the group from which they were drawn. Use the same method to establish unstandardized values for each group formed in step 2.

6. Compare the rankings obtained in steps 2–5 of this procedure with those obtained in step 1. If the rank orders differ, reconsider the ranking and if necessary proceed again from steps 2–6 of this procedure.

Group A	Group B	Group C
$O_4 = 0.60$	$O_2 = 0.09$	$O_1 = 1.20$
$O_5 = 0.50$	$O_7 = 0.35$	$O_3 = 1.00$
$O_{10} = 0.20$	$O_8 = 0.30$	$O_6 = 0.45$
$O_{12} = 0.15$	$O_{11} = 0.10$	$O_9 = 0.25$

7. Standardize the values obtained in step 5 by dividing the value assigned to each objective by the sum of the values assigned to all the objectives.

Design (Morphological) Matrix

Purpose The first step in all organized design processes is to establish and set out the field of investigation. The morphological way of doing this is to produce a design matrix, a visual mapping of alternate ways of achieving design solutions.[29] Parameters are what the object must be or must have and are listed vertically, while the corresponding means of achieving the required characteristics of the parameters are listed horizontally. The ensuing work assumes that the best solution or solutions to the problem must be contained in the field defined by the design matrix.

One column of the field represents one solution or variation of the way in which the problem may be answered and, hence, even a small field will contain a very large number of solutions.

Description The parameters of the field should be as independent as possible from one another. In a good field the parameters will be completely independent so that there will be no connection between the "steps" of one row and the next. A complete "column" solution is then obtained by taking any one "step" from each row, so that the totality of solutions is given by simply multiplying the number of "steps" in the second row, and so on, throughout the field. A complete "column" solution is then obtained by selecting one cell from each row. (See Figure 38.)

Before it is possible to use the design matrix to ar-

Parameter	Description		
Solar Shielding	Shielding of glass	Shielding of glass & walls	Shielding of glass & walls from solar & ground radia- tion
Ventilation	10% of floor area for open- ings	low inlet high outlet	high inlet low outlet
Insulation	high capacity	low capacity	Reflective
Geometry	1:1	1:15	1:2
Roof Slope	Flat	30° shed to North	45° shed to North
Orientation	long-axis North-South	long-axis Northwest- Southeast	long-axis East-West

Figure 38
Microclimatic influences on design.

rive at design solutions, it is necessary to determine the basis of comparison used to make matrix chores. Next, it is necessary to decide upon the factors and assumptions that will be used to make the basis of comparison quantitative. This quantification of the basis of comparison acts as a "filter" or "sieve," and the tolerance of acceptability may be governed accordingly.

Next, it is necessary to reduce the field of investigation by a process of elimination using the basis of comparison and any other means. This reduction may be carried out by means of analysis of rows and analysis of columns.

In analyzing by rows, if each row can be optimized separately from each other row in terms of the basis for comparison, then the optimum from each row gives the overall optimum for the complete chart. Analyzing by columns is more complex in that it implies analysis of all possible combinations and permutations of cells. It is generally useful to reduce

the field of investigation by the process of row elimination.

Evaluation The design matrix is a chart of possible solutions. Its appropriateness is based on the degree to which all cells or compartments can be made quantitative in terms of a given basis of comparison. This technique is a conscious way of carrying out the design process.

Evaluation Matrix

Purpose The evaluation matrix is a graphic display tool for ranking and selecting among alternate design solutions.

Description A list of evaluation criteria should be developed that can be applied to the alternatives generated. For each criterion define a scale for judgment and prepare a table that refers to the various alternatives and various criteria. In the scale for judgment, 1 = good, 2 = barely good, 3 = bare bad, and 4 = bad.

Note that in Figure 39 the evaluation criteria are all equally weighted. It would be possible to assign

	EVALUATION CRITERIA	ALTERNATE SOLUTIONS				
		S_1	S_2	S_3	S_4	S_5
A	daylight desirable during winter months but undesir- able during summer months	1	4	2	2	3
B	cross-ventilation at body zone in all activity areas	3	2	2	1	1
C	orientation of heat and odor producing activities towards the lee side of the building	2	1	3	2	2
D	use of outdoor space during overheated summer months	1	4	2	1	2
	TOTAL	7	11	9	6	8
	RANK ORDER	2	5	4	1	3

Figure 39

relative weights to each criterion. In that case each rating for each alternate solution in each row would be multiplied by the weighted value. The resulting adjusted totals would then indicate the rank ordering of each solution.

Evaluation A primary advantage of the evaluation matrix is its graphic clarity. It is possible to compare a large number of evaluation criteria and to simply arrive at a rank ordering of solutions. Of course, the validity of the ranking is dependent upon the evaluation criteria selected and the validity of each judgment value assigned.

Trade-Off Game

Purpose This game was developed in order to determine people's preferences within a fixed budget. Most preference techniques are not restrictive in this manner. Subjects are able to indicate choices that are unrealistic and unrealizable. As a result, much of the usefulness of many preference techniques are negated.

Description The three-column game requires considerable knowledge about the group taking the test, including their economic capabilities, and typical features that might be included in their environment.

The test is made up of three categories or columns. Each category describes items of relevance to the group being studied. The left column contains items that are considered "above average" for the group. The middle column describes items classified as "average," and the right column describes "below-average" items.

The first step in creating a three-column game is to generate a list of items describing the average for the group. The second step is to determine an above-average and below-average items for each of the initial items. These items are then incorporated into a chart.

There are two possible ways of setting up the game depending on the degree of accuracy desired. The first, and less accurate, method requires that all the items be of equal value. The subject playing the game may select one of the three possible alternatives for each item. For each above-average item selected, he must balance it by selecting a below-average item. The final selections must contain an equal number of above- and below-average items. It is suggested that the items be presented to the subject randomly and that the subject go through the items one time selecting the preferred items without worrying about a final balance. After the initial selection he should be confronted with the fact that he must give up X number of items in order to satisfy the rules of the game.

Another method of playing the game requires more effort in preparing the game but yields more accurate results. Instead of equating the various items, they are assigned a market value. The difference between the average item and the above- and below-average items is computed and indicated on the chart as a plus or minus value.

The subject taking the test is asked to balance not the number of items but the number of dollars he deviates from the average. In this manner, the subjects may not trade in an item of little value for an item of great value. An example of a test aimed at determining items of importance for low income families is given in Figure 40. The values are not indicated due to variances of prices and wages in specific areas.

Evaluation No statistical test has been found that examines the significance of the results. However, it is suggested that the initial selections and the later balancing be recorded. The value of the test comes from the frequencies of which items are retained and given up.

The first step of the evaluation is to total the number of times each item is selected. The second is to total the number of times each item is traded in, in order to balance the game. The third step is to indicate the number of final selections for each item. The percentage that each item has been traded in can be calculated by dividing the second step by the first step.

The game's primary advantage is that it attempts to restrict the subjects within realizable boundaries. However, distinct disadvantages are inherent also. The comprehensiveness of the game will be criticized be-

Above Market Value	Average	Below Market Value
7 room house at 1000 sq. ft. Value	6 room house at 1000 sq. ft. Value	5 room house at 1000 sq. ft. Value
Large Kitchen Area Value	Kitchen-Dining Area Value	Small Kitchen Value
Large Living Space Value	Moderate Living Space Value	Small Living Space Value
Large Front & Rear Yard Value	Small Front & Rear Yard Value	Front Yard Only Value
Carpented Living and Dining Space. Rest of house Asphalt Tile. Value	All Floors Asphalt Tile Value	All Floors Exposed Concrete Slab. Value
One Car Garage Value	One Car Carport Value	Uncovered Driveway Value
1½ Bathrooms Value	1 Bathroom With Tub and Shower Value	1 Bathroom With Tub Only Value
Separate Kitchen, Dining, Living Spaces Value	Living-Dining Space Combination Plus Kitchen Value	Kitchen-Dining Space Combination Plus Living Space Value
1 story house with basement, 1000 sq. ft. Value	1 story house on grade 1000 sq. ft. Value	1 story house off grade, 1000 sq. ft. Value
Shed Roof (Exposed beam) Value	Gable Roof (attic) Value	Flat Roof Value
Porch ___ sq. ft. Value	Entrance Overhang Value	No Door Overhang Value
Wood Finish Interior Value	Sheetrock Interior Value	Fiberboard Interior Value
Alum. Sliding glass door Value	Picture Window Value	Small Windows Value
All Tile Bathroom Value	Tile Wainscot in Bath Value	No Tile in Bathroom Value
Large Kitchen Window Value	Small Kitchen Window Value	No Kitchen Window Value
Service Porch Value	Washer in Kitchen Value	Washer Outside Value

Figure 40

cause usually an individual outside the group creates the game and determines the relevant factors. As a result, important items may be overlooked. Also, it may be argued that the outsider imposes his values on the game and thereby invalidates it.

RATING METHODS

Often there is a need to have access to the beliefs held by clients or user groups about some aspect of the design situation. With a minimum amount of time available and the need for quick, relatively reliable input, rating scales offer a major advantage. Their unique asset is that they allow the researcher to readily quantify and classify information. The choice of particular scale is dependent upon the type of user feedback desired and the size of the user population.

Rating Scales

Purpose Rating scales are used to assign a relative numerical value to the elements of a set. These scales are a class of mathematical types of measurement developed in terms of the distinctive points of correspondence "between the properties of the numerical series and the empirical operations that we can perform" which distinguishes among nominal, ordinal, interval, and ratio measures—with each type adding characteristic properties to the one before it.[30]

Description Nominal scales classify elements into mutually exclusive categories. An essential feature of a nominal scale is that classification can be equally well represented by any set of numbers, and the numbers can be interchanged without altering the essential information.

In an ordinal measure cases are arranged in rank order. It is the characteristic of the ordinal scale that any or all of the numbers applying to the elements can be changed in any way that does not alter their relative ordering.

Interval scales have all of the properties of an or-

dinal scale. In addition, the distances between any two points on the scale are of known size.

In Figure 41, the ordinal scale is formed by asking the question, "Where, on a conveniently numbered scale, would the elements A, B, and C be placed?" This establishes relative distances between the ranked elements. However, the units of this scale are not the units of the basis of comparison. They are simply the units of a convenient scale. In moving to an interval rating scale, a new scale is marked off in units of the smallest distance between any two elements on the ordinal scale. Once this is done, the intervals of the ordinal scale are superimposed on the interval scale with the highest ranked element (A) falling on the first position of the new scale. A hint for constructing the interval scale: place the interval directly under the ordinal to facilitate superimpositioning. Also, start construction of the interval scale with 1 and work toward 100 just far enough to include the position of the last-ranked element. The units of the new scale are the units of the basis of comparison used to rank the elements.

An equivalent rating scale can be constructed from the above mentioned interval scale by making the first ranked element equivalent to 100 and work-

Figure 41

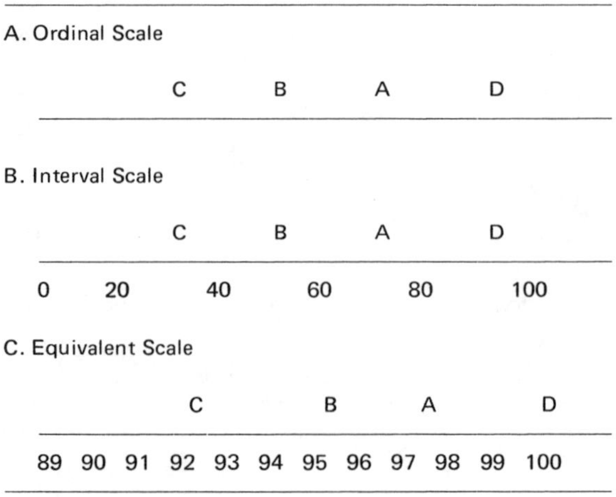

A. Ordinal Scale

	C	B	A	D

B. Interval Scale

	C	B	A	D
0	20	40	60	80	100

C. Equivalent Scale

	C	B	A	D
89 90 91	92 93 94	95 96 97	98 99	100

ing toward 1 just far enough to include the last ranked element.

Evaluation The primary advantage of rating scales is that they quantify subjective data and allow the investigator to use this data in various statistical tests. The investigator can also now talk about elements as *x* number of units of the basis of comparison with other elements.

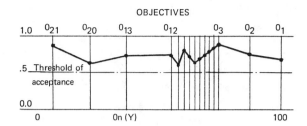

Figure 42
Index of merit.

The Index of Merit

Purpose The index of merit is a technique for evaluating the performance of a design proposal.[31] The performance corresponding to a given proposal is the set of states of properties that are exhibited in the outcome if the proposal were to be implemented. The merit of a performance is the set of degrees of attainment of the set of defined goals. The index of merit of a performance is the ratio of the sum of the rated degrees of fulfillment of the goals to the sum of the ratings.

Description

$O_n(Y)$ = satisfaction of value *n* of goal.
R_{O_n} = rating value of objective *n*.
M = Index of merit.
M_{iY} = Index of merit for the performance *Y* relating to a proposal *i*.
$M_{iY}(t)$ = signifies a particular value *t* of index M_{iY} (where *t* is some number between zero and unity).

When all the goals are fully attained, then $t = 1$. When some of the goals are partly attained, then $t < 1$. When *t* or any one value of *y* is less than 0.5, then the performance is defined as unacceptable.

$$M = \frac{\Sigma[R_{O_n} \times O_n(Y)]}{(\Sigma R_{O_n})}$$

Evaluation The index of merit provides a method for controlling the outcomes of the objectives to be satisfied as well as a comparison between objectives and their attainment. It is a particularly useful tool when objectives, values, and performance lend themselves to quantification.

Guttman Scaling

Purpose A question often raised concerning attitude scales is whether they measure a single attitude. Sometimes it is important to measure the various attitudes toward an object, concept, or value by means of separate scales confined to single dimensions. To accomplish this, the best known is the scale analysis, or scalogram method, devised by Guttman.[32] The scalogram orders items in such a manner that, ideally, persons who answer a given question favorably all have their ranks higher on the scale than the persons who answer the same question unfavorably. From a respondent's rank or scale score, we know exactly which items he endorsed. Thus, ideally, this scale has the property that responses to the individual items are reproducible from the scale scores. It is essential that the items are cumulative.

Description Use of the Guttman scaling method can be best explained by example. Given are six attributes of environment—quietness, homey, greenery, privacy, beauty, and spaciousness—to be tested for dimensionality. These attributes are presented to a number of subjects with instructions to place a plus sign beside those qualities with which they personally agree and a minus sign beside those with which they disagree.

A hypothetically perfect outcome in the Guttman sense involving the seven subjects is shown in Figure 43. For purposes of illustration, assume the six qualities are unidimensional. In general, of course, we do not know in advance that a given set of statements necessarily falls along a single continuum from least to most favorable. It is the sole purpose of the Guttman scaling method to determine whether the responses of the subjects do, in fact, place a given set of statements along a single continuum.

Figure 43 describes favorable (+) and unfavorable (−) responses of seven subjects to six qualities of environment arranged in order from the most to the least favorable.

In this ideal example, a subject who agrees with any one statement also agrees with all statements that express less favorable attitudes. There is no disruption in the internal order of the responses. In a looser scale construction, it would be possible for a person to get a score of three by agreeing with any three statements. But in a perfect Guttman configuration, anyone with a score of three (as subject D) must have agreed with statements 1, 2, and 3 rather than any other combination of three statements. The essential characteristic of a unidimensional scale (Guttman) is that the pattern of responses is reproducible from knowledge of the scale score. Thus, to know the scale score of any subject is to know exactly the statements with which he agreed and disagreed. However, in actual practice, one seldom finds the ideal outcome (Figure 44) described. But the closer the responses approach this ideal, the more likely it is that the scale is not simultaneously tapping several different attitude dimensions. In practice, a certain measure of "error" is allowed. A rule of thumb suggested by Guttman is that the pattern of responses must be 90 percent reproducible in order for a scale to be considered unidimensional.[33] In other words, 10 percent of the responses may fall outside the unidimensional pattern. To calculate the degree to which responses on attempted scale conform to the ideal, Guttman has devised a "coefficient of reproducibility." This measure indicates the percentage of accuracy with which responses to the various statements can be reproduced (or predicted) from knowledge of the total scores. In Figure 43 the coefficient of reproducibility would be 100 percent.[34]

Evaluation The scalogram (Guttman) method and the problem of unidimensionality have been a controversial subject throughout their development. First, an authoritative source on methodology in social psychology has argued that if we wish to predict complex behavior, we need to measure a complex attitude, not a unidimensional one.[35] From a practical point of view this appears to be a sound comment; however, theoretically, if both the attitude and the behavior could be measured unidimensionally, prediction would certainly be enhanced. Second, a scale may be repro-

Figure 43

Subject	Score	Most Favorable Spaciousness	Beauty	Privacy	Greenery	Least Favorable Homey	Quietness
A	6	+	+	+	+	+	+
B	5	+	+	+	+	+	−
C	4	+	+	+	+	−	−
D	3	+	+	+	−	−	−
E	2	+	+	−	−	−	−
F	1	+	−	−	−	−	−
G	0	−	−	−	−	−	−

ducible when taken by one group of persons and not when taken by another. In general, however, the method has appeared useful for certain kinds of scaling problems.

User Rating Test

Purpose If it is desired to evaluate the performance of a building, perhaps one of the most important sources of information comes from the inhabitants or users of the building. It is this group that is affected the most by a malfunction in the building or is in the best position to praise noteworthy features. Visitors, customers, casual spectators, and absentee owners are not in the position to make detailed criticisms. In all buildings, environmental factors should be considered. In many buildings, the users or inhabitants may not agree with the aesthetics, but this is infringing on the realm of the subjective and intangible and can be better evaluated using the semantic differential. The purpose of the user's rating test is to gain some knowledge about the user's feelings and attitudes toward the solution of some of the more important environmental factors in a building.

The degree of specificity may be chosen to fit the particular problem at hand. The test may evaluate the user's feelings about the building as a whole, or the components of the building (living room, bedroom, and so on), or subsystems of the building (circulation, ventilation, lighting, and so on).

Description After a decision has been made concerning the level of specificity, it is necessary to determine what factors are to be studied. The following is a list of some of the more common environmental factors that affect the performance of a building:

Social factors
    Number of people occupying a building
    Behavior of the inhabitants or users
    Behavior of neighbors
Physical factors
    Dimensions of building

    Location of building
    Orientation of building
    Stability of structure
    Building materials
    Light
    Temperature
    Ventilation
    Sound transmission
Natural phenomena
    Wind
    Weather
    Fire
    Earthquakes
Economic factors
    Provision of facilities
    Maintenance

It is desirable to incorporate whichever factors are selected in a matrix or questionnaire that rates them according to the people's values. The selection of scales may vary for different factors. A sample questionnaire is included to illustrate a method of scaling the factors.

The scaled questionnaire in Figure 44 was used to determine employee attitudes toward the College of Environmental Design building on the University of California, Berkeley campus. It was distributed to the clerical employees in the building and returned via mail to the researcher. The raw data were compiled in a series of graphs (Figures 45–48) showing the distribution of feelings about the various factors. Each scale was given a position of ideal performance in order to compare and judge the responses. To illustrate, it was assumed that the maintenance of the building would have to be good for the building to function ideally. When the responses were plotted, it was evident that many considered the maintenance to be poor, thus indicating that the performance was being hindered by this factor.

Evaluation The Kolmogorov–Smirnov one-sample test was utilized to analyze the data. This test compares the degree of agreement between an actual observed distribution of a sample set of values and some speci-

Figure 44
Building performance questionnaire.

1. Please indicate your feelings concerning the density of people occupying the portion of the building with which you are concerned.

 ——: ——: ——: ——: ——: ——: ——: ——: ——: ——:
 too   just   too
 low   right   high

2. Please indicate your feelings concerning the behavior of the people occupying the portion of the building with which you are concerned.

 ——: ——: ——: ——: ——: ——: ——: ——: ——: ——:
 bad   average   good

3. Are there any factors from neighboring buildings or activities (such as noises or odors) that affect the performance of your duties: Yes ____ No ____ If the answer is yes, please state briefly a description of what they are and where they come from._____

   _____

4. To the best of your knowledge, does the portion of the building with which you are concerned function as it was originally intended? Yes ____ No ____ If the answer is no please state the use before and after modifications.

   _____

   _____

5. Has your work space been modified to increase its efficiency? Yes ____ No ____ If yes, what modifications were necessary? _____

   _____

6. Are there any serious mistakes concerning the portion of the building with which you are concerned that you feel the architects should have anticipated? Yes ____ No ____ If yes, please state briefly; _____

   _____

7. To what degree is flexibility important in your work space?

 ——: ——: ——: ——: ——: ——: ——: ——: ——: ——:
 minor   major

8. To what degree is flexibility provided in your work space?

 ——: ——: ——: ——: ——: ——: ——: ——: ——: ——:
 none   average   excessive

9. Please indicate your feelings concerning the temperature in your work space.

 ——: ——: ——: ——: ——: ——: ——: ——: ——: ——:
 cold   just   hot
        right

Figure 44 continued

10. Please indicate your feelings concerning the ventilation in your work space.

——: ——: ——: ——: ——: ——: ——: ——: ——: ——:
bad   average   good

11. Please rate the sound transmission into your work space.

——: ——: ——: ——: ——: ——: ——: ——: ——: ——:
little   average   excessive

12. Please rate the building with regard to keeping out the elements. (Does it leak? Is it drafty? etc.)

——: ——: ——: ——: ——: ——: ——: ——: ——: ——:
bad   average   good

13. To what degree does the orientation of the building affect the performance of your duties? Consider the sun, wind, rain, and views.

——: ——: ——: ——: ——: ——: ——: ——: ——: ——:
adversely   positively

14. What are your feelings concerning the provision of facilities concerned with your job?

——: ——: ——: ——: ——: ——: ——: ——: ——: ——:
poor   average   good

15. Please indicate your feelings concerning the maintenance and upkeep of the building.

——: ——: ——: ——: ——: ——: ——: ——: ——: ——:
poor   average   good

16. How do you like working in the building?

——: ——: ——: ——: ——: ——: ——: ——: ——: ——:
dislike   ok   like

fied theoretical distribution. It is necessary to specify the cumulative frequency distribution that would occur under the theoretical distribution and with the observed cumulative frequency distribution. From these two distributions, the point of greatest divergence can be determined. This divergence is then analyzed to see if the actual curve supports or rejects the null-hypothesis created for the study. A level of significance is established that defines the regions of acceptance and rejection. Usually this figure is 0.05.

Another test of the degree of agreement between the observed performance is to compare the median of the observed distribution to the point of ideal performance. A numerical deviation is obtained, and for good performance the deviation approaches zero. The greater the deviation, the poorer the performance.

The user rating test is good in that it attempts to record and analyze the views of the people most affected by the building. The data and conclusions must be handled circumspectly, however, because the users

76

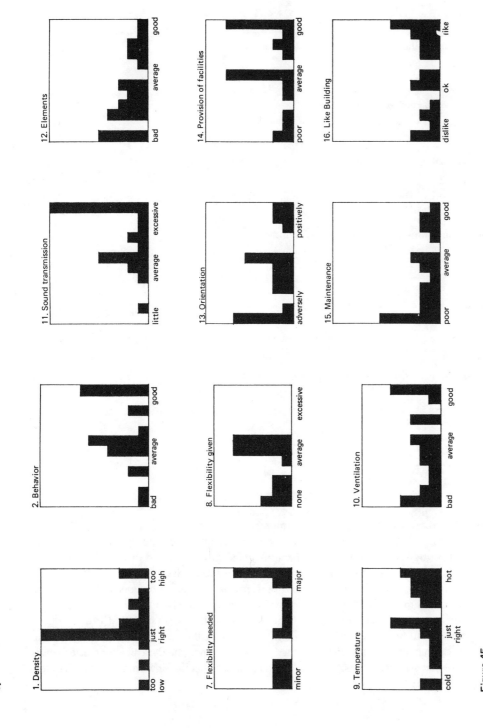

Figure 45
Cumulative frequency distribution.

Figure 46
Tabulation of actual (A) and theoretical (T) results.

							Scale Divisions						
		1	2	3	4	5	6	7	8	9	10	11	12
Density	A	1	0	1	0	1	11	3	1	2	1	0	3
	T	2	2	2	2	2	2	2	2	2	2	2	2
Behavior	A	1	1	0	2	0	4	6	1	0	2	0	7
	T	2	2	2	2	2	2	2	2	2	2	2	2
Temperature	A	2	0	1	1	1	2	5	0	2	3	3	4
	T	2	2	2	2	2	2	2	2	2	2	2	2
Ventilation	A	4	2	1	1	2	2	3	0	3	0	1	5
	T	2	2	2	2	2	2	2	2	2	2	2	2
Sound Trans.	A	0	1	0	0	1	2	5	1	2	1	1	10
	T	2	2	2	2	2	2	2	2	2	2	2	2
Elements	A	5	0	4	3	2	3	0	1	2	2	1	1
	T	2	2	2	2	2	2	2	2	2	2	2	2
Orientation	A	6	1	0	2	2	2	5	0	1	1	2	2
	T	2	2	2	2	2	2	2	2	2	2	2	2
Facilities	A	2	1	1	0	1	1	7	0	1	2	1	7
	T	2	2	2	2	2	2	2	2	2	2	2	2
Maintenance	A	6	2	2	2	1	2	3	0	1	2	2	1
	T	2	2	2	2	2	2	2	2	2	2	2	2
Like Building	A	3	1	2	1	0	3	2	0	2	2	3	5
	T	2	2	2	2	2	2	2	2	2	2	2	2

seem to display a tendency to exaggerate. In addition to magnifying relatively minor problems, they also judge the building for the present only. For example, if the test is administered in the summer and the building is hot, the subjects will say that the building is hot all year long and not consider other seasons of the year. In response to the comment that users magnify minor problems, it may be argued that minor problems to the architect can be major problems to the user.

Semantic Differential

Purpose Semantic rating scales are used to obtain an impression of a group's reaction toward some aspect of the physical environment. Its purpose is to clarify and record attitudes toward concepts and images. Recently this approach has been adopted by architects for the purposes of determining the images people have concerning specific physical environments and building. To date, the evaluative usefulness to architects is derived by determining if the people for whom a structure is intended perceive it similarly or in the way intended by the architect. Research has indicated that architects perceive environments differently than nonarchitects do. This produces inherent problems in the use of the semantic differential.

Description Although the semantic differential is often referred to as a "test" that has a definite set of items and a specific score, this use is incorrect. The semantic differential is a general approach or method

Figure 47
Cumulative totals and deviations. Note that all totals represent fractions of 24,
for example, 5 = 5/24.

Density	A	1	1	2	2	3	14	17	18	20	21	21	24
	T	2	4	6	8	10	12	14	16	18	20	22	24
	D	1	3	4	6	7	2	3	2	2	1	1	0
Behavior	A	1	2	2	4	4	8	14	15	15	17	17	24
	T	2	4	6	8	10	12	14	16	18	20	22	24
	D	1	2	4	4	6	4	0	1	3	3	5	0
Temperature	A	2	2	3	4	5	7	12	12	14	17	20	24
	T	2	4	6	8	10	12	14	16	18	20	22	24
	D	0	2	3	4	5	5	2	4	4	3	2	0
Ventilation	A	4	6	7	8	10	12	15	15	18	18	19	24
	T	2	4	6	8	10	12	14	16	18	20	22	24
	D	22	2	1	0	0	0	1	1	0	2	3	0
Sound Trans.	A	0	1	1	1	2	4	9	10	12	13	14	24
	T	2	4	6	8	10	12	14	16	18	20	22	24
	D	2	3	5	7	8	8	5	6	6	7	8	0
Elements	A	5	5	9	12	14	17	17	18	20	22	23	24
	T	2	4	6	8	10	12	14	16	18	20	22	24
	D	3	1	3	4	4	5	3	2	2	2	1	6
Orientation	A	6	7	7	9	10	13	18	18	19	20	22	24
	T	2	4	6	8	10	12	14	16	18	20	22	24
	D	4	3	1	1	1	1	4	2	1	0	0	0
Facilities	A	2	3	4	4	5	6	13	13	14	16	17	24
	T	2	4	6	8	10	12	14	16	18	20	22	24
	D	0	1	2	4	5	6	1	3	4	4	5	0
Maintenance	A	6	8	10	12	13	15	18	18	19	21	23	24
	T	2	4	6	8	10	12	14	16	18	20	22	24
	D	4	4	4	4	3	3	4	2	1	1	1	0
Like Building	A	3	4	6	7	7	10	12	12	14	16	19	24
	T	2	4	6	8	10	12	14	16	18	20	22	24
	D	1	0	0	1	3	2	2	4	4	4	3	0

A = Actual
T = Theoretical
D = Deviation

of obtaining a certain type of information. Each administration of the test must be designed specifically to the problem for which it is intended.

The first step in creating a semantic differential is to select a concept or aspect of the environment to be studied. Concept is defined by Osgood as the "stimulus" to which the subject's checking operation is a terminal response.[36] The concepts that may be used are practically infinite. They are often visual and usually printed rather than spoken due to the convenience of presentation; however, they are by no means limited to visual concepts. The nature of the problem determines which concepts are applicable. Usually time and subject limitations prevent complete coverage of all the relevant concepts in a given area. Methods of presenting the concepts can include drawings, photo-

Figure 48
Deviations and level of significance.[1]

Density
Ideal =	6.5	p = 0.03 Accept null hypothesis
Median =	6.2	
Deviation =	0.3	D = 7/24 = 0.29

Behavior
Ideal =	12.5	P = 0.08 Reject null hypothesis
Median =	7.7	
Deviation =	4.8	D = 6/24 = 0.25

Temperature
Ideal =	6.5	p = 0.20 Reject null hypothesis
Median =	8.5	
Deviation =	2.0	D = 5/24 = 0.21

Ventilation
Ideal =	12.5	p = 0.20 Reject null hypothesis
Median =	7.0	
Deviation =	5.5	D = 3/24 = 0.125

Sound Transmission
Ideal =	1.5	p = 0.01 Accept null hypothesis
Median =	10.0	
Deviation =	8.5	D = 8/24 = 0.33

Elements
Ideal =	12.5	p = 0.20 Reject null hypothesis
Median =	5.0	
Deviation =	7.5	D = 5/24 = 0.21

Orientation
Ideal =	12.5	p = 0.20 Reject null hypothesis
Median =	6.5	
Deviation =	6.0	D = 4/24 = 0.17

Facilities
Ideal =	12.5	p = 0.08 Reject null hypothesis
Median =	7.8	
Deviation =	4.7	D = 6/24 = 0.25

Maintenance
Ideal =	12.5	p = 0.20 Reject null hypothesis
Median =	5.0	
Deviation =	7.5	D = 4/24 = 0.17

Like Building
Ideal =	12.5	p = 0.20 Reject null hypothesis
Median =	8.5	
Deviation =	4.0	D = 4/24 = 0.17

1. Level of significance (p) determined from Table E of S. Siegel's, *Nonparametric Statistics for the Behavioral Scientist* (New York: McGraw-Hill, 1965).

graphs, and slides as well as actually being in and experiencing the environment being studied.

The next step in the construction of a semantic differential is the selection of appropriate scales. Three areas are of particular importance in selecting scales. These are evaluative scales, potency scales, and activity scales. Most polar adjectives used as scales fall under one of these categories. Osgood suggests using a minimum of three scales to represent each factor. Other criteria in the selection of scales are relevance to the concept being judged, semantic stability for the concepts and subjects in a particular study, and linearity between adjectives or poles which passes through an origin.

Relevancy is important because the test must be efficient. For example, if a senator is the concept being judged, an evaluative scale like beautiful–ugly may be irrelevant while another scale like fair–unfair may be highly relevant.

Semantic stability refers to the interpretation desired by the investigators. The scale large–small is likely to have strict denotative usage in judging physical objects such as a boulder or an ant, but it is likely to be used connotatively when judging concepts like sin or the president.

Sometimes scales will be used that are polar by definition but each pole has acquired either positive or negative meanings. This is called nonlinearity and is to be avoided. One example of nonlinearity is the scale rugged–delicate; both terms tend to be favorable in meaning and therefore are not helpful in defining a concept. An example of linearity can be seen in adjective pairs such as like–dislike and good–bad.

The scales selected are by no means confined to the three major categories mentioned. Often scales of different factorial composition are highly relevant to a particular problem. Only study and experimentation can produce new dimensions in semantic space.

Usually each adjective pair is placed on opposite ends of a scale with seven divisions. Each division stands for different degrees of intensity. An example of a pair of adjectives with opposite meaning on a semantic scale would be "simple" and "complex" (see

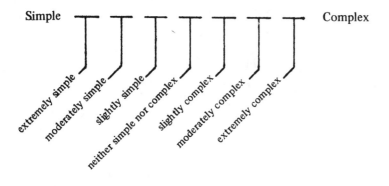

Simple ——————————————— Complex

extremely simple
moderately simple
slightly simple
neither simple nor complex
slightly complex
moderately complex
extremely complex

Figure 49
Paired comparisons. Each individual in the group uses the semantic rating scale to indicate his personal opinion about the environment that is being studied.

Figure 49). The seven steps are defined as extremely, moderately, and slightly simple, neutral and extremely, moderately and slightly complex. There are two accepted forms of organizing the differential. One of these uses a concept for each scale. It is as follows:

Lady   rough __ __ __ __ __ __ __ smooth
Me   fair __ __ __ __ __ __ __ unfair

Each capitalized concept appears on the same line as the scale against which it is being judged. In this way, it is possible to order the items in such a way that a maximum number of concepts and scales occurs between repetitions of each concept and scale. This system is advantageous because the subject is kept shifting from concept to concept and therefore cannot easily compare judgments on one scale with those on another.

The second form uses one sheet of paper for each concept, with all the judgments being made successively:

                    Lady

rough   __ __ __ __ __ __ __   smooth
fair   __ __ __ __ __ __ __   unfair
active   __ __ __ __ __ __ __   passive

With this form, the ordering of the concepts for dif-

ferent individuals may be varied but the form of the differential remains constant. This form has the advantage that it is easy to mimeograph and easy to score.

Evaluation The raw data obtained from the semantic differential are a collection of check marks against bipolar scales. Usually each scale is assigned a digit, either 1 through 7 or –3 through +3, with 0 being the central or neutral position. The arithmetic mean can be helpful in comparing two semantic rating scales. The mean describes the groups' average tendency. In order to calculate the mean, the number of check marks on each step of the semantic scale is multiplied with the value given to that step. When the multiplications for each of the steps have been carried out, these seven numbers are totaled. The mean is the last number divided by the total number of check marks on the semantic scale (see figure 54).

There are a variety of tests that may be applied to the data, depending upon what the investigators desire to determine. Some of the more common investigations are concerned with the following: (1) difference between two different groups in the meaning of the

Figure 50
Adding up the group's check marks.

SIMPLE 3 4 2 1 1 ___ ___COMPLEX

Figure 51
Numerical notation. All the check marks placed on the "extremely simple" step are added up by themselves; then the ones on the "moderately simple" step are added up by themselves; and so on for the seven steps on the semantic scale.

SIMPLE ___ ___ ___ ___ ___ ___ ___ COMPLEX

Figure 52
Bar diagram. The more check marks a particular step has, the taller the bar.

SIMPLE ___ ___ ___ ___ ___ ___ ___ COMPLEX
  -3 -2 -1 0 $+1$ $+2$ $+3$

Figure 53
Numerical values assigned to each step.

$$[3x(-3)] + [4x(-2)] + [2x(-1)] + [1x(0)] + [1x(1)] + [0x(2)] + [0x(3)] = -18$$

$$\text{Arithmetic Mean} = \frac{-18}{3+4+2+2} = \frac{-18}{10} = -1.8$$

Figure 54
Calculating the arithmetic mean.

SIMPLE ___ ___ ___ ___ ___ ___ ___ COMPLEX
-1.8

Figure 55
Graphical presentation of the arithmetic mean.

same concept; (2) difference between the meanings of two concepts for the same group; (3) difference between two individuals in the meaning of the same concept; (4) difference between the meanings of two concepts for the same individual.[37]

Evaluation The semantic differential is a statistical-

Figure 56
Semantic differential.

pleasant ——:——:——:——:——:——:—— :	unpleasant
easy ——:——:——:——:——:——:—— :	hard
happy ——:——:——:——:——:——:—— :	sad
noisy ——:——:——:——:——:——:—— :	quiet
upper class ——:——:——:——:——:——:—— :	lower class
smooth ——:——:——:——:——:——:—— :	rough
cruel ——:——:——:——:——:——:—— :	kind
modern ——:——:——:——:——:——:—— :	old-fashioned
high ——:——:——:——:——:——:—— :	low
relaxed ——:——:——:——:——:——:—— :	tense
violent ——:——:——:——:——:——:—— :	gentle
clear ——:——:——:——:——:——:—— :	hazy
nice ——:——:——:——:——:——:—— :	awful
ugly ——:——:——:——:——:——:—— :	beautiful
dull ——:——:——:——:——:——:—— :	sharp
bad ——:——:——:——:——:——:—— :	good
large ——:——:——:——:——:——:—— :	small
bright ——:——:——:——:——:——:—— :	dark
ferocious ——:——:——:——:——:——:—— :	peaceful
strong ——:——:——:——:——:——:—— :	weak
stale ——:——:——:——:——:——:—— :	fresh
spacious ——:——:——:——:——:——:—— :	cramped

ly weak test because it relies upon nominal verbal scales rather than quantitative scales. In other words, the data that are being manipulated are essentially subjective. There is a significant probability that the researcher places different meaning on many of the scales than do the subjects. The semantic differential takes the subjective introspections on the part of the individuals and deals with them in an objective manner. Therefore, it may be termed objective only with regard to what is done to the data after the test has been administered.

Spatial Performance

Purpose The intent of this test is to obtain a user evaluation of the quantitative elements of the dwelling in which he resides. (This format can be utilized to assess spatial suitability of other building types as well.) This test is an attempt to measure thresholds

82

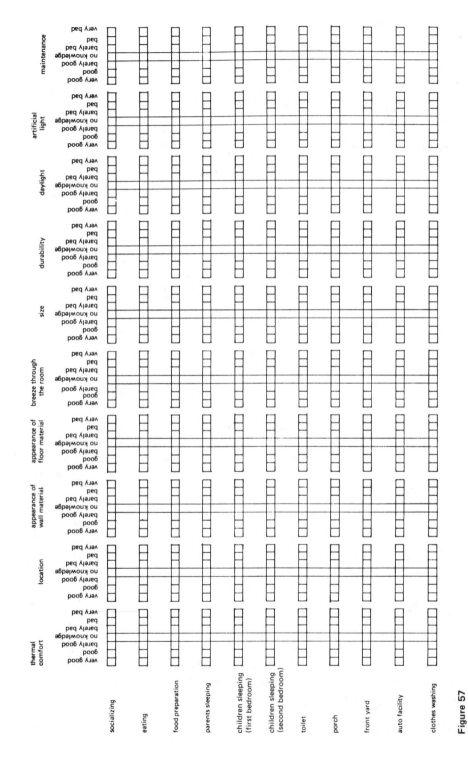

Figure 57
Spatial performance rating sheet.

of satisfaction or dissatisfaction of either innovative solutions or present housing accommodations.

Description Each occupant of the residence evaluates all the spaces in the dwelling according to the variables presented and his knowledge of the degree of satisfaction of each. The respondent must be in the particular space during the period of evaluation, and the results of each variable must be considered independent of the others.

The performance rating sheet (Figure 57) is set up so that each space in the dwelling is evaluated on the basis of comfort, location, size, and maintenance. These variables can be altered to suit particular purposes.

This type of survey requires a number of identical dwelling types for the sample groups to be statistically significant. It may be used also to assess the performance of a single dwelling with periodic change of occupancy.

Many of the variables in this test are influenced by seasonal change, climate, and time of day and require repeated testing.

Evaluation This technique has been pretested to resolve its operational difficulties but has not been tested for reliability, constancy, or significance of results. The evaluation of people's activities and where they occur in housing does not relate to practical limitations of experience. Due to the greater similarities among types of activities people perform than similarities among spaces in which activities are performed, the influence of existing house arrangements is deemphasized.

VISUAL PREFERENCE METHODS

This category of information retrieval methods is particularly appropriate for seeking reactions to visual-spatial information. Visual preference tests have a unique application for designers because of the wide range of visual information that is accessible to them. The types of visual displays developed for response feedback are limited only by the imagination of the designer. They can include drawings or photographs of spaces, buildings, or models. They can be used in conjunction with many of the comparison methods if preferences are desirable. Responses to visual display provide insights into the environment as it is or as it ought to be.

Visual Trade-Offs

Purpose The purpose of a graphic (nonverbal) preference test is the same as that of verbal tests but has the advantage of obtaining responses from illiterate subjects and is less likely to be misinterpreted by the respondents.

Description A graphic or illustrative preference test can take many forms. The test may utilize photographs, perspective line drawings, isometric drawings, plans, sections, or any other visual means of communication. Extra care must be taken to insure uniformity of presentation. If the presentation is not uniform, the subjects taking the test may make their preference decisions on the basis of the nicest or most appealing illustration.

A test was conducted to determine if there are any significant differences between various social classes in the arrangement and size of various rooms. An isometric line drawing questionnaire was developed and was submitted to a random sampling of residents in areas meeting the description of the groups to be studied.[38] The questionnaires were mailed to the investigator, and the results were tabulated on a series of graphs. Statistical tests were applied to see where the various curves diverged and converged, at certain levels of significance. The tests varied according to the data and the information required.

Visual Preference

Purpose This graphic preference test is designed to elicit the best choice for spatial quality of verbally specified activities.[39]

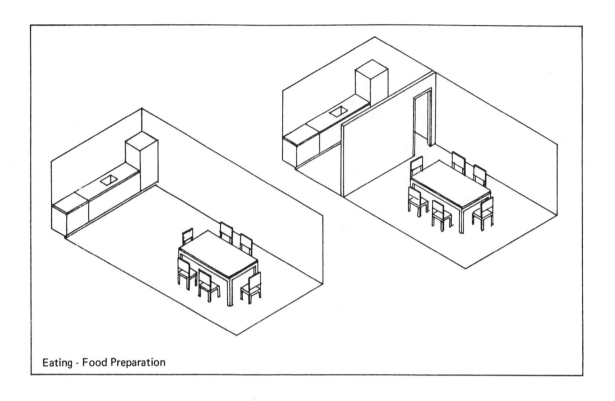

Eating - Food Preparation

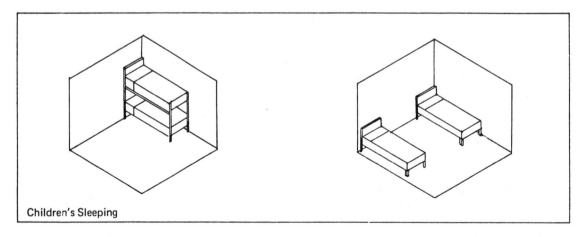

Children's Sleeping

Figure 58
Comparison of alternative spatial arrangements for eating and food preparation
and alternative bed arranagement in children's sleeping space.

Description A set of drawings or photographs is prepared with sufficient alternatives in spatial arrangements so that the respondent is forced to compare and evaluate all selections. The visual displays are developed at the discretion of the designer. Numerous types of spaces, both existing and proposed, can be used to generate a set. The criteria for developing alternative visual displays can be based upon spatial quality, spatial arrangement, or spatial connotation. Similarly, displays can be numerically weighted, based on construction cost, in order to establish trade-offs between preferences.

Evaluation This method is useful for seeking user responses to design alternatives as well as for informing users about spatial options. The development of environmental displays is critical in that they should correspond to the types of visual issues that are most doubtful.

Spatial Preference Gameboard

Purpose This gameboard is an instrument designed to elicit responses concerning preferred spatial arrangements. It is often difficult to impute design criteria from verbal responses. This difficulty is overcome by presenting the respondents with a visual display of spatial choices. In addition, the gameboard introduces trade-offs to force sets of choices. This allows the respondent to establish priorities on his choices.

Description The rules of the game may be oriented toward monetary value; however, the major function is to limit the choice available to force the players into trade-off situations. In a strict sense it is not properly a game since there is no competition involved. The operation of the gameboard, however, is similar to family-type parlor games.

The spatial preference gameboard shown in Figure 60 was used as a part of a study conducted in eastern North Carolina. This media of presentation was selected because of its high level of abstraction and presence of a limited number of cues. It was important that any cues related to texture, material, or color be

omitted at this initial stage of assessment in order to ensure that the respondents were making choices solely on physical form characteristics. This housing game is based on trade-offs between discrete classes of activities. The activity areas of the household were bifurcated for gaming purposes between decisions about sleeping areas for children and adults and food preparation, dining, and living areas. An allocation of sixty-four points was given to the player(s) with two trials to attain this allocation. The points were based on a cost per area ratio with a 2:1 ratio for utility and nonutility areas. The decisions were then based on which of the two classes of activities were perceived as most important by the respondent. The critical decision point is between the need for privacy between food preparation, eating, and living and children's sleeping spaces with an adjacent play space.

Attribute Discrimination Scale

Purpose This scale was designed to rate a particular environmental setting, either real or hypothetical. The scale forces judgments about the attributes of a particular environment. The continuum between each pair of terms can indicate the direction and intensity of each judgment while permitting a wide discrimination of choice. It utilizes linguistic concepts commonly used by designers, which are bipolar in nature.

Description This scale attempts to discover the degree to which a common descriptive language exists; therefore an attempt is made to include "objective" words, though they too have values that vary depending upon the attitudes of the respondents. Several of the terms used to denote properties are value loaded. Thus to many *symmetry* has a negative and *asymmetry* a positive connotation; *novel* may be viewed more favorably than *common*; *static* and *dynamic* seem to be bad and good, respectively.

The street scene depicted in Figure 61 was one of four settings used in a survey of architects to discover which attributes best described the four settings. The "anchor" scale was the like-dislike continuum, which

Figure 59
Alternate spatial arrangements. This set of drawings represents a range of learning places that can accommodate various educational objectives.

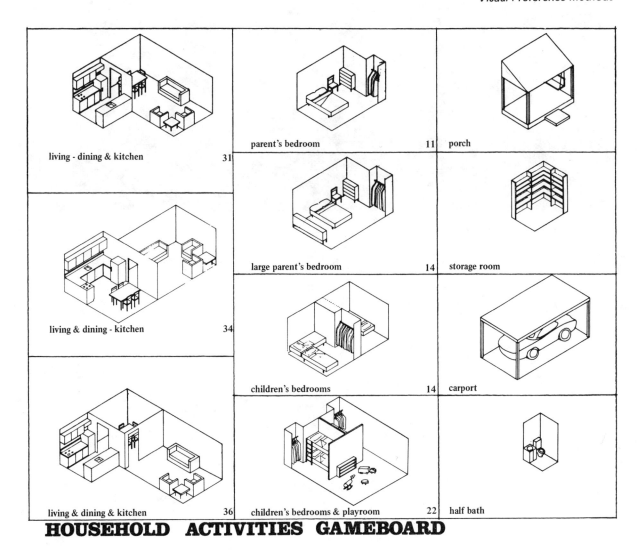

living - dining & kitchen	31	parent's bedroom	11	porch
living & dining - kitchen	34	large parent's bedroom	14	storage room
		children's bedrooms	14	carport
living & dining & kitchen	36	children's bedrooms & playroom	22	half bath

HOUSEHOLD ACTIVITIES GAMEBOARD

Figure 60
Spatial trade-offs.

```
    Simplicity ___'___'___'___'___'___'___' Complexity

   Stimulating ___'___'___'___'___'___'___' Sedative

       Harmony ___'___'___'___'___'___'___' Discord

     Roughness ___'___'___'___'___'___'___' Smoothness

     Ambiguity ___'___'___'___'___'___'___' Clarity

        Formal ___'___'___'___'___'___'___' Informal

      Symmetry ___'___'___'___'___'___'___' Asymmetry

      Boldness ___'___'___'___'___'___'___' Unobtrusiveness

      Interest ___'___'___'___'___'___'___' Boredom

      Hardness ___'___'___'___'___'___'___' Softness

 Individuality ___'___'___'___'___'___'___' Universality

         Unity ___'___'___'___'___'___'___' Variety

       Austere ___'___'___'___'___'___'___' Sensuous

         Novel ___'___'___'___'___'___'___' Common

  Satisfaction ___'___'___'___'___'___'___' Frustration

 Paradoxicality ___'___'___'___'___'___'___' Comprehensibility

   Exhilarated ___'___'___'___'___'___'___' Depressed

          High ___'___'___'___'___'___'___' Low

       Peaceful ___'___'___'___'___'___'___' Disruptive

        Static ___'___'___'___'___'___'___' Dynamic

       Ordered ___'___'___'___'___'___'___' Disordered

       Uniform ___'___'___'___'___'___'___' Divergent

         Tense ___'___'___'___'___'___'___' Relaxed

          Calm ___'___'___'___'___'___'___' Violent

      Intimate ___'___'___'___'___'___'___' Distant

          Like ___'___'___'___'___'___'___' Dislike
```

Figure 61
Attribute discrimination scale. Environmental statements are used to describe the residential setting.

positively or negatively explained each of the respondents' choices.[40]

Evaluation This scale has the distinct advantage of having people respond to many different environmental settings so that comparisons between settings can be made. It is also convenient to dissemenate this type of questionnaire through the mail, provided that a set of instructions accompany the rating request.

CHECKLISTS

Perhaps the most frequently used method of information control is the checklist. It is most appropriately used when operations are normally repeated or habitual. Checklists have become a standard operating procedure for routinized activities such as code and zoning checks, building construction operations, and the like. A frequently used checklist is the code check. It is not a postmortem evaluative tool but a vital preliminary predictive tool. If a proposed building does not meet the requirements set forth in the building codes, it may not be constructed. The edicts set forth in a building code have been adopted by most municipalities as minimum standards for new construction and additions.

The procedure of satisfying the code requirements is a complex and tedious job. It requires a thorough knowledge of the code, its limitations, its intent, and its weaknesses. As a result of the complexity of the task, many architectural offices have established code checklists as aids in fulfilling this requirement. By considering code requirements early, an office may avoid troubles at a later date. Two examples of checklists are included here (Figures 62 and 63) with the intent of systemizing the effort required to accomplish a comprehensive inventory.

SUMMARY

The programmer's kit of parts (Figure 64) is an inventory of the methods that are appropriate during

Figure 62
Zoning and building code checklist.

Zoning Code

1. Be sure legal description on plans is correct.
2. Is property zoned for use indicated on application?
3. Check dimensions of lot on plot plan against maps.
4. Are survey stakes indicated at all corners on plot plan?
5. Check coverage permitted on lot against building area.
6. Check building height permitted in stories and feet.
7. Check for yard compliance—front, side, rear.
8. Check for proper street and alley positions on plot.
9. Does lot meet minimum lot size permitted?
10. Check locations of accessory buildings.
11. Does design meet off-street parking and screening requirements?
12. Be sure parking has proper surfacing and drainage.
13. Driveways and other encroachments over public spaces to be approved.
14. Check for required distances of certain uses from R zones.
15. Must use be in an enclosed or completely enclosed building?
16. Be sure uses subject to variance or conditional hearings are submitted to the board or council for hearing.

Building Code

1. Check for architecture of plans.
   a. Architect's seal and date of same.
   b. If drawn by owner, statement to appear.
   c. Check for completeness of plans.
   d. Index. Door schedule. Finish schedule.
2. Check for building construction classification.
   a. Value of all floors and roofs.
   b. Value of exterior wall construction.
   c. Value of partitions throughout.
   d. Fireproofing of structural frame.
3. Determine use of all areas and be sure such are indicated on floor plans or index.
4. Check area of building against that permitted by building code.
   a. As per construction.
   b. As per number of stories.
   c. Reduction in 1 and 2 fire zones.
   d. Increases based on streets and courts.
   e. Increases based on sprinkler protection.
   f. Areas as based on use of building.
5. Check for height of building based on construction and uses (stories and feet).

(continued)

Figure 62 (continued)

Building Code

6. Check for occupancy separation requirements.
   a. Value of separation.
   b. Extent of separation.
   c. Openings through and at ends of walls.
   d. Parapets required.
7. Check for area division wall requirements.
   a. Value of division wall.
   b. Extent of area division wall.
   c. Openings through and at ends of walls.
   d. Parapets required.
8. Check for required fireproof openings in all exterior walls.
9. Determine person capacity of all areas and total for building.
10. Check for exit requirements based on capacity and other factors.
    a. Number of exits required.
    b. Number of stairways required.
    c. Width of doors.
    d. Width of stairways.
    e. Stairway landings.
    f. Distance of travel and dead-end corridors.
    g. Swing of doors.
    h. Handrails for all stairs and ramps.
    i. Rise and tread dimensions.
    j. Width of corridors.
11. Check for stairway enclosure requirements.
    a. Value of enclosure.
    b. Extent of enclosure.
    c. Smoke-proof stairway requirements.
    d. Value of all openings into enclosures.
12. Check for exit lighting requirements (both path lighting and exit lighting).
13. Check for value of all public corridor walls and doors.
14. Check for fire district location.
15. Check for type of roof covering. Based on construction and roof pitch.
16. Check required ceiling height of all spaces.
17. Be sure temporary partitions are of proper construction.
18. Check furnace and boiler-room enclosure requirements.
    a. Value of walls, floor, and ceiling.
    b. Protection of openings.
    c. Ventilation of room.
    d. Boiler or furnace clearances.
    e. Locations as related to stairways.
    f. Exits from room.
19. Be sure chimney construction meets code requirements.
    a. Materials required.

b. Size of flue.
c. Height above roof.
20. Fireplace construction.
21. Be sure range hood and vent installation meets code requirements.
22. Window area requirements and amount of operations sash provided.
23. Shaft construction, elevator, dumbwaiter, duct shafts, and others.
24. Penthouse construction.
25. Access to roof and when stairway to roof is required.
26. Balcony areas and construction of balcony.
27. Marquees and platform construction.
28. Arcade and bridge construction and protection of openings in same.
29. Incinerators and their enclosure rooms.
30. Interior finish requirements for all areas. Finish schedule should be on plans of importance.
31. Lowered ceiling constructions.
32. Attic divisions for floors and under roof areas.
33. Check all fireproof opening requirements.
    a. Value of doors required.
    b. Number of doors to openings
    c. Check for labels.
    d. Closing devices and hardware.
    e. Type of frames for doors.
    f. Check for types of fire windows.

different stages of a design project. Clearly there are methods suitable at particular stages of a project as there are methods relevant for more than one stage. Since the domain of this book is programming, the column corresponding to preliminary design and production was left vacant since other types of methods would be employed during this phase of a project.

	Living Room	Dining Room	Kitchen	Adult Bedroom	Children's Bedroom	Children's Bedroom	Children's Bedroom	Guest Room	Basement	Porch	Front Yard	Back Yard	Garage
Taking a Nap													
Loafing or Taking it Easy Around the House													
Reading Newspapers or Magazines													
Reading a Book													
Watching TV or Listening to Radio													
Individual Study, Writing, Composing													
Music (Playing or Listening to Radio)													
Visiting With Friends Over the Phone													
Crafts and Hobbies (Woodworking, Knitting)													
Entertaining Neighbors													
Entertaining Friends at Home (Includes Supper, Cards)													
Family Casual Conversation													
Gossiping													
Watching People in the Street													
Housework													
Sewing and Mending													
Food Preparation													
Meals at Home													
Washing Dishes													
Washing Clothes													
Home in Bed (Upset Stomach, Colds)													
Overseeing Children's Study, Practicing													
Overseeing and Participating in Various Forms of Home Recreation													
Children's Indoor Play (Toys, Games)													
Children's Sleeping													
Adults Sleeping													
Overnight Visitor													
Grandparents or Relatives Sleeping													
Yard Maintenance													
Car Maintenance													

Please Indicate the Amount of Time and Place (In Each Cell) Devoted to Each Activity

Figure 63
Household activities checklist. This is used to identify which household activities occur in different rooms of the house.

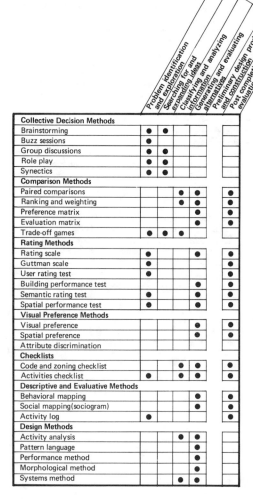

Figure 64
The programmer's kit of parts.

NOTES AND REFERENCES

1. Irwin Bross, *Design for Decision* (New York: The Free Press, 1953), p. 37.
2. See W. J. J. Gordon, *Synectics* (New York: Collier Books, 1961).
3. Bross, *Design for Decision.*
4. L. B. Archer, "An Overview of the Structure of the Design Process," in *Emerging Methods in Environmental Design and Planning*, ed. G. Moore (Cambridge: MIT Press, 1973).
5. H. A. Simon, *Models of Man* (New York: John Wiley & Sons, 1957), p. 198.
6. H. Sanoff, S. Christie, D. Tester, and B. Vaupel, "Building Evaluation," *Build International* 6 (May–June 1973): 261–297.
7. H. Sanoff, "Behavioral Settings in Residential Environments," *Journal of Architectural Education* 25, no. 4. (1971): 95–97.
8. R. Barker, *Ecological Psychology* (Stanford: Stanford University Press, 1968).
9. H. Proshansky and B. Seidenberg, eds., *Basic Studies in Social Psychology* (New York: Holt, Rinehart & Winston, 1965).
10. E. Willems, "Place and Motivation: Independence and Complexity in Patient Behavior," in *EDRA-3: Proceedings from the 3rd Annual Environmental Design Research Association Conference*, ed. W. Mitchell (1972), 4.3.1–8.
11. G. Winkel and G. Hayward, "Some Major Causes of Congestion in Subway Stations," unpublished manuscript, 1971.
12. R. Bechtel, "Human Movement in Architecture," in *Environmental Psychology*, ed. H. Proshansky, W. Ittelson, and L. Rivlin (New York: Holt, Rinehart & Winston, 1970), pp. 642–645.
13. H. Sanoff and J. Dickerson, "Mapping Children's Behavior in a Residential Setting," *Journal of Architectural Education* 25 (1971): 98–103.
14. B. Wells, "The Psycho-social Influence of Building Environment: Sociometric Findings in Large and Small Office Spaces," in *People and Buildings*, ed. Robert Gutman (New York: Basic Books, 1972), pp. 93–118.
15. W. Moleski, "Environmental Programming for Offices Based on Behavioral Considerations," in *Proceedings of Conference: Architecture for Human Behavior*, ed. J. Lang, C. Burnette, and D. Vashon (Philadelphia: AIA, 1971), and W. Moleski and R. Goodrich, "The Analysis of Behavioral Requirements in Office Settings," in *EDRA-3*, ed. Mitchell, pp. 41–47.
16. L. Goldblatt, "Architecture, Prisons and People," unpublished manuscript, 1972.
17. J. Moreno, *Who Shall Survive?* (New York: Beacon House, 1934).
18. Wells, "The Psycho-social Influence."
19. J. Gullahorn, "Distance and Friendship as Factors in the Gross Interaction Matrix," *Sociometry* 15 (1952): 123–134.

20. J. Adams, T. Alford, and T. Raper, "Environmental Planning Study," unpublished manuscript, North Carolina State University, 1970.

21. Wells, "The Psycho-social Influence."

22. S. Van der Ryn and M. Silverstein, *Dorms at Berkeley: An Environmental Analysis* (Berkeley: University of California Press, 1967).

23. A. Edwards, *Techniques of Attitude Scale Construction* (New York: Appleton-Century-Crofts, 1957).

24. By means of Table 1 in the appendix to ibid.

25. The ranking chart is described in Bruce Archer, "Systematic Method for Designers, Part Four: Examining the Evidence," *Design* 179 (Nov. 1963): 68–72.

26. For a complete analysis and description of the Kendall coefficient of concordance, see S. Siegel, *Non-Parametric Statistics for the Behavioral Sciences* (New York: McGraw-Hill, 1956), p. 229.

27. R. Ackoff, *The Design of Social Research* (Chicago: University of Chicago Press, 1953).

28. Ibid.

29. K. W. Norris, "A Morphological Approach to Engineering Design," in *Conference on Design Methods*, ed. J. C. Jones and D. G. Thornley (New York: Pergamon Press, 1963).

30. L. B. Archer, "An Overview of the Structure of the Design Process," in *Emerging Methods in Environmental Design and Planning*, ed. G. Moore (Cambridge: MIT Press, 1973); M. Riley, *Sociological Research* (New York: Harcourt, Brace & World, 1963).

31. Archer, "An Overview of the Structure."

32. L. Guttman, "The Basis for Scalogram Analysis," in *Measurement and Prediction*, ed. S. A. Stouffer, L. Guttman, E. A. Suchman, P. F. Lazarsfeld, Shirley A. Stor, and J. A. Gardner (Princeton: Princeton University Press, 1950), pp. 60–90.

33. Ibid.

34. See B. W. White and E. Saltz, "Measurements of Reproducibility," *Psychological Bulletin* 24 (1957): 81–99, for an excellent discussion of this technique.

35. Clair Selltiz, Marie Jahoda, M. Deutsch, and S. W. Cook, *Research Methods in Social Relations*, rev. ed. (New York: Holt, Rinehart & Winston, 1959).

36. W. Osgood et al., *The Measurement of Meaning* (Urbana: University of Illinois Press, 1957).

37. For a more complete discussion of these objectives, see C. Osgood, G. Suci, and P. Tannenbaun, *The Measurement of Meaning* (Urbana: University of Illinois Press, 1957), p. 100.

38. Milne Murray, research paper, University of California, Berkeley, 1964).

39. H. Sanoff, "Relating Learning Objectives to Education," in *Designing the Method*, ed. D. Tester (Raleigh, N.C.: Learning Environments, 1974), p. 231.

40. For a detailed description of the study, see H. Sanoff, "Measuring Attributes of the Visual Environment," in *Designing for Human Behavior*, ed. J. Lang, C. Burnette, W. Moleski, and D. Vachon (Stroudsburg: Dowden, Hutchinson & Ross, 1974), pp. 244–260.

3

Methods of Transforming Design Information

DESIGN PROCEDURES AND METHODS

There are undoubtedly numerous methods for gathering information, so too are there many procedures for transforming this raw information into codifiable, communicable, spatially related material for a design program. These transformation procedures or design models, as they are frequently referred to, exist in varying stages of utility to the designer and correspond to various classes of design problems.

All design models advocate information about the user as central to their purpose. Each introduces concepts, procedures, and often a vocabulary unique to the model. Generally all models rely upon some subset of information-gathering methods conceptually organized to offer the designer an opportunity for a fresh look at the process of designing. The advocates for new and improved methods of designing seek to enhance the quality of the designed artifact through the development of procedures that are conscious and communicable. It is argued that the self-conscious awareness of the designer's process provides the designer with control over his destination as well as the opportunity to learn. Only through repeated use of various methods and strategies can the designer learn about their effectiveness and modify them to a wide variety of purposes.

SYSTEMATIC DESIGN

This design procedure is intended to function in the area between the "traditional methods, based on intuition and experience, on the one hand, and a rigorous mathematical or logical treatment, on the other"; in a sense, to have the best of both. It is intended also to have the following effects: to reduce design error, redesign, and delay, and to make possible more imaginative and advanced designs.[1]

The imagination works best when it is allowed to alternate freely between all aspects of the problem without restraint of any type. Logical analysis fails if it departs from a systematic step-by-step sequence. Existing logical methods depend on keeping such diverse options apart by conscious and unnatural effort of the designer. Systematic design emphasizes the use of logic and intuition kept separate by an awareness of which approach is appropriate. The method develops in the usual three stage of analysis, synthesis, and evaluation.

The following is a detailed outline of the method. Jones usually refers to meetings of people—thus, plural or committee design stages—but indicates that the same procedure could be utilized by an individual. However, the discipline of sequential study obviously must be maturely self-administered, whereas in the group attack a leader or administrator would control this. The thrust of systematic design uses a team approach and multidisciplinary in nature.

Analysis

In the initial analysis stage of systematic design, requirements are identified, listed, and subsequently reduced to a parsimonious few, which are then organized into a set of interrelated performance specifications. The subsequent stages can be categorized.

Random list of factors At this and subsequent participants record all the thoughts that occur to them about the problem. Each person then reads his list, and each item is serially recorded. This is basically a brainstorming session free of criticism of ideas and with no attempts made to avoid duplication. The purpose of this first meeting is to generate as many ideas and collect as much information as possible in an open atmosphere.

Classification of factors At this and subsequent stages where the information does not appear to disclose any general pattern it may be useful to use a classification chart, which is an aid to relate factors to corresponding categories (Figure 65). Additional charts can be used for listing facotrs in each category when the lists become lengthy and complex. This stage in the analysis process is one where further additions as well as omissions can be identified.

Factors	Catagories				
	1	2	3	4	n
1........		●			
2........			●	●	
3........		●			
4........		●			
n........					

Figure 65
Classification chart.

A new category should be developed to separate ideas and solutions from information and requirements. There are many methods of recording this information, ranging from a notebook with idea sheets and information sheets to index cards that can be sorted into categories.

Sources of information The design team has now generated a large quantity of information, much of which may be conflicting and in need of verification. The classification process also identifies where information gaps occur. The use of libraries, information services, and technical and trade journals is valuable but often time-consuming and expensive. In order to minimize retrieval time, it is useful to identify and seek out what specific information is not known and request it as precisely as possible. The use of experts and consultants can also fill information gaps, particularly when there is a systematic attempt to distinguish between facts and opinion. It may also be necessary to resolve a controversial issue by experimentation or research.

Interactions between factors The factors affecting design are highly interactive and should therefore be diagrammed in order to discover and understand patterns of relationships. The most frequently used

Factors	1	2	3	4	5	6	7	n
1			●		●			
2				●	●		●	
3					●		●	
4							●	
5								
6							●	
7								
n								

Figure 66

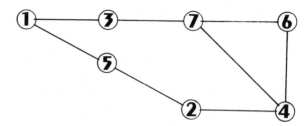

Figure 68
Interaction net.

method for finding relationships is the interaction matrix where all the possible combinations, by pairs, of the factors are recorded in the cell grid (Figure 66). Where every pair of factors interacts, there will be a design requirement that will be expressed as a performance specification. The pattern of relationships between intersecting factors can then be graphically replotted to form an interaction net, which is obtained in two stages. First, write out the numbers in a circle and draw connections corresponding to the crosses plotted on the interaction matrix (Figure 67). Second, redraw the net, keeping groups of interconnected numbers apart with as few crossed lines as

possible (Figure 68). This interaction net clarifies spatial connections so that the designer can see patterns of relationships, for example, between 7, 4, and 6.

Performance specifications In order to distinguish between the requirements of the problem and the solution, with no reference to shape or materials, performance specifications are written. An illustration of a P spec for roofing might be: "To prevent the penetration of water from outside, either by transfer through the material or by leakage and wind driven rain." A complete set of P specs for roofing would include weather resistance, wind resistance, fire endurance, impact-puncture resistance, slippage resistance, rupture resistance, thermal movement resistance, and resistance to water–vapor transfer.

Obtaining agreement The complete listing of performance specifications should be reviewed by all individuals whose agreement to the final design will be required.

Synthesis

The second stage of systematic design is synthesis, where solutions are sought for individual P specs so that a completed design is built up from partial solutions. It is the stage of integration and transformation of raw information and concepts with partial solutions.

Creative thinking It is again necessary to explore the fantasies of a number of people with different backgrounds in a situation free of criticism. Brain-

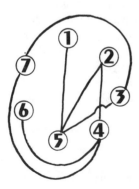

Figure 67
Interaction net.

storming can be utilized to review each P spec, and participants should respond to each statement. This meeting can generate conditions, amendments, and the like that can assist the design team in further clarifying the P specs.

Partial solutions Most traditional approaches to designing result in a solution conceived of as a whole with the subsequent resolution of details. The systematic approach is diametrically opposite: partial solutions to P specs are sought first, and then they are combined to generate several alternative whole solutions. Thus, each partial solution is considered independently of the others. In this way, the process of combining partial solutions has the least compromise insofar as satisfaction of P specs is concerned. As partial solutions are refined, it is necessary to establish parameters that circumscribe the limits of acceptability.

Combined solutions This stage of combining partial solutions is one of seeking compatibility and resolving conflicts. In order to determine the compatibility of partial solutions, an interaction matrix

and then an interaction net can be used. Since it is unlikely that compatible solutions will meet all P-specs, the problem is to decide which combinations are least compromising.

Solution plotting A systematic approach to designing seeks a range of alternatives that satisfy the specifications through clearly charted evidence of the solution's acceptability. It is often desirable to graphically plot relationships between all possible solutions and the degree to which they posses the desired characteristics. In Figure 69, seven alternative solutions are compared with their acceptability for both shape and performance. The relative range of desired characteristics can be shown on the graph so that their intersection demarks an area of satisfactory solutions.

Evaluation

Evaluation is that final stage where alternative designs are judged on how well they fulfill performance specifications.

Methods of evaluation Judgment by experience is the most effective method of evaluation, particularly when the right kind of experience is available and when more scientific methods are too costly or time-consuming. In new areas of design where experience is not applicable, the task then consists of devising tests where the designs are checked against P specs. Other possibilities include the formation of a design review committee whose responsibility might include the identification of possible consequences of the solutions.

Evaluation for operation The primary concern is for the prediction of the behavior of the physical artifact developed by the designer. The methods included for prediction are the collection of available experience and judgment, simulation of the solution by model making, drawings, and experimentation, and anticipation of circumstances and changes the solution may be required to withstand. With production items, the development of prototypes and

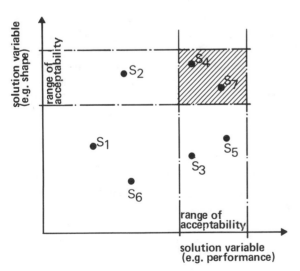

Figure 69
An array of solution(s) is compared by acceptability to shape and performance.

market pretesting are valuable approaches for predicting sales.

PATTERN LANGUAGE

Christopher Alexander succinctly states that there are two things wrong with design programs: "First of all, even if you state clearly what a building has to do, there is still no way of finding out what the building must be like to do it. The geometry of the building is still a matter for the designer's intuition; the program does not help. Second, even if you state clearly what the building has to do, there is no way of finding out if this is what the building ought to do. It is possible to make up an arbitrary program for a building. There is, at present, no way of being sure that programs are not an arbitrary program for a building. There is, at present, no way of being sure that programs are not arbitrary; there is no way of testing what the program says."[2] The underlying issue for Alexander is the rightness or wrongness of a program, which he states "is not a question of value, but one of fact." This model of pattern language attempts to provide a program that is objectively correct and that yields the actual physical geometry of a building.

The idea of a pattern is based on the premise that typical systems of connections exist. As an example, the relationship between entry, receptionist, and the waiting area in offices seems to occur frequently with very slight variations. While there are many people who do not believe that typologies of solutions exist, the pattern concept seeks to identify those typological situations.

The program model is behaviorally oriented; it replaces the concept of user needs with the concept of user tendencies, or what people are trying to do. The statement of tendencies is a hypothesis requiring careful specificity. Multiple meanings or ambiguity can confound the resolution of tendencies. Although people are continuously trying to do something, there are numerous occasions where the environment is not resilient enough to permit human tendencies to occur simultaneously. When conflict occurs, the environment needs design. A good environment, then, is one in which there are no conflicting tendencies. This requires the identification of all conflicts that might possibly occur in the environment. This process is a difficult one since it requires the designer to deliberately search for conflicts. It is also based on the premise that designing is an error-correcting process. This view is a major departure from other approaches since it begins with existing geometrical arrangements of relationships in the physical environment. The approach presumes that features of the building can help to prevent conflicts. The organization of building features is called patterns.

The pattern process encourages invention since tendencies are not inherent in conflict, but are brought into conflict by the condition in which they occur. The resolution of conflicts requires an invention of an arrangement in which the conflict would not exist. The context is the environmental setting in which tendencies come into conflict. These forces in conflict are perceived as the effect of an inadequate or fragmented environment. The primary goal of the designer, then, is to rearrange the environment so that there is a mutual coexistence of all forces. The basic philosophy of patterns is that there can be a satisfactory environment only when all forces coexist.

Although patterns should be universal, it is evident that they are culture based and, because of inherent value differences among individuals, they may be viewed differently. Similarly, the impact of patterns on the total design problem is variable. Since they are not equally influential, the combinatorial process is vague due to the numerous possible combinations and linkages generated from joining patterns.

Patterns do, however, complement the skills of the traditional designer in that they transmit notions of possible solutions. Patterns also require data, yet the pattern format specifies data related to design problems and permits input from a wide range of fields.

Clearly, the major advantage of the pattern approach is that it can save the designer the wasteful labor of working out solutions each time from the beginning.

To understand the way patterns are generated, used, and combined, consider the following case study, which illustrates the use of this method.

Two alternative designs for the same bank on the same site were prepared by Duffy and Torrey.[3] One design solution was based on the principle of a centralized forum, while the other solution employed a forum encompassing two-street frontages of a corner site. The experimenters indicate that initially there was no reason to select either alternative over the other, except for formal, nonpattern reasons.

A corner site of 104 feet by 99 feet was selected for both alternatives. The western street was assumed to be busier than the southern, whereas the other two sides of the square were adjacent to other buildings. Six officers and their four assistants required accommodations as well as seven tellers, three specialist tellers, and eleven clerks. Based upon the existing bank, the following space standards were adopted:

Entrance and forum space	2,230 square feet (34%)
Officers' area	1,230 square feet (19%)
Tellers' area	580 square feet (9%)
Clerical area	1,150 square feet (18%)
Vault and access	430 square feet (6%)
Staff lounge and storage	900 square feet (14%)

The length of the tellers' counter was set at seventy-five feet, or seven and one-half feet per person. A public writing shelf, thirty feet long, was also provided. Figures 70 and 71 illustrate the patterns and standards employed in two different situations. (Figures 72 and 73 show a further example.)

Although this case study of a bank merely summarizes the pattern concept, it does suggest that pattern usage does not result in one unique solution. Clearly, the two solutions were intuitive leaps to new combinations of patterns.

THE ACTIVITY ANALYSIS

The design process prescribes the establishment of the method by which the problem becomes identified.[4] In many problem situations, this can be a difficult task. One strategy for minimizing the difficulty is the articulation of the goal-setting process and the development of an activity analysis. The activity analysis comprises an assortment of techniques that are concerned with the goals for which that system is required to satisfy as well as provide the basis for defining the overall goals of the project. A systematic procedure for designing the program elements follows.

1. Identify and list the goals of the problem (statements about needs that a design tends to satisfy) and the constraints imposed on the solution from the problem statement. Brainstorming is a useful technique during this phase because it permits many uninhibited ideas to be voiced in a short time. The designer or group should permit full freedom to develop many possible design concepts. Every idea, fact, or question related to the problem should be listed, while judgment and criticism are restrained. Evaluation of the ideas occurs after the generation phase by establishing their order of importance as well as their relevance. The order of importance or ranking can be achieved by the paired comparisons method,[5] which consists of sets of paired statements that require comparative judgments as to which member of each pair is more favorable (Figure 74). The frequency with which each statement is judged more favorable is a result of the column totals.

2. Find the tacit goals and constraints (threshold of acceptance)—that is, those that are not explicitly mentioned because they are self-evident. The context may impose constraints that the designer must operate within.

3. Find the evaluation criteria that are relevant to the problem.

The problem now requires dissection into a possible set of subproblems whose restrictions and goals

Numbers	Topic	Problem	Tendencies conflicting
1	Entrance to architect's office—transparent	Visitors feel that they are not welcome when they approach the office.	1. Visitor feels uncomfortable about entering an alien professional world. 2. "Architects" fear complete exposure to public realm.
3	Entrance—position of reception desk in relation to entrance	Office has to control entrance of visitors.	1. Visitors want a route. 2. Some visitors want to come into office unobserved 3. Visitors want to prepare "face." 4. Receptionist wants to observe visitor as soon as he enters and be unobserved. 5. Receptionist wants another direction to face.
5	Staff and path to drawing office	In many offices there is nowhere for the staff to get together. There is nowhere to go (except at the work table), nowhere to sit, nowhere to prepare coffee, snacks, etc.	1. Staff tend not to meet each other except when they are actually collaborating on a problem. 2. Staff tend to learn more from each other if they meet informally away from workplace. 3. Staff tend to get jaded, need breaks, light relief.
6	Partners and contact with staff	Partners must keep in contact with staff yet want a place of their own in the office.	1. Partners tend to make special "places" for themselves in the office 2. Staff tend to lose contact with partners.
8	Two workplaces	People want to work in groups as well as work as separate individuals	1. People tend to want relief from a single task. 2. People tend to want to work in groups—realize that it's more efficient for certain kinds of arch. problems.
9	Conference room	Not all meetings can be held in the drawing office.	1. Need for meetings with limited outside contact. 2. Need for staff and partners to keep in touch (see pattern 6).
12	Group proximity	Group work is impossible without proximity.	1. Tendency for groups that are geographically separate to act separately. 2. Tendency for proximity interchange to increase sentiments of solidarity.
13	Privacy and access with the group	Solitary work is often necessary within a working group—the problem of interruptions becomes critical.	1. Tendency to want solitude. 2. Tendency to want contact within group.

Figure 70
Patterns and transformations for architects' offices.

Pattern	Transformations		
	A	**B**	**C**
If: Entrance to any architect's office. Then: Entrance facade has transparent surfaces on either side of *door* and/or door can be transparent also.			
If: Entrance to any architect's office that maintains a reception desk. Then: Visitor faces wall as he enters, then turns right angle. Receptionist nearest to entrance has clear view of entry; can turn in 2 directions faces visitor, no way ino office except by R desk.			
If: Any architect's office. Then: Kitchen near receptionist, breakplace in center of office where all circulation joins & BETW. All workplaces and entrance, library niche can be used as breakplace but should be opposite BP if have both, breakplace near R & K.			
If: Office where partners and staff are in danger of being separated. Then: Common circulation for each and staff and partners work together in teams in drawing office.			
If: Any architect's office. Then: Library is equipped with carrels for individual study & is large enough to store books and materials. Open on one side of main circulation route. Space large enough for 1/3 maximum office staff at any time.			
If: Any architect's office. Then: Conference room just off main circulation route. entrance not through workplace. receptionist can give easy directions to it, distractions controllable to and from workplace.			
If: Any architect's office. Then: Cluster workplace tables in work groups for any size job. Semi transparent screens drop from ceiling grid enable any group to totally enclose itself.			
If: Any architect's office. Then: Option for closure on at least 2 sides of each workplace. Use existing walls or screens.			

2. Combination of patterns
Local condition—
Example A: Small office
Local condition—
Example B: Medium office

The Architects' offices examples show that local conditions (three existing structural shells in this case) affect the order in which patterns are used and that individual patterns vary where applied in different circumstances.

1. Entrance facade has transparent surfaces on either side of *door* and/or door can be transparent also.

2. A part of the display area in waiting space explains architect's design approach.

3. Visitor faces wall as he enters. Then turns right angle. Receptionist nearest to entrance has clear view of entry; can turn in 2 directions faces visitor, no way into office except by R desk.

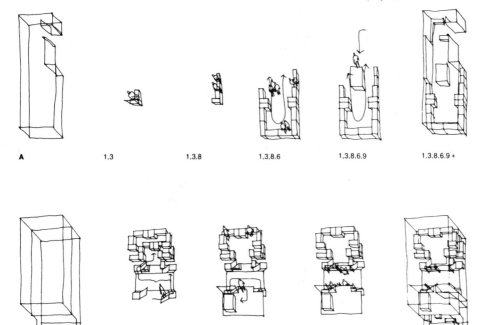

A   1,3   1,3,8   1,3,8,6   1,3,8,6,9   1,3,8,6.9 +

B   6,13   6,13,9   6,13,9,8   6,13,9,8 +

Figure 71
A progress report on the pattern language for architects' offices.

4. Route from waiting area to conference room includes whole view of office.

5. Kitchen near receptionist, breakplace in center of office where all circulation joins and between all workplaces and entrance, library niche can be used as breakplace but should be opposite BP if have both, breakplace near R & K.

6. Common circulation for each and staff and partners work together in teams in drawing office.

7. Central location for library shelves on main circulation route.

8. Library is equipped with carrels for individual study and is large enough to store books and materials. Open on one side of main circulation route. Space large enough for 1/3 maximum office staff at any time.

9. Conference room just off main circulation route, entrance not through workplace, receptionist can give easy directions to it, distractions controllable to and from workplace.

10. Destroy all non-current drawings; use microfilm and store in library provision for scanning in ind. study space in library.

11. Common circulation for partners and staff; partners and staff work together in teams in office (see pattern 6).

12. Cluster workplace tables in work groups, for any size job. Semi transparent screens drop from ceiling grid enable any group to totally enclose itself.

13. Option for closure on at least 2 sides of each workplace. Use existing walls or screens.

14. Provide two surfaces as shown.

15. Provide for slide out surface as shown.

16. Provide for quick reference (technical) books as shown.

17. Provide adjustable drawing surface as shown.

18. Provide for a 4' minimum back up space as shown.

19. Provide for range of acceptable workplace layouts—workplaces rearrangeable.

20. Provide flat file (4' × 5' × 4') under layout surfaces whenever 2 layout tables come together. One layout table must belong to partner.

3. Final configurations—architects' offices

A

0   5   15   30

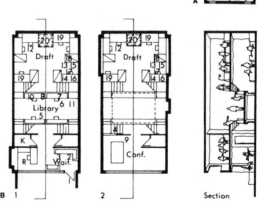

B   1   2   Section

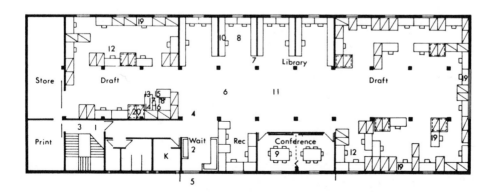

Numbers	Topic	Problem	Tendencies conflicting
3	Entrances to banks	Banks are anxious that people should feel at ease when coming off the street.	1. Banks want people to feel free to stand around without interception by receptionists or other checking devices. 2. People want to locate quickly the part of the bank they are looking for.
4	Bank forums	Banks want to guide but not propel people towards their services.	1. Banks want people to feel free to enter 2. People demonstrate the desire to hesitate a little before launching into their business.
6	Writing out and calculations by customers	Banks want to permit people to write out checks etc. but don't want blocked circulation.	1. People write out checks etc. after they have entered the bank. 2. Banks don't want such people blocking free circulation.
8	Internal circulation	Banks permit the public to enter freely but want to limit their access to certain sections of the bank.	1. Public circulates freely unless checked 2. Bank staff wish to go about their business without distraction from unauthorised public.
9	Bank officers and the public	Banks want to attract the public to their officers but control access.	1. Banks want public to feel free to talk to its officers. 2. Public may either miss altogether or inundate officers.
10	Tellers and the public	Banks want to attract the public to their tellers and yet ensure security.	1. Banks want public to feel easy and friendly when dealing with tellers. 2. Banks want to protect their tellers and cash.
13	Contact between officers	Bank officers need to be separate from each other and yet keep in contact.	1. Bank officers deal with limited ranges of decisions and may wish to pass a problem to a colleague quickly and without fuss 2. Public wants privacy in dealings with bank officers.
14	Tellers and administration	Tellers need to be in contact with both the public and bank administration.	1. Tellers deal with public 2. Tellers seek records, statements, etc. from administration constantly. 3. Administration supervises tellers.

Figure 72
Patterns and transformations for banks.

Pattern	Transformations	
	A	**B**
1. Public enters the bank without check. 2. Entrance point permits an overview of all bank services. 3. All bank services are clearly marked and distinct from one another.		
1. Public enters bank without check. 2. Waiting or hesitating space is provided both immediately outside and inside the bank. 3. Exhibits may be used to mask hesitation.		
1. Writing space is provided near the entrance but in a position out of the main flow of circulation and which does not impede vision.		
1. Clearly defined circulation for public. 2. Entirely separate circulation for staff.		
1. Clear visual link between public and officers. 2. Distinct separation between officers area and public forum. 3. Guides stationed on border to sanction access to officers.		
1. 4'6" high continuous bench 2' wide separates public and tellers. 2. Tellers can control moveable and lockable cash boxes.		
1. Bank officers are open to each other as well as to the public. 2. Sufficient separation between officers to ensure private individual dealings.		
1. Tellers are sandwiched between public and administration.		

5. Combination of patterns

Example A: Formal scheme

Example B: Formal scheme

The Bank examples show that the same patterns combine in the same circumstances (1 structural shell) in different ways. Two different formal schemes (two variations of pattern 8) influence the way in which shapeless pattern material can be organized in the design process.

1. Banks on corners or on other conspicuous sites (at a certain frequency). Sidewalk and entrance to bank is designed to permit loitering.

2. Public may glimpse bank activities from outside but are not permitted to register any great detail.
Certain bank activities are screened from the public eye.

3. Public enters the bank without check. Entrance point permits an overview of all bank services.
All bank services are clearly marked and distinct from one another.

4. Public enters bank without check. Waiting or hesitating space is provided both immediately outside and inside the bank.
Exhibits may be used to mask hesitation.

5. Counter design permits variation in number of tellers. Space provided for lines of 6 but no more.
Customer at entrance point can survey all lines equally easily and select the shortest.

6. Writing space is provided near the entrance but in a position out of the main flow of circulation and which does not impede vision.

7. More than enough space and height is provided in the public part of the bank. Materials are chosen which connotate richness.
A limit is set to both space extravagance and richness in accordance with public notation of what is fitting.

8. Clearly defined circulation for public. Entirely separate circulation for staff.

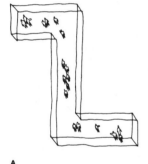

A

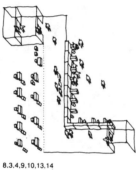

8,3,4,9,10,13,14

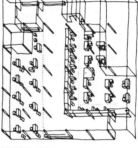

8,3,4,9,10,13,14 +

B

8,3,4,9,10,13,14

8,3,4,9,10,13,14+

Figure 73
A progress report on the pattern language for banks.

9. Clear visual link between public and officers.
Distinct separation between officers area and public forum.
Guides stationed on border to sanction access to officers.

10. 4'6" high continuous bench 2' wide separates public and tellers.
Tellers can control moveable and lockable cash boxes.

11. Security is achieved by appropriate low barriers and also by overall openness and visibility.

12. Vault is near entrance. Vault is easily visible at night from outside the bank for police checks.

13. Bank officers are open to each other as well as to the public.
Sufficient separation between officers to ensure private individual dealings.

14. Tellers are sandwiched between public and administration.

15. Officers may be separated from administration but no request for a piece of information whether requested by telephone or secretary should be the cause of delay.

16. Officers are arranged in rank order. Space and equipment is sufficient to indicate that officers are of managerial status.

17. A hidden rest area is provided where staff can go occasionally to relax or eat lunch or exchange informal conversation.

6. Final configurations—banks

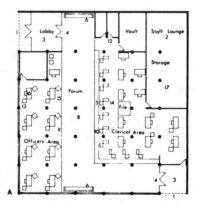

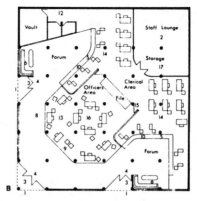

Figure 74
Paired comparisons.

A	B	C	D	E
B	C	D	E	F
A	B	C	D	
C	D	E	F	
A	B	C		
D	E	F		
A	B			
E	F			
A				
F				

are more clearly defined. Two examples of sub-problems or subsystems are described here, with the conceptual tools and techniques for their analysis.

Activity System Analysis

An activity is an occurrence in which there is a spatial connection between people and place. Any recognized activity or unit of activity should be considered in respect to the necessary relations between other activities and the basic physical requirements. Activities and activity systems are so closely related to our understanding of the physical facilities that condition them that we sometimes describe an activity in terms of the type of physical "place" or facility in which it is performed without fully understanding the relationship.

In order to realize the relation between the organization and employment of physical elements in space and the human activities that determine their employment, an independent or abstracted view of the activity itself should be conducted, free of any preconceived spatial attitudes. The activity analysis is essentially a study of the boundary conditions of the system and the enveloping environment.

1. Identify the activities for which the artifact is primarily to be designed. (These primary activities define the purpose of the artifact.)

2. Identify and list those activities that take place as consequences of the primary activities (secondary activities or derived activities).

3. For each of these activities determine the requirement to be fulfilled in order to make them possible. Indicate whether the requirement is based on fact, intuitive fact, or assumption. (A requirement is a quantifiable statement about a proposed behavior.) This indication is a useful guide for future decisions and the degree of their uncertainty.

4. Determine dimensional and area standards between persons and objects likely to be used in the object study (anthropometric analysis).

5. Analyze activities and predict alternate tentative optimal arrangements. This is conducted through the analysis of organizations and relationships between activities. For example, privacy is an important factor that can influence spatial proximity. This factor, however, has two important distinctions: visual and acoustic. Visual privacy is primarily the need to mask eye contact between two or more activities, whereas acoustic privacy is the requirement

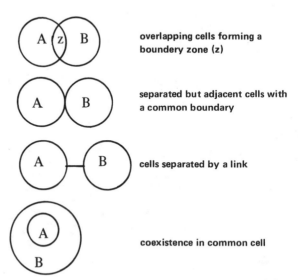

overlapping cells forming a boundery zone (z)

separated but adjacent cells with a common boundary

cells separated by a link

coexistence in common cell

Figure 75
Topological relationships for activity analysis (relative position of two cells).

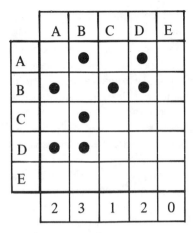

Figure 76
Ranking interaction matrix.

for separation of activities because of unwanted sound. Generally, satisfying an acoustic requirement subsumes visual separation as well; however, the reverse is not true. Another factor influencing arrangements is the traffic between activities. Traffic is measured by the flow of people between places and the frequency of that flow.

6. Rank activity relationships in order of importance and rate the ranking. This is best accomplished by utilizing a matrix to identify the relationships (Figure 76). List all the activities on both the horizontal and vertical axis of the matrix. Then compare each activity with all of the others to determine if there is a dependency between any of the pairs. A notation in the cell grid indicates a relationship between the pair of activities. The summation of marks in the vertical columns of the matrix indicates the number of connections between activities, as well as an order of importance. This discussion is based on binary decisions between two activities; either there is a relationship or there is not. It is possible to assume that there is some connection between all the activities in the matrix so that the important distinction is the magnitude of the dependency between each pair. In this case it would be appropriate to substitute a numerical scale value from one to five to

indicate potency, rather than a notation to indicate dependency. An interaction matrix can be made to ensure that all possible interactions or dependencies are discovered. A matrix can also be used to exhibit relationships for each of the variables to be investigated and to establish orders of importance.

7. Synthesize the analysis.

Design Alternatives

In this part of the process, principal conceptual alternatives are to be found for the layout of the system to be designed. As a first step, it is sufficient to find the various possibilities that are consistent with the previously determined requirements and constraints.

1. Determine which of the activities identified above should take place in a common cell (a spatial unit for multipurpose and combinative use). Refer to the types of relationships in Figure 75 to produce a diagram similar to that in Figure 77.

2. Find the alternatives for arranging primary activity cells as they result from the analysis of activities and traffic studies.

3. Find the meaningful alternatives for laying out the entire environmental complex, thus combining the multiple primary cells with secondary cells, each

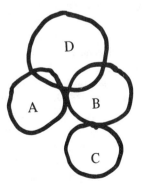

Figure 77
Topological relationship.

of them corresponding to a complex activity space. A topological analysis is suffient at this stage.

4. Check the design alternatives for their compatibility and exclude those that have to be rejected according to your preliminary criteria. Design a display (Venn diagrams, for example) of these alternatives that shows their similarities and differences.

5. From your previous considerations, try to derive metrical restrictions and prescriptions to all of the alternatives. The result will be a set of semitopological alternatives for the design concept of the object.

6. From the list of evaluation criteria, find those that can be applied to the alternatives. For each criterion define a scale for judgment and prepare a table that refers to the various alternatives and criteria.

THE PERFORMANCE CONCEPT

The performance concept is a procedure used to describe desired attributes of a material, component, or system in order to fulfill the requirements of the intended user. It provides for the incorporation of technological alternatives and the opportunity for innovation. A statement of performance suggests conditions that must be met rather than standard rules of thumb. The performance concept is industry oriented. It is proposed to bring production costs of products within the demand capability of the market. It is an orientation calculated to make the direction of industry freer of constraints by providing industry the incentive to develop new products.

The performance concept consists of a set of elements sequentially developed and begins with the performance requirements, statements about the users whom the environment tends to accommodate. User needs embrace the entire sociopsychological spectrum. Performance criteria are those characteristics used to assess the degree of fulfillment of the requirements. Once criteria are identified, there is a need to develop a method of evaluating solutions

prescribed to satisfy the requirements against such criteria. These are referred to as performance evaluative techniques. Statements that indicate which criteria are to be considered and how they are to be measured are described as performance specifications. To the extent that the specifications can be generalized, they can, by an authoritative body, be considered a performance standard. A collection of specifications and standards adapted by law is called a performance code.

John Eberhard, formerly with the National Bureau of Standards, has described the performance approach:

> The performance concept is an organized procedure or framework within which it is possible to state the desired attributes of a material, component or system in order to fulfill the requirements of the intended user without regard to the specific means to be employed in achieving the results. This is true of any product or system produced for use by humans, from shelter to weapons. We are concerned in this report with the development of performance statements for the system and sub-systems of a house, a dwelling unit, a collection of dwelling units in a high rise building, or a community of units in low rise buildings, but not with systems of the city or beyond the concerns of a community development. We are concerned with community systems and services only as they interact with our prime considerations listed above.[6]

The performance concept consists of a set of elements that are more or less sequentially developed and that normally become more rigorous at each stage of their development. This range of elements is shown in Figure 78, and we will expand on the terms used.

Performance Requirements

At the fundamental level, performance requirements are derived from the characteristics of users that the physical environment can affect. Some of these are physiological needs (the life processes), psychological needs (the mental processes), and

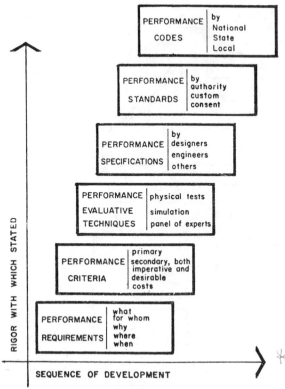

THE PERFORMANCE HIERARCHY

Figure 78
From J. P. Eberhard, *The Performance Concept: A Study of Its Applications to Housing* (Washington, D.C., 1969), 1: 38.

sociological needs (the interactions between people and groups and the effects of commonly held beliefs).

Needs are not dependent on particular materials, devices, or systems but are derived from the following questions: What is the use or function being considered? For whom is the requirement posed? Why is there a need? (This helps explain the background consideration out of which the need has grown and will assist in determining the anticipated benefits.) Where will the needs exist, or what are the limits and context of the needs? When will the needs exist and for how long?

Performance Criteria

Performance criteria are attributes or characteristics that are to be used in evaluating whether the requirements are being met. They may or may not be measurable in any rigorous way but can be evaluated by some appropriate method. There are secondary but imperative criteria with respect to public health and safety that may be present because of the context of the requirement. There are secondary but desirable criteria related to the interface between solutions and the larger subsystems or systems of which they will be a part. Criteria related to costs of alternative solutions will enter into the evaluation of performance potential versus benefits.

Performance Evaluative Techniques

Once criteria are identified, there is a need to develop some method of evaluating solutions advanced to meet the requirements against such criteria. The most reproducible evaluative techniques are those based on physical tests. But some criteria do not lend themselves to numerical evaluation so that simulation techniques will have to be utilized to determine if the solution is satisfactory. In other cases the judgment of experts may be the only evaluation possible.

Performance Specifications

Performance specs are statements that are rigorous enough to indicate which criteria are to be considered and how they are to be measured. Upper or lower limits, established according to the selected measurement technique, are used to indicate the range of values of the criteria that are considered acceptable or unacceptable. They may be used or required by owners or their agents, including architects and engineers.

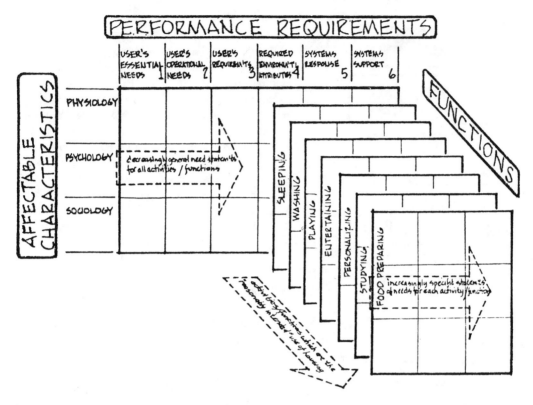

Figure 79
Performance requirements development methodology. From J. P. Eberhard,
The Performance Concept: A Study Of Its Applications to Housing **(Washing-**
ton, D.C. 1969), 1: 53.

Performance Standards

If the measurement techniques are reproducible and the requirements are reasonably common ones, a duly constituted (authoritative) body may issue the specifications as a standard to be referenced by others, or it may become a de facto standard by common usage.

Performance Code

A performance code is a collection of specifications and standards adopted by a process of law and enforceable by the police power of a government.

Codes are promulgated by national model code groups and by state and local governments. A code is usually intended for impartial regulation of an area of activity to protect the safety, health and general welfare of the public.

Performance Requirements for Housing

There are two methods for developing performance requirements for housing. The first is to develop statements of users' needs—those "satisfactions" the user desires or needs from housing. The second method is to use currently available building component parts and systems as models and to abstract from these their important and desired performance characteristics. Both methods can be developed into performance specifications used to procure housing. The first method is more difficult, implying evaluative techniques and a data base not completely available now. It does offer a wider range of alternative responses to user needs as the statements are essentially stated in terms of the user and not the item of hardware. The second method offers, in a number of cases, an easier transition to the performance "way" of designing and procuring housing because the evaluative procedures are relatively well developed.

Because user satisfaction is given foremost consideration in the performance approach, it is acknowledged that for each function and activity, criteria must be described for each user. Since there are many users who change over time as individuals or families, and as communities grow and influence each other, all users have been aggregated into a generic "user" to accommodate the performance approach at this time. It has been previously stated that the characteristics of users that the physical environment can affect are physiological, psychological, and sociological needs. The user's responses to these needs largely depends on his resources, social group, location, and unit size.

Although it is desirable to describe the environment as a function of these characteristics, and to develop "needs" statements since they do influence the quality of the environment, performance requirements can be developed only for psysiological needs for the typical user. This approach advocated by the authors of *The Performance Concept* was based on the limited time frame and state of the art, which precluded any focus on the psychological and sociological needs. It has been argued that by developing a pshysiological orientation, performance statements could be generated for factors such as gravity, illumination, helath, and safety, while privacy, personalization, and aspirations will markedly vary for different users and user groups.

The organization of the performance approach is based on four major features. The *requirements of the user* are those essential needs that must be met by the environmental system. *Environmental attributes* is the link between the user and the environmental system of housing. This statement describes the qualitites the environment must possess in order that the user requirement can be satisfied. *Environmental responses* are descriptions of how the attributes can be supplied. *Environmental systems support* describes the energy sources, spatial and structural support, or removal of unwanted output.

In pursuing performance characteristics for housing, specific activities and functions need to be developed into clear statements of user requirements, environmental attributes, systems response, and support. The activity of *food preparation* was selected to illustrate the features of the performance approach. Although the consideration for food preparation would include a myriad of considerations such as cooking facilities, preparation surfaces, water supply, storage, serving, waste removal, physical arrangement, light, ventilation, and acoustic characteristics in addition to health and safety, the illustration will be the "sensory" environment. The ingredients included in the sensory environment are thermal, illumination, acoustical, tactile, and aesthetic, as shown in Figure 80.

If the function is reading, the reader must be able to see the material. The environmental attribute then is light and appropriate levels of illumination. The systems response of how light is supplied might take the form of lighting fixtures, windows, or some unique light source not yet known. Environmental systems support describes the energy sources and spatial and structural adequacy as well as any unwanted or controllable side effects, such as heat generated by light.

BUILDING PERFORMANCE SYSTEM

The Building Performance Research Unit (BPRU) was originally conceived out of the long-standing conviction that building designers were accumulating little collective experience as a profession and were

REQUIREMENTS OF THE USER 3	ENVIRONMENTAL ATTRIBUTES 4	ENVIRONMENTAL SYSTEMS RESPONSE 5	ENVIRONMENTAL SYSTEMS SUPPORT 6
"PROPER" SENSORY ENVIRONMENT FOR FUNCTION MUST BE PRESENT DURING THAT FUNCTION	Provide proper thermal environment for user engaged in food preparation - Conduction - Convection - Radiation reference: B.3:4.3	- Supply System - Control System - Removal System for unwanted output	
	Provide proper illumination for food preparation: - Light levels appropriate to tasks, e.g.: reading, cutting - Color Fidelity - Direction of light to task areas - Controlled Contrast - Controlled Glare reference: B.3:4.4	- Supply System - Control System - Directional Controls - Surfaces to achieve such illumination needs	
	Provide proper acoustical environment for food preparation - Ambient Noise e.g., equipment, mechanical - Low transmitted sound from adjacent spaces - Low reverberation in food preparation space - "Signals" audible to the user to aid food preparation reference: B.3:4.1	- Absorptive or non-reverberant surfaces in use contact with "hard" objects - Adequate sound attenuation with adjacent space	
	Provide proper tactile environment for activity Textures for use during function 1. With attention to rate of activity and position of user during activity	- Surfaces which are comfortable to the touch and permit food preparation and related activities - Information transmitted by texture, e.g., surfaces which should be used for cutting, etc.	
	Provide proper esthetic environment, i.e., one which clarifies and enhances use	Surfaces, edges, shapes and organizing principles, which - Perception of food preparation activities and clarity - Information transmittal e.g., hot surface - Focus on activity	*B*
	Provide consistancy of sensory environment		

A

PHYSIOLOGY | ACTIVITY SUPPORT

PERMIT (OR ENHANCE) THE OCCURRENCE OF ACTIVITIES AND FUNCTIONS

Figure 80
Typical performance requirement data sheet.

subsequently prone to replication without assessment. BPRU started work in 1967 at the University of Strathclyde in Scotland when architects, engineers, the Ministry of Public Works, and the *Architect's Journal* joined together to provide the necessary financial support for design research and development, primarily in the area of educational facilities.

Frequently investigations are not subject to feedback prior to or during the research process by the larger professional community, whom the results will ultimately serve. Therefore, to lessen the probability of relevance and communications problems, feedback was considered a necessary component of agreement through explicit presentation and discussion of the BPRU projects at all points in their conceptual development with their sponsoring body. It was subsequently found that feedback of this sort was much more helpful if it were used to locate areas that needed research or that had problems and if it were offered at key points in the research scheme, specifically, after the problem was perceived and properly modeled, prior to secondary data collection, after a synthesis route was perceived, and in the evaluative phases of each study.

The outcome of this kind of conception can serve only to break the design-research barriers. Upon review of its activities, BPRU determined this feedback process somewhat counterproductive to the research process but realized that it did considerably increase the use of or interest in research at the practicing professional level. "It is obvious that buildings are for people. People use them; peoply pay for them; and people design them. Therefore, an understanding of design and the subsequent performance of its products must logically start with an understanding of people."[7]

A statement of beliefs about people was put forth as an orientation to help the reader understand the Building Performance Research Unit's descriptive *Model of the Building/People System*, which formatively helped in the specification and development of its research work in the United Kingdom. This statement of premises can be summarized as follows:

1. People are goal oriented and subsequently modify their environment in ways that will enable them to achieve their goals more readily.
2. People work toward the achievement of many goals to fulfill their long-term aims or objectives. It is at the goal-oriented level, though, that we can most readily see the relevance of the physical environment.
3. In a systematic sense, people can be considered adaptive organisms. People modify their environment in order to achieve their goals, and, subsequently, the resulting environment acts to modify their initial goals.
4. This individual–environment system (to the designer) is most usefully described in terms of the processes that constitute it.
5. People (and, hence, the organizations to which they belong) can be regarded as forming together with the environment a set of systems that themselves are goal oriented.
6. These systems interact with each other in an open rather than a closed fashion.

Conceptual Model of the System of Building and People

The design of buildings is contingent upon numerous subsystems. The BPRU constructed its descriptive model (which is at building scale) to serve as a framework for the examination of implicit and explicit relationships between these contingent subsystems. (See Figure 81.) "For purposes of decision-making, this model has two interesting and unusual features. First, it enables the whole system, or any part of it, to be explained in terms of at least five different yet related categories of description: (1) Objective; (2) Activity; (3) Environment; (4) Hardware; (5) Resources. Thus, for instance, in describing the provision of illumination one could describe an actual fixture, with its dimensions, materials, lamp, physical characteristics (4); or one could describe the performance of the fixture in appropriate units of

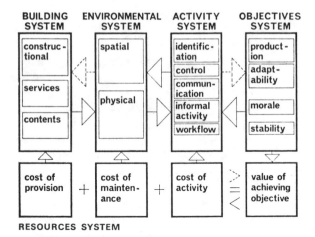

Figure 81
Conceptual model of the system of building and people.

physics and photometry-total flex emission, luminous intensity in a given direction, surface luminance, etc. (3); or one could describe the effects of the illumination and photometric characteristics on activity or behavior-glare assessment, or one could describe the objective which the illumination achieves—a level of morale, profit, or self-identity in a work group (1). Finally, one could describe the costs and benefits of the system at any of the four levels (5)."[8]

Specification of this variety can thus be seen as providing a metalanguage by means of which intention is translated into achievement parameters. The performance specification can, therefore, be viewed as a prescriptive statement expressing the required properties of a product within a range of different descriptive categories.

The second characteristic of the model is that each of its four parts has costs or values related to it. These can be stated in either subjective or objective terms, depending on the level of related information extant. Thus, by attributing a relative cost to all aspects of the building system, genuine cost-benefit analysis and optimization within a given resource envelope can be obtained.

Using the specification form implicit in this model, it is probable that the building industry will have to subdivide design roles into a client/design analysis group to initially specify what is needed or wanted, and a product design/producer group to design a product to meet these specifications. This model can also be extended into a third dimension,—time (Figure 82). A cross-section through the solid in Figure 81 shows a snapshot, at any moment in time, of the whole system, which is dynamic. The generative subsystem of design (control) is the connecting link between these layers, which determines the way one changes into the next. The whole of this is concerned with the birth, life, and death of one scale of system—a building and its occupants, for example.

The Design Process and Appraisal[9]

Most descriptions of the design procedure recognize two basic patterns in the process: morphologically "vertical" and "horizontal" processes.[10] The vertical is a management process, whereby a critical path is worked up to divide the total time available into stages that follow linearly (abstract to concrete). The Royal Institute of British Architects' plan of work, stages A to B, is a well-know example of such a structure.[11]

The horizontal process is essentially the same as the vertical except its weaknesses are to some extent remedied by using an open-ended, iterative decision process at each of its stages. This process appears to have three main parts to it that are not clearly separable and may occur in any sequence. (See Figure 83.) These are:

1. Understanding the problem (analysis): This includes the gathering of all relevant information: the establishment of relationships, constraints, objectives, criteria.
2. Producing a design solution (synthesis): The designer appears to select or combine three strategies: predicting on the basis of a body of

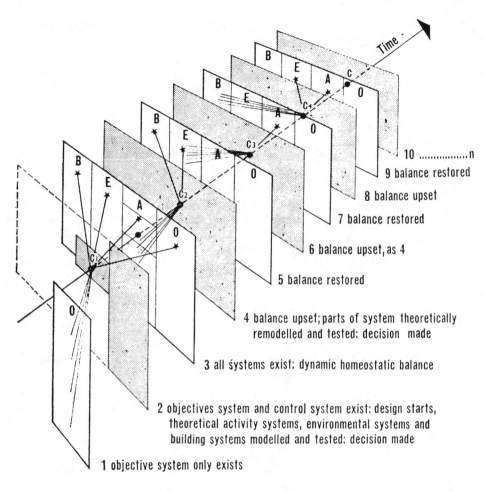

10 ....n

9 balance restored

8 balance upset

7 balance restored

6 balance upset, as 4

5 balance restored

4 balance upset; parts of system theoretically
remodelled and tested: decision made

3 all systems exist: dynamic homeostatic balance

2 objectives system and control system exist: design starts,
theoretical activity systems, environmental systems and
building systems modelled and tested: decision made

1 objective system only exists

$$C = \begin{cases} \text{control of activity} \\ \text{control of environment} = \text{design} \end{cases}$$

Figure 82
The system model extended in time.

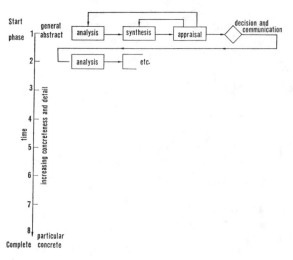

Figure 83
Model of the design process.

knowledge; testing out an idea, largely unaware of its consequences until after the test; and designing and building a solution that embodies a range of related solutions in hopes that at least one will work.

3. Establishing the performance of the solution (appraisal): There are three basic steps: representation (modeling the solution in a suitable way); measurement (the performance of the model is obtained on as wide a variety of counts as necessary); and evaluation (obtained via cost-benefit analysis; subjective valuing; comparison with the ideal or initially specified performance standards; conformity to constraints recorded in analysis; and so on).

There are three basic sequences in design (see Figure 84). Choice and combination of these sequences depends on the personality of the designer, the complexity of the problem, and the organizational pattern of the design office. These are:[12]

1. A problem may be analyzed in full detail from beginning to end before any design concept is attempted.

2. The solution is designed via an iterative agglomeration or reclustering procedure.

3. Each stage of analysis is followed by synthesis at its own level before proceeding to the next.

The Use of Resources

All design is concerned with finding solutions to problems within a resource envelope.

Resource partitioning Characteristic of Western political systems is that resources for building (publicly and privately) become available through the sequential allocation of funds in a chainlike, diminishing fashion. For the building designer and owner, a segment of the last slicing operation above him results in his slice of the original allocation. This slice is both a functional and territorial one. Money available for maintenance and alteration usually lands in the system via a different route. This divisional route-slicing operation makes comprehensive cost-benefit analysis an unattractive appraisal technique to the client.

To make the best use of limited resources (not only initially but over the life of the system), the control activity must unite physical design and the redesign of activity systems with that of hardware and must be free to allocate resources across the board. Otherwise, only diseconomic solutions can result.[13]

Resource models Designers need to have not only conceptual models of the system but ways of representing the resources they require for their creation and maintenance and the losses and gains (benefits) yielded. There are four basic types of resource models available to us. They are:

1. Capital cost model: This is the predominant mode. It works for small economic matters because there is enough feedback due to the repetitive nature of these situations to continuously readjust purchasing policy; on larger economic matters this feedback is absent.[14]

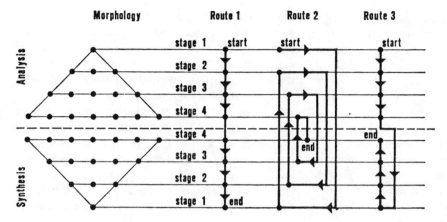

Figure 84
The three sequences in design.

2. Cost-in-use model: This model allows projection into the future to determine cost that will be accrued through time allowing comparisons to be made on an equal basis.[15]

3. Cost-effectiveness model: In addition to the cost-in-use projections, the cost of activity, in the activity system of the model, are treated as part of the total cost system and the value of the objectives as the effects. The solution is selected that, at the stated cost, results in effects of the highest value.

4. Cost-benefit model: This model expresses all terms in the cost model in a single unit (cash). If all functional relationships in the system are known, it is possible to set up equations that express these and to generate an optimum (maximum return) solution.[16]

Optimization A single criterion must be adopted to explore the possibilities in the context of contemporary economic theory (as in the cost-benefit model above). The two variables being compared can then be expressed as nonlinear equations and graphed (Figure 85). A summary curve can then be derived representing total cost and the optimum value read as the ordinate that intersects the summary curve at the point where its slope is 0 relative to the X axis.

To extend this procedure into the realm of subjectively derived criteria (obtained via semantic scales or other response variable methodologies) attach cost figures to the various levels of performance initially gleaned (the amount of money that is required to provide for this variable versus the amount of money required to shift responses by a measureable amount). Using this method, optimum performance criteria can be derived in related variable situations—for example,

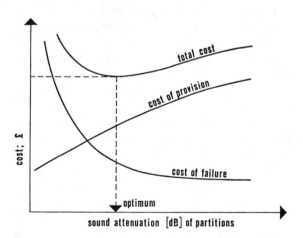

Figure 85
Optimization of attenuation of partitions and cost.

noise versus speech interference, thermal environment versus productivity, and corridor width versus risk of accident.

Boundaries

In the development of an adequate performance model, it is necessary to discuss the issue of bounding spatial elements. We frequently refer to a wall or partition to describe the vertical divisions between spaces. In this approach the word *boundary* is used in preference to conventional references because it includes definitions of space by furniture groupings, change in floor level, and color differences, in addition to partitions.

The concept of boundaries is useful in that it permits a restatement of their primary functions. Vertical boundaries, for example, act as a filter to selectively admit or diffuse vision; they may identify one area from another; they act as a containment of air, noise, light, heat, or other potential disturbances.

Since all primary activities are concerned with various levels of privacy of people, an appropriate boundary should admit only the required information and exclude what is not wanted. Boundaries also change their function. At one time a boundary may expand separate spaces or it may become a barrier to an environmental condition. The BPRU has identified a list of boundary attributes and how they are measurable (Figure 86). This was developed in recognition of the various performance characteristics required of boundaries to satisfy a variety of conditions. The listing explicitly states the wide range of considerations necessary for designing a boundary. The design of boundaries is crucial to the success of spatial layout and was chosen as a key study area for further research by the BPRU.

Response to boundaries Through user satisfaction studies, size and shape available in the class room (a quality closely related to the boundaries provided) was found to be a key variable. A number of proper-

ties of classroom space were examined. They are: wish for a bounded space that has continuity over time (a room of one's own); the psychological properties of the boundaries that define the room; and the effects of noise on children's behavior. A result of each of these studies follows below.

To study the need for bounded space, teachers' reactions to drawings of standard classrooms were studied. Both formal and informal seating arrangements were portrayed in the drawings similar to those in Figure 87. Each of the rooms was analyzed in terms of cost and sound attenuations with the general finding that teachers regarded walls as necessary to keep out sounds.

Summary of the results of study of vertical boundaries.[17] 1. There is a good correlation between the attributes of sound insulation and cost in use, all other things being equal. In other words, it is possible to predict the cost of boundaries from the degree of sound attenuation required of them with sufficient accuracy to be useful at an early stage in the design process without waiting for "post hoc" pricing or tendering.[18]

2. Significant differences exist between the calculated average sound attenuation values and the values measured in the sample of schools. Differences due to flanking, opening, and so on, resulting in lower than calculated attenuation were expected, but more surprisingly, some results are considerably better than had been calculated because of the presence of absorbent surfaces in the rooms. This suggests that closer attention to securing a short reverberation time within teaching spaces may provide an acceptable acoustic environment with relatively poor sound attenuation in the boundaries. Inadequate attenuation is aggravated by overreverberant classrooms.[19]

3. Boys are more affected by noise than girls. The effects of noise on performance are complex. For instance, an earlier finding that high and low noise levels produce less error than medium levels is supported by the results of the experiment. It was not possible to measure the effects of exposure to high noise levels over a long period.[20]

Boundary attributes and measures

Attribute in respect of	Description and measure	Unit
1 Air	Permeability. The rate of flow of air through the boundary for a given pressure difference per unit area	m^3/h m^2
2 Cost	Cost in use compounded of cost of provision and of maintenance	£
3 Durability	The life of the boundary under specified conditions of use	years
4 Fire	Combustibility, i.e. ability to support combustion. Surface spread of flame (Class grading). Fire resistance, i.e. the length of time a standard fire test can be resisted. All as described in BS 476, Part 1	yes/no; Rank position; hours
5 Flexibility	The ease of handling, taking down and re-erecting: (a) in the same place, i.e. operable or temporary boundaries; (b) in another place, i.e. demountable partitions, etc. Weighted in both cases for any loss and replacement involved: 0 = not possible without major works 1 = possible when building closed for holidays but requiring tradesmen or special plant 2 = possible over weekends, by janitors or other non-specialists 3 = possible between days, by janitors or other non-specialists 4 = possible between periods by teachers	Rank position; Rank position
6 Maintenance	Ranks to be developed to measure variables of materials, plant and labour required for routine maintenance	Rank position
7 Optical	(a) Transmission of light (b) Reflection from surface: diffuse specular (c) Colour (d) Vision through	percent; Munsell designation; visual acuity measure
8 People	(a) Flow of people through boundary. The number of people who can pass through in unit time (b) Security: 0 = break-in possible without trace 1 = break-in possible with bare hands 2 = break-in possible with furniture (chair) 3 = break-in possible with light tools 4 = break-in possible with heavy tools	person(s)/sec; Rank position
9 Services	What services can be concealed within the boundary thickness, what outlets are possible and what constraints are imposed on the services: 0 = no services 1 = light, flexible wiring or piping up to 30 mm dia. in vertical direction only 2 = ditto in both directions; flexible services possible in both directions 3 = rigid services possible in one direction only, up to 30 mm dia. 4 = flexible and rigid services possible in both directions up to 30 mm dia. 5 = no restriction	Rank position
10 Shape	Geometrical description of the run of the boundary on plan, assuming always that the section is vertical. Lengths of straight run and angles	mm number; degrees
11 Sound	(a) Absorption (b) Attenuation of sound energy passing through the boundary (normalised sound pressure level difference) measured at high, medium and low frequencies and quoted as an average, weighted where the slope of the curve is abnormal	sound absorption coefficient; dB or grade curve
12 Strength	(a) Impact resistance. Resistance to indentation or breakage by impact (BS 3760 describes a suitable test rig) (b) Ability to support furniture load, measured by variable load on standard cantilever (wash basin bracket) at standard height (DES Performance Specification for Partitions) (c) Ability to hold nails or screws; resistance to driving and extraction of standard nail and screw sizes, with plugs if necessary. Safe lateral load on standard nail. Safe lateral load on standard screw (d) Ability to support structural loads: safe distributed load per unit length	Rank position; kg or N; kg kg kg; kg/m
13 Surface	(a) Evenness. Deviation from plane over, 3 m square (b) Texture (c) Pattern or surface configuration (d) Warmth to touch	mm
14 Thermal conductance	The amount of heat energy conducted through unit area in unit time with unit temperature difference	c = W/m^2 deg C
15 Water	Solubility Water resistance Water vapour resistance	yes/no; m^2s MN/g-m
16 Weight	The mass density per unit area	kg/m^2

Figure 86
The physical performance of boundaries.

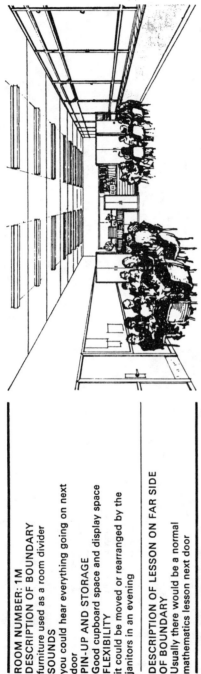

ROOM NUMBER: 1M
DESCRIPTION OF BOUNDARY
furniture used as a room divider
SOUNDS
you could hear everything going on next door
PIN-UP AND STORAGE
Good cupboard space and display space
FLEXIBILITY
it could be moved or rearranged by the janitors in an evening

DESCRIPTION OF LESSON ON FAR SIDE OF BOUNDARY
Usually there would be a normal mathematics lesson next door

GENERALLY SPEAKING WOULD YOU LIKE TO TEACH IN THIS ROOM?

1. I would love it
I would be enthusiastic about it
I would like it very much
I would like it a good deal
I would like it on the whole
I would like it fairly well
I would like it a little
I would be indifferent to it
I would not like it on the whole
I would dislike it a little
I would dislike it
I would dislike it very much
I would dislike it very much indeed
I would hate it

HOW WOULD YOU DESCRIBE THE CLASSROOM?

2. Extremely interesting
Very interesting
Moderately interesting
Hardly interesting at all

3. Extremely pleasant
Very pleasant
Moderately pleasant
Hardly pleasant at all

4. Extremely lively
Very lively
Moderately lively
Hardly lively at all

5. Extremely cosy
Very cosy
Moderately cosy
Hardly cosy at all

HOW MUCH PRIVACY DO YOU THINK YOU WOULD HAVE IN THIS CLASSROOM?

6. A very great deal of privacy
A lot of privacy
A moderate amount of privacy
Very little privacy

HOW DISTRACTING DO YOU THINK THE CLASS ON THE OTHER SIDE OF THE BOUNDARY WOULD BE?

7. Very little distraction
Moderately distracting
Very distracting
Very distracting indeed

HOW MUCH MORE EFFORT THAN USUAL WOULD BE NEEDED TO KEEP ATTENTION IN THIS ROOM?

8. No extra effort
A little more effort
More effort
A lot more effort

Figure 87
Drawing of standard classroom used in testing teachers' reactions to boundaries.

4. Considerable space savings are possible if movable partitions can be used in conjunction with a continuous process of matching the variables of role, options, teachers, and time—and hence class size—to the areas required for the classes. The seat utilization in the average comprehensive school with fixed partitions is only about 60 percent, so that maximum space saving theoretically possible would be on the order of 40 percent.[21]

5. Teachers show a preference for partitions that they think have good sound attenuation. This property is highly correlated to a number of judgments, such as satisfaction, distraction, attention, disturbance, privacy, and pleasantness.[22]

6. There is every indication that, at the present time, teachers regard having their own classroom as essential and that they would not be adequately compensated by having a small private office instead.[23]

7. Multiple linear regression techniques applied to up to five variables in boundary attributes show that the relationships that exist enable cost to be predicted from performance with an error in the order of $\pm$ 30 percent, far too large a margin for practical design purposes.[24]

8. In the design context of a comprehensive school, it appears that the operable partition is rarely an economic proposition. The removable partition, on the other hand, shows considerable advantage in cost in use over the fixed partition although the latter may be much cheaper in its initial cost.[25]

9. Due to the great complexity of the interaction of the various attributes and the consequent errors in cost prediction from them, it is not possible to predict usefully at a strategic level what the unit cost of a boundary with defined levels of performance in all attributes will be. Where one attribute is of paramount importance it is possible, however, to make such a prediction.[26]

Spatial Elements

Reasons for studying comprehensive schools The BPRU's interest in developing an understanding of, and techniques for, building performance appraisal led to the need to select a building type in which a large number of similiar examples could be easily reached; background information on the buildings could be readily obtained, there was some hope of assessing the actual product of the organization that the building housed;[27] research findings could actually be incorporated into future designs; and a centralized administration existed. All these considerations pointed to schools.

Selection of a sample A sample of forty-eight schools was drawn (with the help of the Scottish Education Department) that fulfilled the following requirements: all were within the central belt of Scotland; all were fully utilized (near capacity); and all were built in the last ten years or remodeled substantially during this ten-year period.

Primary areas of focus for the study In schools, three major areas within the spatial environment were identified.

(a) Spaces for activities. What space do the various activities of teaching and learning require? What is the optimum group size, how much space does equipment need, how far is shape of the space critical? When the interactive nature of spaces and activities is understood it is immediately apparent that many of the immediate and obvious answers to these questions are highly suspect. For instance, the traditionally "right" size of a class of children with one teacher is 30. This appears to be due more to the fact that 30 children can conveniently be fitted at desks into a room of about 500 square feet, and that rooms of about this size are commonly found in schools, than to any adult/child group communication, teaching/learning theories. Further, the "half" class of 15 for practical subjects is obviously derived arbitrarily from the figure of 30 for administrative convenience. The spatial requirement of activities in schools open very wide-ranging questions.

(b) Divisions between spaces. Traditionally the division between spaces within the spatial environment is the wall or partition. Other divisions are possible, some of them merest suggestions such as changes of floor finish or ceiling level. Others are ephemeral like curtains or movable screens. What are divisions for? What do they do? How does their presence affect the activities they separate?

Can their performance requirements be specified accurately and can such specifications be accurately met? We hardly need to go into schools at all to know that noise transmission between rooms is a major concern of teachers and that walls between teaching spaces are frequently said to be inadequate on this account. But there are much more subtle effects concerned with status, control, territory and privacy about which we know little.

(c) The groupings of spaces. Once a decision has been made, usually early in the design process, that one pattern of juxtaposition of spaces rather than another shall be adopted, a pattern of activities is encapsulated in the building form. The variety of groupings can be very large, e.g. by departments, or by houses, or by year groups, or by social or pastoral care groups, or by grouping together those spaces requiring similar environmental or structural characteristics and so on. Whatever the basis chosen, the decision is permanent but its validity endures only so long as the activity pattern it represents or so long as it is robust enough to accommodate variations in the activity pattern.

Parts of the investigations have been concerned at different levels in all three of the above areas.[28]

Space for activities   "Most current ideas about the appropriate size of groups of children taking part in any specified activity in the process of learning appear highly conditioned by the environment of the traditional school building."[29] Traditionally class size is based on the number of children that can be conveniently fitted into a standard classroom, rather than on the purpose of the activity and the preferred mode of interaction between teacher and child.

Due to a lack of statistics on the sizes of teacher-formed activity groups engaged in curricular subjects, the BPRU conducted a survey based on a histogramming technique previously developed by the Scottish Education Department. After collecting this information for a variety of subject areas and transposing it to histogram graphs, an alternative graphing technique was developed to determine the approximate percentage of spatial overprovision.

This graphing technique, called an "activity pattern," is an alternative technique of ordering the same data. Group size is plotted on the vertical axis

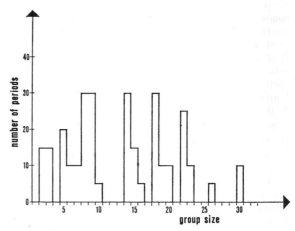

Figure 88
Histogram of group sizes in English.

versus the number of periods cumulatively plotted on the horizontal axis, with group size decreasing from left to right. Spatial overprovision can be determined by superimposition by dividing the horizontal axis by the number of periods in the curriculum cycle. Plugging in the per pupil allocation of space in each subject, as found in applicable hueristics afforded by the Scottish Education Department, the vertical can be changed into units of area.

Computer application to space use   A computer-aided technique was developed by BPRU to incorporate normal design constraints and to satisfy teaching activity needs as well. The package, known as SECS, contains three flexible programs that can be used independently or in conjunction with each other. The first program (SECS A) computes a space use schedule for any set of group activities. The information required to schedule space use is an inventory that includes every class period in a week, subjects taught, grade level, and class size. In addition, the computer will require the floor area per student relevant to each of the subjects and the number of periods per week per subject. The machine can then provide the best schedule for each subject in terms of the number and area of rooms required.

A second component part of the package is SECS

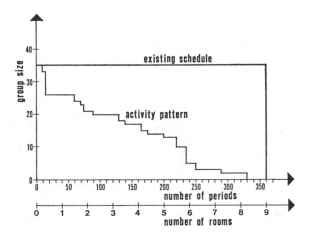

Figure 89a
Activity pattern: mathematics.

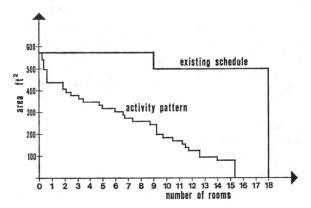

Figure 89b
Combined activity pattern compared with schedule of accommodation.

B, which examines existing class schedules and the amount of space allocated for each subject. The program then computes the provision of space within each range of class size and indicates whether it is over or under the desirable amount.

Recognizing that both teaching methods and curricula change over time, new school buildings are required to incorporate some degree of flexibility to accommodate scheduling changes. Another program, SECS C, was designed to determine the degree of

flexibility necessary to satisfy present and future sets of group activities. There are two design approaches for accommodating building change over time. The first is described as redundant space where projected space needs are based on a replication of existing spaces. The second is the physical flexibility strategy where demountable partitions are used to accommodate future changes. BPRU conducted a cost comparison of the two strategies, which basically compared overprovision of space in the redundant strategy against the extra cost of demountable partitions over conventional partitions in the physical flexibility strategy; the results indicated advantages in adopting the latter. Although SECS C has been developed for school design, it is equally applicable to any building type where requirements will vary over time.

MORPHOLOGICAL APPROACH

The morphological approach, as in other methods, involves problem definition, analysis, synthesis, and presentation. If the desire is to seek out new or peculiar solutions, the field of inquiry should include all acceptable and reasonable or possible solutions. The morphological way of doing this is to produce a table or matrix where all the parameters (characteristics) concerned are listed vertically and the corresponding parameter "steps" (how to achieve the characteristics) are listed horizontally. The parameters of such a morphological chart describe in general the features and functions of the subject considered.

In determining the boundaries of the field of investigation, the parameters and parameter steps are important since they represent the field that contains the solution.[30] In a good field the parameters should be as independent as possible from one another; there should be no connection between the steps of one row and the next. One column of the field represents one solution to the problem. Any one step from each row can be selected to generate the column. Certain

Figure 90a
Morphological approach to design*

Subject must have or be PARAMETER (characteristics)		Means of achieving what subject must have STEP					
		A	B	C	D	E	F
1. Part of body supported		none	foot	leg	bottom	back	hand (etc.)
2. Orientation of body		none	vertical	horizontal	skew		
3. Nature of cushioning element adjacent to part supported		none	hard	soft			
4. Number of cushioning elements adjacent to part supported		none	one	two	three	four	more than four
5. Load spreading element adjacent to part supported	form	none	flat	curved			
6.	nature	none	rigid	flexible			
7.	number	none	one	two	three	four	more than four
8. Positioning element	form	none	fixed	variable			
9.	nature	none	rigid	flexible			
10.	number	none	one	two	three	four	more than four
11. Resilience element	nature	none	hard	soft			
12.	number	none	one	two	three	four	more than four
13. Damping element	form	none	friction	velocity			
14.	nature	none	deadbeat	oscillatory			
15.	number	none	one	two	three	four	more than four
16. Load spreading element adajcent to support reaction	form	none	flat	curved			
17.	nature	none	rigid	flexible			
18.	number	none	one	two	three	four	more than four
19. Cushioning element adjacent to support reaction	nature	none	hard	soft			
20.	number	none	one	two	three	four	more than four

To find (design or develop) a comfortable, inexpensive, easily used and maintained means of support (against gravity) for the human body to replace occasionally or supplement the existing means of support.

*From Murray Milne, "Morphological Method Illustrated," unpublished manuscript, University of Oregon, 1967.

Solution: A1, A2, A3, A4, A5, A6, A7, A8, A9, A10, A11, A12
A13, A14, A15, A16, A17, A18, A19, A20

FREE FALL

Solution: D1, D2, A3, A4, A5, A6, A7, B8, B9, B10, A11, A12,
A13, A14, A15, A16, A17, A18, A19, A20

PROP

Solution: H1, B2, A3, A4, A5, A6, B8, C9, B10, A11, A12, A13,
A14, A15, C16, B17, F18, A19, A20

NOOSE AND GIBBET

Solution: F1, C2, A3, A4, A5, A6, A7, B8, B9, B10, A11, A12,
A13, A14, A15, C16, B17, F18, A19, A20

STRAP HANGING

Solution: B-F1, C2, A3, A4, A5, A6, A7, B8, B9, F10, A11, A12,
A13, A14, A15, B16, B17, B18, A19, A20

BED OF NAILS

Solution: B-F1, C2, A3, A4, C5, C6, B7, B8, C9, C10, A11, A12,
A13, A14, A15, C16, B17, F18, A19, A20

HAMMOCK

Solution: D-F1, D2, A3, A4, B5, B6, B7, B8, B9, E10, A11, A12,
A13, A14, A15, A16, A17, A18, A19, A20

CHAIR

Solution: B-F1, C2, C3, B4, B5, C6, B7, B8, B9, E10, A11, A12,
A13, A14, A15, A16, A17, A18, A19, A20

BED

Figure 90b
Morphological Process

of the column solutions from the field may be eliminated because of the variance of one parameter step with another. The total number of viable solutions will be less than the total number of mathematical combinations.

There still remains an inordinate number of solutions displayed on the morphological chart, suggesting the need to reduce the field of investigation. The concept employed is called "basis of comparison" where judgments are made to determine the best solution(s).

In the field of engineering design, basis of comparison is seen as a viable tool to eliminate solutions from the field. While there is no doubt that the basis of comparison needs to be realistic and searching, the criteria usually employed in the engineering field are highly quantitative, such as cost/ton payload.

Whether the criteria are highly quantitative or qualitative, it is necessary to reduce the field of investigation by means of analysis of rows and analysis of columns. By analyzing rows independently, each row can be optimized to provide the overall optimum solution for the complete chart.

Analyzing by columns implies an analysis of all possible solutions, which is impractical. Sample column solutions may be chosen to acquire a "feel" for trends.

NOTES AND REFERENCES

1. J. Christopher Jones, "A Method of Systematic Design," in *Conference on Design Methods* (New York: Macmillan, 1963), pp. 53–73.
2. Christopher Alexander and Barry Poyner, "The Atoms of Environmental Structure," in *Emerging Methods of Environmental Design and Planning*, ed. G. Moore (Cambridge: MIT Press, 1973), p. 308.
3. F. Duffy and J. Torrey, "A Progress Report on the Pattern Language," in *Emerging Methods*, ed. Moore, pp. 270–277.
4. An example of the design process is described in Morris Asimow, *Introduction to Design* (Englewood Cliffs, N.J.: Prentice-Hall, 1962).
5. A. Edwards, *Techniques of Attitude Construction* (New York: Appleton-Century-Crofts, 1957.
6. John Eberhard, *The Performance Concept: A Study of Its Application to Housing* (Washington, D. C.: U.S. Department of Commerce, 1969), 1:3.
7. T. A. Markus, ed., *Building Performance* (New York: Halsted Press, 1972), p. 1.
8. Ibid., p. 19.
9. Ibid., pp. 21–25.
10. Asimow, *Introduction*.
11. *RIBA Handbook of Architectural Practice and Management* (London, 1967).
12. Markus, *Building Performance*, pp. 21–25.
13. Ibid., pp. 29–30.
14. See P. A. Stone, "The Economics of Building Design," *Journal of the Royal Statistical Society* 123 (1960), for a discussion of the deficiencies of this.
15. P. A. Stone, *Building Economy* (Oxford: Pergamon Press, 1966).
16. Markus, *Building Performance*, p. 31.
17. Ibid., pp. 112–113.
18. BPRU, "The Relationship between One Performance Criterion and the Cost of Some Boundaries Separating School Teaching Spaces," Report GD/27, University of Strathclyde, Glasgow, 1968.
19. BPRU, "Sound Attenuation of Some School Boundaries," Report GD/26, University of Strathclyde, Glasgow, 1968.
20. BPRU, "Psychological Studies," Report GD/28. University of Strathclyde, 1968.
21. BPRU, "The Implications of Choice of Boundary on Accommodation Scheduling," Report GD/29, University of Strathclyde, 1968.
22. BPRU, "Psychological Studies."
23. BPRU, "The Relationship between One Performance Criterion."
24. Ibid.
25. BPRU, "Design Appraisal—Extract from RIBA Conference Paper, Part 2," Report GD/24, University of Strathclyde, Glasgow, 1968.
26. BPRU, "The Relationship between One Performance Criterion."
27. The assumptions that background information on the buildings could be readily obtained and that assessing the actual product of the organization that the building housed later turned out to be troublesome.
28. Markus, *Building Performance*, pp. 55–56.
29. Ibid., p. 56.
30. K. W. Norris, "The Morphological Approach to Engineering Design," in *Conference on Design Methods*, ed. J. C. Jones and D. G. Thornley (New York: Macmillan, 1963).

4

Applications of Programs

The previous chapters of this book have illustrated the vast reservoir of technical resources available to generate and synthesize information. This large inventory only reflects the flexibility necessary for the designer to accommodate to the diversity of situations frequently confronted.

The selection of information generating and organizing methods is referred to as the strategy for developing the program. This section illustrates different types of field applications of a program. Particular program types included are *representative* of an approach; they do not inventory the wide range of program types currently being developed.

Each of the program approaches varies considerably to the degree that users participate in the process; yet each has a developed, communicable format for extracting the expertise of the users. The characteristics common to all approaches are shown in Figure 91, which outlines the goals, activities, needs, and options sequence. The questions of environmental purpose and behavioral supports are answered in the diverse program strategies presented in this section.

PAK (PLANNING AID KIT)[1]

The process of programming and planning for community mental health facilities is a complex one and influential upon the success of local mental health programs. The National Institute of Mental Health (NIMH) has been gathering information and experience about problems facing all communities in their delivery of mental health services. In order to systematically gather and disperse information about the process of mental health programming to aid local communities, the Planning Aid Kit (PAK) was developed to enhance community planning processes. PAK is not an attempt to derive standards but to place the responsibility for providing certain services on the community. PAK was developed by the Buffalo Organization for Social and Technological Innovation, Inc. (BOSTI).

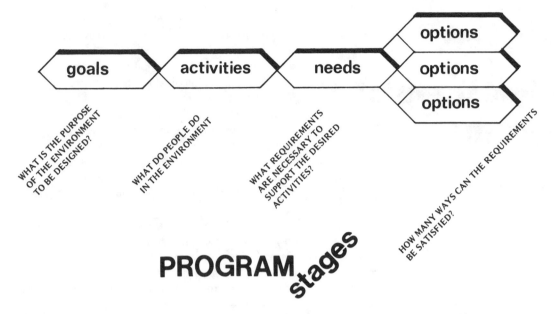

Figure 91
Program stages.

Underlying Logic

Mental health treatment is now based on needs that are related to the user's interaction with social conditions and physical attributes of the environment. Treatment can be aimed at the community, so it becomes the delivery mechanism for a range of explicit and implicit mental health programs.

PAK has been designed to help community mental health services articulate the environmental implications of the mental health treatment programs under their supervision. It sets up a self-perpetuating system of user-directed information retrieval aimed at establishing a data base for individuals interested in mental health planning and man–environment relations. Participation in this process is generated on the basis that an instrument will be provided that builds a time-tested procedure into the mental health planning process and shares the vast body of knowledge that has been assembled about other communities' experience if participants carefully monitor the mental health planning process, collect data about it, and provide feedback.

Participation

The process requires maximum feasible representation of various points of view held by community members and professionals who serve them. In order to use the PAK, different groups of participants, each with a defined role and type of input, are required. They are:

1. *The planning group,* composed of users of available mental health services and people who deliver or perform these services. They go through the steps of PAK and select and weight problems to be run through the PAK.
2. *Professional consultants,* aid or represent members of the planning group but they have no decision power.
3. *Public authorities* are primarily overseers who have whatever authority accrues to them in

130

their official capacity. They have no vote or decision power in the PAK.

The Process

The PAK premises itself on a performance concept, a technique of describing goals in terms of their desired performance. Stated in this fashion, a range of alternative solutions yielding this performance can be generated that fulfills the initial goal statement. Group discussion, role-defined participation, and a detailed procedural scheme are used to develop these alternative solutions and describe their environmental characteristics. Once this descriptive information has been obtained, it can be used as either selection criteria for potential renovations in the community or programming criteria for new facilities.

Participants are the decision makers in the process of using the PAK. It is their concerns (as users) that are displayed, discussed, argued, and made part of the ongoing programming and planning process. After a participant group that agrees to work in accordance with the PAK is assembled, the members select a discussion leader using criteria explicitly stated in an introductory PAK training session. It is the discussion leader's responsibility to direct the group's flow of ideas and discussion, aid the group in the negotiation of conflicts, and record all the decisions made during the planning process.

Through discussion, issues regarding mental health are introduced, and their implications are expanded; then information is recorded on sheets provided by the planning group. For a problem area to be pursued, it must be perceived of as either implied as the objectives of a service now provided, inferred from community demographic data, a recurrent abernant behavior in the community, of specific interest to the professional group, or a recurring national problem that may erupt locally. Problems are recorded on sheets and through discussion expanded into linearly related causes and effects (Figure 93). Related thoughts that occur to participants are also recorded

for future reference. These may entail treatment programs, settings for programs, or people to carry out programs.

After the group has discussed a range of problems, it completes a matrix (of problem versus participant opinion of priority). Participants mark all problems either low, medium, or high (each having a corresponding numerical value), and scores are collated along the problem axis to obtain a problem priority index (PPI). This technique is used to select critical problems (those having a PPI above a given cutoff point). Each remaining problem is typed on a course

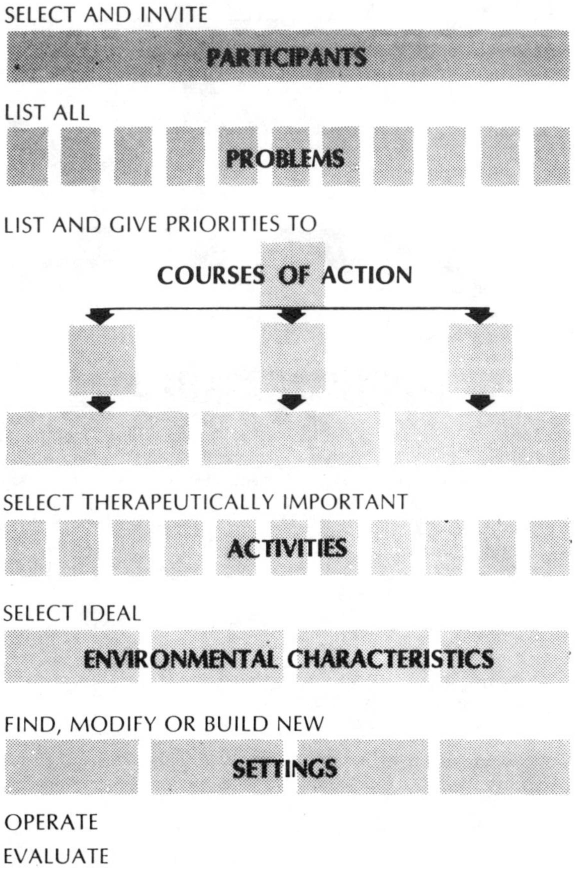

Figure 92
Planning aid kit (PAK) process.

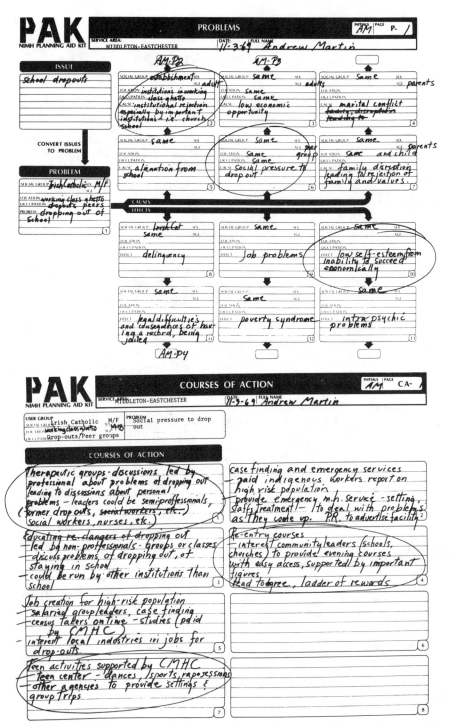

Figure 93

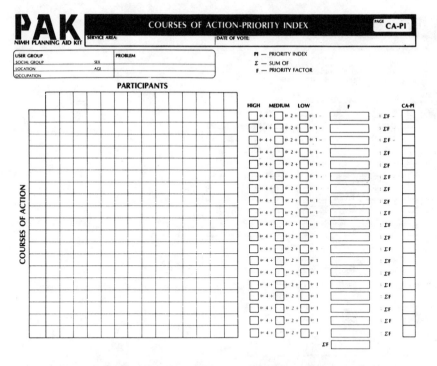

PAK
NIMH PLANNING AID KIT

COURSES OF ACTION-PRIORITY INDEX

PAGE **CA-PI**

SERVICE AREA:

DATE OF VOTE:

USER GROUP
SOCIAL GROUP — SEX
LOCATION — AGE
OCCUPATION

PROBLEM

PI — PRIORITY INDEX
Σ — SUM OF
F — PRIORITY FACTOR

PARTICIPANTS

COURSES OF ACTION

HIGH   MEDIUM   LOW   F   CA-PI

PAK
NIMH PLANNING AID KIT

PROBLEMS -PRIORITY INDEX

PAGE **P-PI**

SERVICE AREA:

DATE OF VOTE:

PI — PRIORITY INDEX
Σ — SUM OF
F — PRIORITY FACTOR

PARTICIPANTS

PROBLEMS

HIGH   MEDIUM   LOW   F   P-PI

PAK
NIMH PLANNING AID KIT

COURSES OF ACTION-FINAL PRIORITY INDEX

SERVICE AREA: ___   FULL NAME ___

PAGE **CA-FPI**

CA-PI — PRIORITY INDEX OF COURSE OF ACTION
P-PI — PRIORITY INDEX OF PROBLEM
OP-PI — PRIORITY INDEX OF OTHER PROBLEMS RELATED TO CA
CA-FPI — FINAL PRIORITY INDEX OF COURSE OF ACTION

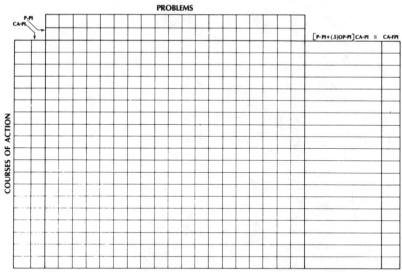

PROBLEMS

$[\text{P-PI}+(.5)\text{OP-PI}]\text{CA-PI} = \text{CA-FPI}$

COURSES OF ACTION

PAK
NIMH PLANNING AID KIT

ENVIRONMENTAL CHARACTERISTICS

INITIALS **AM**   PAGE **E.C.'s-/**

SERVICE AREA MIDDLETON-EASTCHESTER   DATE 4-3-69   FULL NAME *Andrew Martin*

USER GROUP	PROBLEM	COURSE OF ACTION	ACTIVITY
SOCIAL GROUP Irish Catholic, M/F / SUB AGE working class ghetto 14-18 / OCCUPATION Drop-outs/Peers	social pressure to drop out	therapeutic groups	discussion to stimulate ability to accept institutional responsibility

RANK	ENVIRONMENTAL CHARACTERISTICS	MOST	SOME	NEUT	SOME	MOST	ENVIRONMENTAL CHARACTERISTICS	MEASURES FOR E.C.'s	REQUIREMENTS
7	PRIVACY	X					COMMUNALITY	SEE PAGE 29	Personnel *discussion leader (professional or semi-professional)*
2	SOCIOPETALITY	X			X		SOCIOFUGALITY	SEE PAGE 30	
8	INFORMALITY		X				FORMALITY	SEE PAGE 30	
3	FAMILIARITY		X				REMOTENESS	SEE PAGE 31	
4	ACCESSIBILITY	X					INACCESSIBILITY	SEE PAGE 31	
9	AMBIGUITY		X				LEGIBILITY	SEE PAGE 32	Equipment — *Furniture for sitting comfort, not boisterous activity should compel seating*
11	DIVERSITY	*irrelevant*					HOMOGENEITY	SEE PAGE 32	
10	ADAPTABILITY				X		FIXITY	SEE PAGE 33	*—phonograph, tape recorder A.V. equipment*
6	COMFORT	X					DISCOMFORT	SEE PAGE 33	*—accomodate 5-20 people*
5	*intimacy*			X			*vast*	SEE SHEET 28	
1	*warm & pliable*	X					*austere & hard*	SEE SHEET 29	Access *large facility containing this Activity should be near the daily routine of the user.*

WHAT SETTINGS ARE CURRENTLY USED FOR THIS ACTIVITY? *Store front; church rooms; school rooms, Y.M.C.A., neighborhood action center*

WHAT SETTINGS MIGHT BE USED FOR THIS ACTIVITY? *lounge or special teen facilities (hopefully near other teen activities; spaces usable for dances, large meetings, and other small group spaces) back room of candy store (Pop Morgan)*

This activity should be remote (within that facility

134

Figure 94

SERVICE AREA: MIDDLETON-EASTCHESTER	DATE: 11-3-69	FULL NAME: Andrew Martin

USER GROUP	PROBLEM	COURSE OF ACTION
SOCIAL GROUP Irish Catholics M/F	social pressure to	therapeutic groups
LOCATION working class ghetto 14-18	drop out	
OCCUPATION Drop-outs/peers		

THERAPEUTIC GOALS | ALTERNATIVE ACTIVITIES

SEQUENCE

THERAPEUTIC GOALS	ALTERNATIVE ACTIVITIES		
getting compatible people together to form group [1]	pay workers to select appropriate members [2]	recruit through word-of-mouth & use "exclusivity" as incentive [3]	recruit through incentives such as activity opportunities, school credit, money [4]
having members learn to gain group cohesion [5]	employ active and effective group leader/s [6]	develop "gang" orient identification (jackets, insignia, etc.) - control exclusive "turf" eg. an inner sanctum [7]	develop common group goals - eg. educate younger people [8]
getting members to work together [9]	discuss problems of the group members in accepting institutional allegiances & understanding personal problems [10]	create manageable goals to do constructive or communally effective projects [11]	carry out programs [12]
getting group to gain achievements, realize goals [13]	find jobs or proper social roles outside group for its members school or proper job alternatives [14]	carry out goals - eg. change environment construction, protests, petitions [15]	give diplomas or get drop-outs back to school or understand that school is not necessary [16]
termination (or perpetuation of group [17]	parties reunions recruit new members [18]	→ Ditto [19]	Ditto [20]

135

of action (COA) sheet (Figure 93), and copies of each sheet are distributed to the members of the planning group.

Individually, each participant generates as many courses of action as he or she can for a given problem. The sheets are then collected, and all COAs generated by the group are placed on priority matrixes to determine how well each COA solves its corresponding problem (rating matrix) and whether a given COA solves other problems as well (hybridizing matrix). Using a low, medium, and high rating system in each case a final group of COAs is established. (From this point on in the PAK process, participants receive advocacy consultation from professionals.)

Using the COA sheet (Figure 93) as a framework, the participants develop corresponding therapeutic goals for each remaining COA. Each goal is then expanded into a group of sustaining activities necessary to sucessfully carry out each goal statement (Figure 94–Activities). These activities should: be able to be performed in a single kind of setting; state exactly what is taking place and who it affects; and be expanded to cover who is delivering the service, what the setting is it is being delivered in, and over what time period it is being delivered.

Participants circle all of the activities on the sheet that they would like to see as part of the program. Each activity that is circled is considered in the next step of PAK when the discussion leader distributes an activity-designated environmental characteristic sheet to each participant. Using the catagories provided on the sheet as a framework (Figure 94–Environmental Characteristics) each activity is expanded into personal requirements, equipment requirements, access requirements, and corresponding environmental characteristics needed for the operation of that particular activity. A rank-ordered semantic differential containing specified bipolar opposites (privacy-commality, familiarity-remoteness, accessibility-inaccesmality, familiarity-remoteness, accessibiltiy-inaccessibility, legibility-ambiguity, diversity-homogeneity, adaptability-fixity, comfort-discomfort, and any other groups decided should be added) is employed to qualitatively and quantatively describe the environmental characteristics that the group deems necessary for the performance of a given activity. Using these environmental considerations as a medium of communication between mental health professionals and designers, a wide range of alternative settings found in the community (some not traditionally thought of as mental health delivery program settings) can be examined as possible settings for the delivery of mental health services.

This final information is used by the community mental health service to develop new delivery systems, and it is fed back into the PAK data base to be used by the larger PAK network. Since any one of the component parts comprising the totality of our social system may be responsible for the occurrence of a mental health problem in an individual, all should be considered as a resource for the prevention and delivery of mental health services.

COMPUTERS IN ARCHITECTURAL PROGRAMMING

The widespread recognition of the architect's new domain dealing with the social and environmental needs of an unpredictable future has stimulated experimentation in the field of automation. Computer augmentation and design assistance methods have found their way into the daily office practice of various design organizations throughout the United States.

Resistance to computerization has taken the form of caution and skepticism for fear of being replaced by a machine as well as concern about sterility of design solutions. The first fear was well founded; in fact, many routine and repetitive tasks can be augmented by computer assistance. Insofar as quality of design is concerned a brief look through your window will call attention to the unimaginative characteristics of most buildings that have been created—without the use of computers.

Clearly the two critical factors influencing the use of computer methods are the complexity and the scale of building operations. Computerization offers the potential of storing and retrieving vast quantities of information, as well as analyzing and simulating an almost infinite number of different solutions. It is now possible for the architect to conduct a more rigorous analysis of design factors by computer than would normally be possible using manual methods in the same period of time. One of the more recent advantages of computerization is to explore complex program relationships that previously were beyond the scope of human mental processes.

The architectural firm of Perry, Dean, and Stewart has been involved in computer applications for several years.[2] Its inhouse computer system ARK/2 (architectural kinetics/man-machine interaction) has been integrated into all phases of architectural design. PDS states that "ARK/2 has enabled multifaceted, multilayered approaches which generate sets of alternatives for different design issues. The logical selection of these alternatives and their combinations develops alternative total design possibilities which may be evaluated against specially developed functional and nonfunctional criteria." Through constant man-machine interaction, many aspects of the design process can be handled by computer, more design issues can be faced, and more criteria can be investigated.

The ARK/2 system is composed of groupings of three program types: arithmetic logics, interactive graphics, and text manipulation. Each of the sets contains further possibilities for creating something new, editing the existing, and storing for further work.

The planning process PDS employs has four parts: inventory, goals, program, and proposal. PDS has described how it used the system in designing the expansion of an existing hospital:

> We collect data related to the existing function. We then try to establish goals of the hospital, operational, medical, human, environmental, and community goals—all those responsibilities that the hospital must fulfill. Next, we develop alternative architectural programs including written descriptions, numerical programs, graphic programs and drawing of all spaces, and, of course, construcion cost. Inventory, goals, and program lead finally to the proposal. We set down the alternative solutions and establish some criteria based on the goals of the hospital for selecting the most appropriate solution. We can then phase the soltuion for future development.

Other computer programs can also be applied to the planning process. The diagram in (Figure 95) illustrates how various programs are integrated into the design process and how the structure of the process is enhanced by providing the continuing design and data base. We will, however, only discuss three of the programs: Comprograph, Comprorelate, and Comproplan.

Comprograph provides a mathematical model of spatial alternatives for building design, interior layout, and inventory control for various sizes of projects. Pertinent qualities and characteristics of the space are described in detail from dimensional use to probable cost and environmental characteristics (see Figure 95). These data are provided for each programmed space on an input sheet. Comprograph recognizes three hierarchical levels within a project: programs, departments, and items. A project is made up of programs. Each program is composed of departments, which contain several items.

Comprograph includes the following data about each programmed space (Figure 95) in terms of area and cost requirements:

1. Program name: The name of the general functional zone in which space resides, such as surgery, administration, and so on.
2. Department name: The name of the subgroup to which it belongs, such as staff area, social services, and so on.
3. Room name: The name of the space itself, such as radiology treatment, storage, conference room, and so on.
4. Number: The quantity of such similar rooms in the groups.

Group	Program	PREDESIGN			PROGRAMMING				SCHEMATIC DES				DES DEVELOPMENT					WORKING DRGS				SPECS		BID	CONSTRUCT		
		Checking similar projects	Estimate schedules	Estimate manpower needs	Review similar room types	Model area program	Work out relationships	Establish parameters	Develop plan layouts	3-dimensional studies	Establish cost goals	Start outline spec	Review room details	Mech studies	3-dimensional studies	Revise cost goals	Redo outline specs	Plans sections elev.	Mech. studies	Construction network	Estimate	Edit master spec	Print specifications	Cost review	Construction monitor	Cost monitor	Shop drawing monitor
DRAW	COMPROSPACE	o			o			o	o			o	o					o					o	o			
DRAW	COMPROVIEW							o		o				o	o				o								
COLLECT/SORT	COMPROGRAPH	o			o	o			o			o	o					o				o					
COLLECT/SORT	COMPROPLAN								o				o					o									
MANIPULATE/MANAGE	COMPROWORK		o	o					o				o					o				o		o			
MANIPULATE/MANAGE	COMPROMAN			o				o				o					o				o		o	o	o		
MANIPULATE/MANAGE	COMPRONET		o					o												o			o				
MANIPULATE/MANAGE	COMPROAREA	o			o	o					o		o			o					o			o	o	o	
MANIPULATE/MANAGE	COMPROCOST	o									o					o					o	o		o		o	
MANIPULATE/MANAGE	COMPROSPEC	o						o			o	o				o	o				o	o	o	o			
SPECIAL	COMPROSTAIR								o																		
SPECIAL	COMPROLINK							o						o					o								o
SPECIAL	COMPROPARK	o								o						o											
SPECIAL	COMPROSIGN																	o									
SPECIAL	COMPROGRAM	o			o	o		o																			

Matrix of Computer Programs and Tasks in an Architectural Design Process

Figure 95
Matrix of computer programs and tasks in an architectural design process.

COMPROGRAPH INPUT FORM
PERRY DEAN & STEWART, ARCHITECTS & PLANNERS

JOB: MARLBORO HOSPITAL   JOB NO.: 1334   CODE:
DATE: MR 5, 71   MARL

INPUT	PHASE	FORM	EXPANSION	CEILING	FLEXIBILITY	EQUIPMENT	CONTROL	SPACE CHARACTERISTICS
1..project	0. existing	1. square	0. none	7=7' 2=12'	0. none	0. none	0. open	P. privat W. nat lgt
2. program	1. one	2. dbl sqr	1. yes	8=8' 3=13'	1. internal	1. average	1. stf only	S. social D. no nat
3. dept	2. two	3. gld horz		9=9' 4=14'	2. use	2. spl elec	2. stf-user	Q. quiet V. view
4. room	0. future	4. gld vert		0=10' 5=15'	3. dimensnl	3. spl plmb	3. stf-publ	N. noisy C. cntg out
5. subtotal	(use one 0)			1=11' 6=sp.	4. struct	4. loading	4. isolat	O. sun G. at grade
6. continue								

input 5: indicate % curculation under quantity; lgth & width in feet

INPUT	NO.	CODE	DESCR	QUANT	LGTH	WIDTH	COST SQ FT	PHASE	FORM	EXPAN	CEIL	FLEXB	EQUIP	CONTR	CHRCT	SPARE	COMMT
1			MARLBORO HOSP														
2	6		SURGICAL	1													
3	A		DELIVERY SUITE														
4	1	O/R	OPERATING ROOMS	4	20	20	90	1	2	0	0	1	2	4	P		
4	2	D/R	DELIVERY ROOMS	2	20	20	90	1	2	0	0	1	2	4	P		
4	3	SP	PR SPECIAL PROCEED	1	20	25	70	1	4	0	0	1	2	4	P		
4	4	SP	PR SPECIAL PROCEED	1	20	25	90	2	4	0	0	1	2	4	P		
4	5	INST	SPEC INSTRMT RM	1	9	10	80	1	4	1	9	2	3	1	P		
4	6	STCOR	STAFF CORRIDOR	1	12	90	75	1	3	2	9	2	3	1	P		
4	7	STCOR	STAFF CORRIDOR	1	12	20	76	2	3	1	9	2	3	1	P		
4	8	ACTS	ACTS CLEAN TERM	1	8	10	75	1	1	1	9	1	2	1	P		
4	9	SCRUBS	SCRUB ALCOVES	4	8	10	80	1	1	0	9	0	3	4	P		
4	10	SOIL	SOILED HOLDING	4	10	12	70	1	1	0	9	1	0	1	P		
5			CIRCULATION	65													
3	B		NURSING SUPPORT														
4	1	STO	GAS STORAGE	1	5	10	70	1	3	0	2	0	4	1	O		
4	2	MONIT	MONITOR ROOM	1	9	12	100	1	1	1	1	0	1	2	O		
4	3	EQUIP	EQUIPMENT STOR	1	10	20	50	1	3	1	2	2	0	2	O		
4	4	NLOKMD	NURSE LOCKER	2	20	50	60	1	3	1	8	3	3	2	P		
4	5	TECH	TECHN LOUNGE	1	10	20	50	2	3	1	8	1	0	2	W		
4	6	ANEST	ANESTHESIA WORK	1	10	15	70	1	1	0	0	2	1	1	W		
4	7	AOFF	ANESTHESIA OFF	1	10	12	50	2	4	0	8	1	0	2	W		
4	8	ORSUP	O/R SUPERVISOR	1	10	12	60	1	4	0	8	1	0	2	G		
4	9	OBSUP	OB SUPERVISOR	1	10	12	70	1	1	2	9	1	0	2	W		
4	10	CSURG	CHIEF SURGERY	1	10	12	70	2	1	0	9	1	0	2	W		
4	11	COBG	CHIEF OB/GYN	1	10	12	70	2	1	0	9	1	0	2	W		
5			CIRCULATION	15													
9	6																

Figure 96
Comprograph input sheet.

```
                    MARLBORO HOSP




                      SURGICAL      : NUMBER  1

DELIVERY SUITE

                 NUM LEN WID UNS PH FO EX CE FL EQ CO CH SP     UNAR     ITAR      ITS


OPERATING ROOMS   4  20  20  90  1  2  0  0  1  2  4     P      400.    1600.   $144000.
DELIVERY ROOMS    2  20  20  90  1  2  0  0  1  2  4     P      400.     800.   $ 72000.
SPECIAL PROCEED   1  20  25  90  1  4  0  0  1  2  4     P      500.     500.   $ 45000.
SPECIAL PROCEED   1  20  25  90  2  4  0  0  1  2  4     P      500.     500.   $ 45000.
SPEC INSTRMT RM   1   9  10  80  1  4  1  9  2  3  1     P       90.      90.   $  7200.
STAFF CORRIDOR    1  12  90  75  1  3  2  9  2  3  1     P     1080.    1080.   $ 81000.
STAFF CORRIDOR    1  12  20  75  2  3  1  9  2  3  1     P      240.     240.   $ 18000.
ACTS CLEAN TEAM   1   8  10  75  1  1  1  9  1  2  1     P       80.      80.   $  6000.
SCRUB ALCOVES     4   8  10  80  1  1  0  9  0  3  4     P       80.     320.   $ 25600.
SOILED HOLDING    4  10  12  70  1  1  0  9  1  0  1     P      120.     480.   $ 33600.
CIRCULATION      65%          0


                      NET PHASE 1    4950.    $   414400.
             CIRCULATION PHASE 1     3217.    $        0.
                 SUBTOTAL PHASE 1    8167.    $   414400.

                      NET PHASE 2     740.    $    63000.
             CIRCULATION PHASE 2      481.    $        0.
                 SUBTOTAL PHASE 2    1221.    $    63000.

                 TOTAL ALL PHASES    9388.    $   477400.
```

Figure 97
Comprograph output in tabular format.

5. Length and width: The desirable dimensions of the room.
6. Equipment: Whether there will be special building to be built in five years (phase 1), ten years (phase 2), or in the foreseeable future.

The pertinent qualitites and characteristics of the space are classified as follows:

1. Cost: Up-to-date costs are obtained from professional estimators and are developed at the programming stage of development.
2. Form: When the dimensions of the space are not obtainable, an approximation of the form of the space is established.
3. Expansion: Whether the space needs to be thought of as fixed or expandable.
4. Ceiling: The desirable ceiling height of the space.
5. Flexibility: Whether the need for flexibility is in internal layout, for different use, dimensional, or structural.
6. Equipment: Whether there will be special electrical demand, special plumbing demand, or heavy loading due to equipment.
7. Control: Whether the space needs control for staff only, for staff and users, or staff and public.
8. Characteristics: Whether the space is private,

NURSING SUPPORT

	NUM	LEN	WID	UNS	PH	FO	EX	CE	FL	EG	CO	CH	SP	UNAR	ITAR	ITS
GAS STORAGE	1	8	10	70	1	3	0	2	0	4	1	0		50.	50. $	3500.
MONITOR ROOM	1	9	12	100	1	1	1	0	1	2	1	0		108.	108. $	10800.
EQUIPMENT STOR	1	10	20	50	1	3	1	2	2	0	2	0		200.	200. $	10000.
MD NURSE LOCKER	2	20	50	60	1	3	1	8	3	3	2	P		1000.	2000. $	120000.
TECHN LOUNGE	1	10	20	50	2	3	1	8	1	0	2	W		200.	200. $	10000.
ANESTHESIA WORK	1	10	15	70	1	1	0	0	2	1	1	P		150.	150. $	10500.
ANESTHESIA OFF	1	10	12	50	2	4	0	8	1	0	2	W		120.	120. $	6000.
O/R SUPERVISOR	1	10	12	60	1	4	0	8	1	0	2	G		120.	120. $	7200.
OB SUPERVISOR	1	10	12	60	1	1	0	8	1	0	2	G		120.	120. $	7200.
CHIEF SURGERY	1	10	12	70	1	1	0	8	1	0	2	W		120.	120. $	8400.
CHIEF OB/GYN	1	10	12	70	2	1	0	8	1	0	2	W		120.	120. $	8400.
CIRCULATION	75%			0												

NET PHASE 1	2868.	$	177600.
CIRCULATION PHASE 1	2151.	$	0.
SUBTOTAL PHASE 1	5019.	$	177600.
NET PHASE 2	440.	$	24400.
CIRCULATION PHASE 2	330.	$	0.
SUBTOTAL PHASE 2	770.	$	24400.
TOTAL ALL PHASES	5789.	$	202000.

PROGRAM NET PHASE 1	7818.	$	592000.
PROGRAM CIRCULATION PHASE 1	5368.	$	0.
PROGRAM SUBTOTAL PHASE 1	13186.	$	592000.
PROGRAM NET PHASE 2	1180.	$	87400.
PROGRAM CIRCULATION PHASE 2	811.	$	0.
PROGRAM SUBTOTAL PHASE 2	1991.	$	87400.
PROGRAM TOTAL ALL PHASES	15177.	$	679400.

social, quiet, or noisy; needs sunlight, no light, or a view; to be contiguous to the outside or must be on grade.

9. Special: An extra criterion to associate with the space at the designer's option.

10. Evaluation: A percentage to increase net areas and net cost to gross areas and gross costs.

Depending on the use of Comprograph, the output can be represented in two different formats. The first alternative is presented in alphanumeric tabular form in Figure 97. This table identifies the unit area for each space as well as the item area and cost for all the similar spaces. Summaries of net and gross area and cost are presented according to phases, and department, program, and project summaries are all tabulated. The second alternative output has the ability to display every space graphically to scale and toned to indicate phasing (Figure 98). A total block can be drawn to scale illustrating the sum of each department and divided by tone into the various phases. PDS indicates that a seventy-five-page program can be obtained in less than ten minutes of computer time. A similar size Comprograph, hand done in 1966, required thirty-three weeks to complete, and it was impossible to edit.

Another feature of Comprograph is its sorting flexibility. Comparisons can be made among different

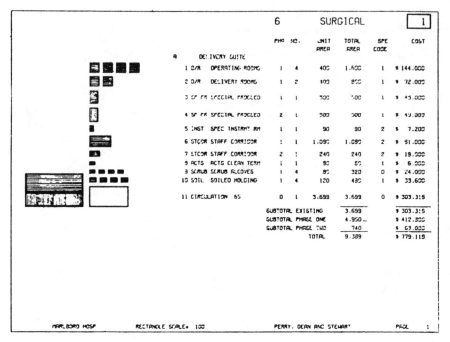

Figure 98
Comprograph graphics output.

situations under design consideration and existing conditions. Other kinds of sorting for specific spatial features, such as common ceiling height and perimeter locations, are also possible. When the ingredients of the architectural program are understood, the sets of rooms in each department become the data for the *Comprorelate* program.

Comprorelate is a relationship program based on relationship data entered in a matrix, which is automatically displayed via a cathode ray tube from the Comprograph data. The client and architect can then rate the importance of the relationship, comparing each space with every other space.

The relationships are related on a scale of from one to six, based on the importance of their connection or proximity. When the matrix is completed, a graphic bubble diagram is displayed on the cathode ray tube representing the results after considering the results of all the paired comparisons. Sets of

different bubble diagrams can be generated by considering different relationship criteria such as adjacency, visual connection, distance, frequency of interaction, or hierarchy of privacy.

The client and the architect have the opportunity to edit the data base; they can delete a room or change its size, and they can alter the relationship ratings due to judgmental errors entered in the matrix. Diagrams are quickly produced to reflect these changes.

Having arrived at a suitable relationship scheme, the designer can ask the computer to replace the bubbles in the Comprorelate diagram with the area and dimensions to scale stored in the Comprograph data base. This program is called *Comproplan*.

Since the data structure of Comproplan output is compatible with the Comprospace program, all the facilities of Comprospace can be included in the resulting drawing. Also, the drawing can be zoomed to

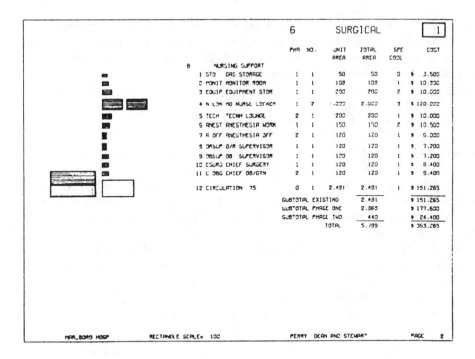

any scale, and hard copies are available for further study. There is, however, no actual floor plan at this time. A carefully manipulated Comproplan can be used for further study by the designer. It has the appropriate room and space dimensions arranged in a functional manner and a known and acceptable gross square footage. Many of the basic requirements for a successful design have thus been insured.

ANALYTIC SPACE PROGRAMMING

While I will not attempt to treat problems by building typology, it is important to realize that many advances in programming methods have come from those designers involved in office planning from the Burolandschaft (office landscape) of the 1960s to the present computer-aided office layout programs. Substantial development can be accounted for as a result of two major factors. The first was the speculative office builder and his need to predict the adequacy of speculative space in order to ensure a return on his investment. The second is the unique specificity of organizational objectives requiring spatial layouts that support human activities and their relationships.

It is common practice, in the planning of most buildings, to consider two central factors: pedestrian movement and paper flow in the office. More recently, communication or the transmission of messages, face to face or by telephone, has been introduced as an alternative information flow model.

Open Space Layout

For the successful office layout, certain data are necessary for making layout decisions. Colin Cave itemizes the following factors: number of staff in groups and departments, now and for some years ahead; grades of staff; planned changes in method of work (for example, new equipment); patterns of contact within groups; patterns of contact between groups; patterns of contact with visitors; use of meetings of various kinds; use of communication devices; management style; equipment used by individuals; equipment shared by groups; existing method of work; and informal social groupings among staff.[3]

Various techniques can be utilized to gather this information, among them, interviews with management and staff, questionnaires, or both. Analyzing and retrieving information on area requirements, relationships between departments and groups in order of priority, individual palce relationships as well as identifying key design issues has usually been a cumbersome manual process. A computer-aided office layout program, SCION, has been developed to aid in the analysis of organizations to facilitate spatial planning. This program essentially interprets questionnaire data about face-to-face contacts with people and goes through the stages outlined in Figure 99. Clearly, relationships in work flow that are not face to face are not considered in the program, which begins its work by resolving conflicts among respondents who disagree about the frequency of their weekly contacts.

The data base consists of plotted "closeness ratings," recorded on a matrix called a relationship chart (Figure 99). Each "closeness rating" has to be supported by a reason. To the relationship chart are added the physical details of space required by each activity. From this information a best-relationship diagram can be produced. One method for accomplishing this is to select the activity with the highest "total closeness rating," place it in the center, and arrange all others in relationship to it. The next stage is to add areas to the model and manually fit it into the building space (if it exists) or use it as a planning basis if a new building is required.

Another organizational method is through the use of sociometric analysis where face-to-face contact data are organized into clusters of five or six people with a value assigned to each cluster on the basis of intense interaction. Space data and cluster data are then combined to be fed into the available building space.

Activity Site Model[4]

Walter Moleski of the Environmental Research Group developed the activity site concept to relate behavioral and physical components in an office setting. The activity site has a behavioral component that is influenced by the task at hand and by the participants involved. From these descriptions, performance requirements are generated, which form the basis for the design of the physical support system.

The task descriptors, which are numerically weighted and ranked, are used to differentiate people's behavior. The following descriptors are used in this system:

1. *Level of activity*: The degree of muscle control required to perform the task.
2. *Level of thinking*: The range of neutral activity from problem solving to rote tasks.
3. *Level of routineness*: The habitual nature of the task.
4. *Level of attention*: A measure of intensity necessary to perform the task.
5. *Orientation of the performer:* The degree of focus that must be maintained to accomplish the task.
6. *Volume of work*: The completed work load for a given time period.

There is also a social component to the activity system that relates individuals to social groups. The social structure comprises those behavioral patterns that reflect the rules governing interdependent behavior. The nature and intensity of the task influences the type of interaction patterns generated by the task or as a result of the task. Another pattern is the communication network that connects individuals and groups by the frequency and flow of informa-

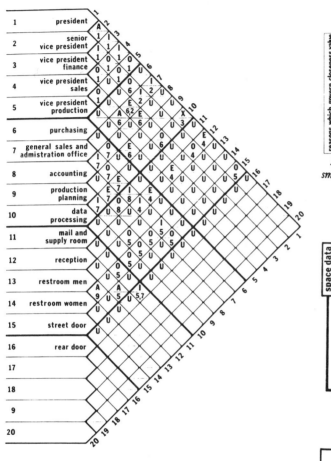

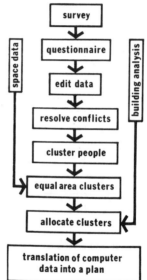

reason		
	code	reason
	1	personal contacts
	2	use of steno pool
	3	noise
	4	number of visitors
reasons which govern closeness value	5	convenience
	6	supervisory control
	7	movement of paper
	8	use of supplies
	9	share same utilities

Relationship chart for a small firm.

importance		
	value	closeness
	A	absolutely necessary
	E	especially important
closeness rating	I	important
	O	average satisfies
	U	unimportant
	X	undesirable

Figure 99
Stages in SCION's program.

perceptual elements—all of which are familiar to designers, solutions can be more consistent with organizational goals.

LEARNING ENVIRONMENTS PROGRAM[5]

Learning environments is a program for open classroom planning designed to furnish guidelines for creating learning environments for centers for children. It can be used to create new centers, to redesign existing centers, or to remodel existing buildings. The intent is to stress the interrelatedness of the goals of children's developmental programs and the physical environment in which they are housed.

In order to clearly present design guidelines, each of the activity areas that might be contained in a center is described in terms of objectives, design requirements, participants, and the molecular activities children engage in. The objectives attempt to clarify the way in which the activities support and nurture the child's development. The design requirements merely state relationships for the appropriate functioning of the activity area. Various education approaches, whether emphasizing free choice or highly structured programs, can be accommodated by the way in which the activity areas are organized. The molecular activities describe what the expected range of behaviors might be in the activity areas.

Diagrams are used to illustrate, but not determine, the way in which the activity areas should be organized. The organizational diagrams, however, only suggest relationships between the participants and aspects of the physical environment. Differing community needs, programs, and objectives should serve as criteria that will modify the way in which these guidelines are employed.

Goals

The recognition of children's needs and learning processes is a prerequisite to the formulation of goals for a child development program. These goals are first defined in terms of the major areas of learning and growth that are regarded as crucial; then they can be adapted to provide a stimulating environment that encourages children to respond and develop their specific needs and capacities for successive stages of development.

The center and the home share in the development of the individual in all stages of childhood. Stated in general terms, the center should bring competence in the physical-motor, social-emotional and intellectual skills; encourage creative expression and invention; and nurture individuality in ways that contribute to feelings of worth and self-identity. These goals need to be reformulated in terms of differences between successive developmental stages. It is the enhancement of the developmental processes that are the most appropriate concept of educational goals. This means that increasing the children's self-understanding, learning, reasoning, and basic skills and helping them achieve appropriate and enduring relationships are all intrinsic to the goals.

The following set of goals has been reformulated in developmental terms and includes factors within the environment that foster these goals.

Individual development In order to facilitate the development of an image of self as a unique and competent person, the school environment should provide for an increasing knowledge of self through identity, family, ethnic membership, and awareness of skills. It should also provide constructive, manipulative activities with a variety of materials like sand, clay, block, and wood.

Social development To help the child develop controls for appropriate handling of drives and internalize impulse control and conflicts, the school environment should communicate a clear set of non-threatening controls, such as limits, rules, and regulations; create a functional adult authority role, which sets understandable restraints, nonpunitive sanctions, and alternative behavior patterns; and foster special relations of child to adult and guidance in learning to share things as well as people.

To advance and develop the child's functioning knowledge of his environment, the school environment should provide for: observation of the community environment through visitation and demonstration; story reading about work processes and people's roles and functions; and discussion of contemporary events that children are aware of—for example, war demonstrations, and space activities.

To provide a positive emotional climate in which the child learns to trust others and himself, the school environment should provide for: building informal, communication channels, verbal and nonverbal, which include adult–child and child–child; cooperative and collective child-group discussion periods and joint work projects; and creating supportive adult role where the adult is a source of comfort, troubleshooter, and has an investment in the child's learning.

Intellectual development To promote the potenial for ordering experience through cognitive strategies, the school environment should provide for: developing and extending receptiveness by a variety of sensory-motor-perceptual experiences (such as color, shape, texture and sound patterns), which focus on observational discrimination; extending modes of symbolizing through gestural representation and graphic representation (such as pencil, paints, clay, block, and wood); developing facility with language through word meanings and usage, scope of vocabulary, meaningful verbal communication and expression, and mastery of syntax; and developing verbal-conceptual organization of experience and problem-solving skills though accent on classification, ordering, relationship, and transformation concepts in varied experimental context and through very selective play materials.

To support the play mode of incorporating experience, the school environment should provide an atmosphere that nourishes and sets the stage for dramatic play activity by providing experiences, materials, and props, and freedom to go beyond the restraints of reality in representing experience.

Activities

An activity area is a section of the learning environment described by specific materials and physical boundaries. The environment is subdivided into areas to order the room, limit chaos, and encourage children to pursue an activity that excites their interest for a maximum length of time and with minimum interference from other activities or other children. The important factors in organizing activity areas are the relative noise levels of activities, patterns of traffic within and among areas, the potential for interfering dirt or mess from surrounding activities, the number of children likely to participate in an area at a given time, and the need for adequate storage space.

Flexibility is an essential ingredient in spatial planning because needs and activities of children will change and thus create the necessity for rearrangement. Flexibility implies creating areas with portable, functional parts so that teachers and children can determine what the environment will be.

The activity chosen for a children's center should be selected on the basis of teaching style, the known and anticipated needs of the children, and the physical space of the classroom. The life of the activity centers is in the learning materials they house. Given freedom to learn and the innate inquisitiveness and fascination with the world they possess, children learn for and by themselves or with each other's help through the materials in the activity centers. A child can choose his own learning activities and build confidence by doing so. The environment should be prepared so that there are options for learning by personal exploration or in conjunction with others. The provision for quiet work is important because the environment should not generate competitiveness, frustration, or boredom. The staff would be available to help children select and use materials in the appropriate activity areas. From this prepared environment children can derive positive feelings and confidence— the confidence to run and jump and dance; to build and paint; to count, compute, and read letters and words and then books. The activity areas provide spaces where children work on tasks important to them that convey messages about the outside world of things and processes, of problems and ways of working on problems. The environment that activity centers provide furnish the children with options in the choice of learning materials.

The basic arrangement of a learning environment figures significantly in the kind of activity that is stimulated. There are three major categories of stimulation to be considered in designing the environment: sensory stimulation, activity stimulation, and cognitive stimulation. Sensory stimulation excites the senses. Activity areas should be colorful while containing children's art and literature. Within each activity area there should be appropriate visual material generally relevant to that area. Sensory stimulation is enhanced by diversity in the environment through patterns, textures, object shapes, and forms where children have the opportunity to touch, smell, listen to, and even taste a variety of materials. Activity stimulation comes from spatial arrangements that encourage children to participate in activities yet define the scope and limitations of the activities. Cognitive stimulation refers to the teachers' utilization of the environment to encourage children to work in areas and at levels that will promote their intellectual development. The physical environment can be an effective catalyst for children's learning.

A graphic notation system can be used to describe relationships between qualities of surfaces, screens, and objects, which represent the physical parts that shape the activity centers. Diagrams are also used to describe the many activities that can occur in a children's center. They represent a graphic code for identifying and describing the activity areas. The graphic notation system is a diagrammatic aid for use in conjunction with the design requirements. (See Figure 104.)

Any recognized activity or unit of activity should be considered in respect to the necessary relations between other activities and to basic physical requirements. Activities and activity sets or systems are so closely related to our understanding of the physical facilities that condition them that we sometimes describe an activity in terms of the type of physical "place" or facility in which it is performed without fully understanding the relationship.

A disciplined approach was developed to liberate conventional thinking methods. This approach is illustrated by a case study of its application to a particular environmental problem.

In order to realize the relation between the organization and employment of physical elements in space and the human activities that determine their employment, an independent view of the activity itself was conducted, free of any preconceived spatial attitudes. Therefore, the activity analysis is essentially a study of the boundary conditions of the system and the enveloping environment.

A graphic method was selected for describing the basic relationships. A simple coding system was used to suggest qualitative differences between activities so that a wide array of alternative relationships would be possible.

The diagrams, sometimes referred to as Venn or bubble diagrams, describe three basic relationships. Intersecting or overlapping circles describe compatibility between activities, while a line connecting two or more circles (activities) suggests separation by a circulation link.

The criteria used for establishing the nature of the relationships were "privacy," both visual and acoustic and frequency of circulation, or "traffic." While other criteria may be used, these two seem to be the most important in influencing relationship decisions.

The method employed in producing the relational diagrams has two stages. The first is described as an interaction matrix where each activity is compared with the remaining activities in terms of compatibility and proximity (Figure 102). Each cell in the matrix is coded to indicate the nature of the interaction: low (L), medium (M), or high (H). In Figure 102, the computer program Compograph was used to generate the final diagram.

The interrelationships between the learning centers and supporting activities were based on the proximity and compatibility of molecular activities within each center. The spatial sets provide a guide for clustering the children's activities and a preliminary organizational step in the development of the solution.

	ART	VISUAL AIDS	LISTENING	WATER	MANIPULATIVE	MUSIC	DRAMA	READING	LARGE GROUP	CONCEPT FORMATION	SCIENCE	MATH	BLOCKS	INDOOR ACTIVE	CONSTRUCTION	NAPPING	CUBBY	LOCKERS	EATING	COOKING	TOILET	WASHING	ENTRY
ART																							
VISUAL AIDS	L																						
LISTENING	M	H																					
WATER	H	L	L																				
MANIPULATIVE	M	M	H	L																			
MUSIC	L	L	L	L	L																		
DRAMA	L	M	L	L	L	H																	
READING	L	H	H	L	H	L	L																
LARGE GROUP	L	H	H	L	L	H	M	L															
CONCEPT FORMATION	L	M	H	L	H	M	L	H	H														
SCIENCE	M	M	M	H	L	L	L	H	L	H													
MATH	L	M	L	M	H	L	L	H	L	H	H												
BLOCKS	L	L	L	L	L	M	M	L	L	L	L	M											
INDOOR ACTIVE	L	L	L	L	L	M	M	H	L	M	L	L	H										
CONSTRUCTION	L	L	L	L	L	L	L	L	L	M	M	M	H	H									
NAPPING	L	L	M	L	M	H	L	H	L	L	L	L	L	L	L								
CUBBY	M	M	M	L	L	H	L	M	L	L	L	L	L	L	L	H							
LOCKERS	L	L	L	L	M	L	M	L	M	L	L	L	L	L	L	L	M						
EATING	L	L	M	M	L	L	L	L	M	L	L	L	L	L	L	L	H	L					
COOKING	H	L	L	H	L	L	L	L	L	L	M	L	L	L	L	L	L	L	H				
TOILET	M	L	M	M	L	L	L	L	L	L	L	L	L	L	M	L	H	H	H	M			
WASHING	H	L	L	H	L	M	M	L	L	L	M	L	L	L	H	H	H	H	H	H	H		
ENTRY	L	L	L	L	M	L	L	L	L	M	L	L	L	L	L	L	H	H	L	L	M	M	

INTERACTION SCALE
L=LOW
M=MEDIUM
H=HIGH

Figure 102
Interrelationships between children's activities based on proximity and compatibility of activities.

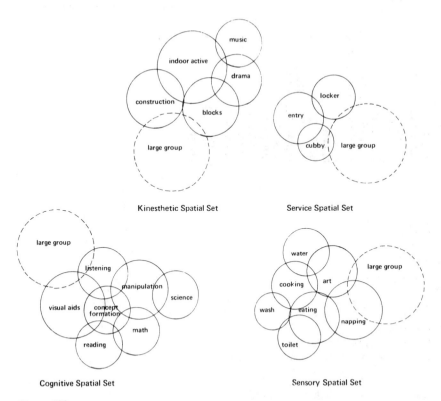

Kinesthetic Spatial Set

Service Spatial Set

Cognitive Spatial Set

Sensory Spatial Set

Figure 103
Children's activity areas subdivided into spatial sets. The large group area is
indicated by dotted lines to represent the focal point for each spatial set.

The computer diagram was altered into four spatial sets—kinesthestic, cognitive, sensory, and service—representing activity clusters that are mutually dependent (Figure 103).

Two other critical areas of information may modify the set of tentative relationships; the first is the age distribution of the children and the second is the program needs and emphasis.

In the consideration of varying age levels of children that may participate in a program, an attempt was made to describe the relative amounts of time children of various age groups may be involved in the various activities. These frequencies are relative and based on a set of systematic observations made by teachers of three age groupings of children.

Figures 104–111 illustrate the development and use of a graphic notation system in support of a verbal specification system. Each activity area in a children's center is identified by a functional symbol that acts as a code for organizing the program and as a graphic aid in the design of the activity centers. The graphic notations represented in Figure 105 and 106 describe the spatial features and physical supports necessary for each of the learning centers. The information contained in Figures 107 through 111 illustrates a method for organizing verbal and visual requirements for twenty primary activity centers in an early learning facility. Each center is briefly described by a scenario and accompanying design requirements, by an identification of secondary

activity diagrams

Health	Locker/Wrapping	Cubby/Locker	Observation	Large Group	Toilet	Director
Washing	Kitchen	Eating	Sleeping	Visual Aids	Listening	Entry/Reception
Water Play	Dramatic Play	Art	Blocks	Manipulative	Science	Staff/Lounge
Reading	Construction	Sand	Climbing	Swinging	Open	Parent/Community
Concept Formation	Mathematics	Indoor Active	Music	Cooking	Protected Outdoor	Laundry

Figure 104
Activity area diagrams. Each activity area is identified with a graphic symbol.

Sitting Apparatus	Resting Apparatus	Climbing Apparatus	Swinging Apparatus
Parking	Stationary Storage	Records Storage	Portable Storage
Vertical Work Surface	Horizontal Work Surface	Mirror Surface	Weather Protection
Telephone	Visual Aids	Dramatic Props	Science Materials
Audio Aids	Manipulative Toys	Art Tools	Art Supplies
Art Drying Apparatus	Animals	Television	Typewriter
Clothes Storage	Sand	Vegetation	Math Materials
Water Play Props	Construction Tools	Napping Pads	Blocks & Props
Drinking Water	Sink	Toilet	Garbage
Towels	Clothes Washing Equipment	Refreshments	Refrigeration Equipment
Cooking Apparatus	Food Preparation Equipment	Food	Potential Darkness
Musical Instruments			Reading Material

Figure 105
Functional symbols. All of the physical elements for the activity areas were graphically described notations.

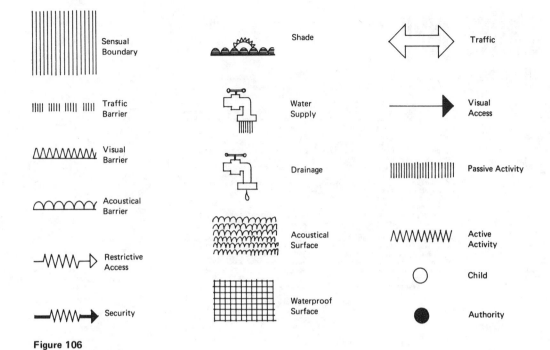

Figure 106
Legend of physical factors.

Sensual Boundary

Traffic Barrier

Visual Barrier

Acoustical Barrier

Restrictive Access

Security

Shade

Water Supply

Drainage

Acoustical Surface

Waterproof Surface

Traffic

Visual Access

Passive Activity

Active Activity

Child

Authority

manipulative play

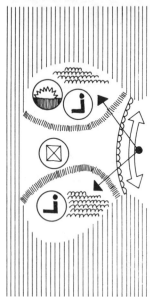

An area especially for manipulative toys is an important provision in a child development center. In this area, children can play with these toys and learn from them without being distracted by other activities in the center. Manipulative toys are intended to present discreet concepts to children. Usually they are designed to eliminate any variables that tend to interfere with their specific purposes. For example, if the concept of shape is intended to be associated with and discovered from a toy, then irrelevant factors such as color and texture are kept constant in the toy so that children cannot confuse shape with other concepts. Such simplification makes learning easy and enjoyable for children. Manipulative toys often require children to operate them manually and with some degree of precision. Puzzles, pegboards, and construction sets are familiar examples of toys that encourage somewhat complex operations. Children learn both about their physical manipulations, and about the relationships resulting from these actions. As a result they develop eye-hand coordination as well as perceptual skills and conceptual knowledge. A manipulative area functions best if it allows privacy for individually oriented activities.

Design Requirements:
1. Provide for quiet, individual play in the manipulative toy area.
2. Provide an open space for small group interaction in the area.
3. Provide a wide variety of manipulative toys.
4. Provide storage that displays these toys and makes them easily accessible to children.
5. Provide movable, comfortable, child sized furniture in the area.
6. Provide flooring in the area that encourages lounging.
7. Provide a high level of lighting in the area.
8. Provide protection from circulation and other activities.

Objectives:
concept formation   positive self-image
sensory and perceptual acuity
eye-hand coordination
visual discrimination   problem solving
small muscle development

Participants:
children
teacher
teacher assistant

Molecular Activities:
handling   listening
arranging   grouping
stacking
ordering
combining
taking apart

concept formation

Although concept formation is a consequence of many different activities in the child development center, a special area devoted to the presentation of specific concepts is an important part of the center. In the concept formation area, exhibits and relevant books emphasize a single concept isolated so that children can understand its meaning clearly. Geometric shape, color, and distance are a few of many concepts that can be presented. Children can relate these specific concepts to their discoveries in other activities. Exhibits in the area are changed periodically so that children can be exposed in depth to a variety of different concepts. Concept formation is a somewhat individual activity. However the area must accomodate varying numbers of children and can well be a focal point of the child development center.

Design Requirements:
1. Provide for the formation of a variety of specific concepts by periodically changing the displays in the concept formation area.
2. Provide books in the area to emphasize the particular concept being presented.
3. Provide for quiet, individual activities in the concept formation area.
4. Provide enough space in the area so that numbers of children can participate simultaneously.
5. Provide ample horizontal and vertical display surfaces in the area.
6. Provide protection from circulation and other activities.

Objectives:
concept formation language development
sensory and perceptual acuity

Participants:
children
teacher
teacher assistant

Molecular Activities:
sitting
handling
displaying
taking apart
feeling
tasting
looking
listening

Figure 107
Activity centers.

listening

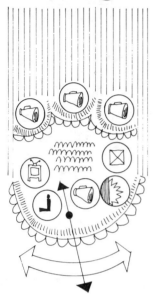

Spoken language is the basis of communication among people. Dependent upon it is practically all childhood socialization and subsequent education. Children cannot begin to learn beyond a physical realm of understanding until their listening and speaking abilities are strong enough to permit them to understand abstract thought. Parents usually train their children to a great extent in understanding and using words as a medium for expression and comprehension. However, the child development center must reinforce for children the listening and speaking abilities they have learned from their parents, polish these abilities, and direct them toward further development. In order to accomplish these goals, it is necessary that a listening area be included in the center. An area specifically for listening helps to broaden children's experiences with sounds and spoken words. Especially important is the provision of tape recorders to allow children to hear their own voices. The area must be somewhat private, but it also must be usable by groups as well as by individuals.

Design Requirements:
1. Provide for quiet individual and group activities in the listening area.
2. Provide listening equipment that is easy for children to operate such as

language masters, tape recorders, and a television.
3. Provide cubicles for individual listening in the area.
4. Provide comfortable and movable seating in the area for children and teachers.
5. Provide flooring in the area that encourages lounging.
6. Provide vertical display surfaces in the area.
7. Provide for adult supervision of the listening area.
8. Provide that visual access to the outside does not interfere with listening activities.
9. Provide protection from circulation and other activities.

Objectives:
concept formation
sensory and perceptual acuity
language development
rhythm development

Participants:
children
teacher
teacher assistant

Molecular Activities:
listening   watching television
speaking   operating equipment
taking out/putting away equipment

science

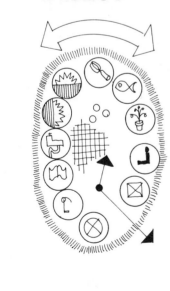

Children come to the child development center equipped with an imaginative curiosity about the world around them. They want to know about heat, water, light, living things, and a wide range of other items and phenomena. A science area integrates natural and man-made objects into the world of children and nurtures their curiosity and understanding of the environment and the inter-relationships within it. The information presented to children by displays of plants, animals, and scientific measuring equipment is accentuated by relevant reading material in the science area. Activities in a science area are usually oriented to the individual. For this reason, privacy is an important provision for scientific learning.

Design Requirements:
1. Provide a variety of experiences for investigation of the natural world in the science area.
2. Provide for quiet, individual activity.
3. Provide ample space for display and experimentation that is easily accessible to children.
4. Provide laboratory facilities and equipment in the area.
5. Provide separate containers for different animals.
6. Provide for a minimum of physical contact between children and living things.

7. Provide for all around viewing of natural displays.
8. Provide natural lighting for plants.
9. Provide ample horizontal work surfaces in the science area.
10. Provide comfortable, child sized seating in the area.
11. Provide a sink in the area that is easily accessible to children.
12. Provide lockable storage for some scientific equipment.
13. Provide protection from circulation and other activities.
14. Provide an outdoor space for gardening and animals.

Objectives:
concept formation   problem solving
sensory and perceptual acuity
perpetuate inquiring nature
experimentation

Participants:
children
teacher
teacher assistant

Molecular Activities:
reading
observing
manipulating displays
measuring
maintaining animals and plants
experimenting

water play

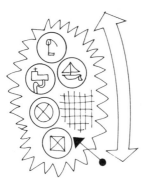

Flexibility in form and function is a primary characteristic of water, and because of its flexibility, it offers children many opportunities for experimentation. Water play, therefore, is important for concept formation. While children splash, they can observe the phenomenon of waves. Playing with toys in the water and measuring introduce to children concepts of floating, sinking, and quantity. These activities are only a few examples of the discovery and learning that occur during water play. Just as important is the pleasure children have in stimulating their senses and feeling. Water play tends to be a group activity. For this reason, an area for this activity requires enough space to accommodate varying numbers of children.

Design Requirements:
1. Provide a water receptacle as deep and as large in water surface area as possible.
2. Provide enough area around the receptacle so that numbers of children can participate in water play simultaneously.
3. Provide an ample supply of props for water play.
4. Provide storage for props that is easily accessible to children.
5. Provide for a minimum of water spillage.
6. Provide waterproof and slip-proof surfaces in the area.
7. Provide some means for keeping children's clothing dry such as waterproof aprons.
8. Provide towels that are easily accessible to children.
9. Provide facilities for hose connection.
10. Provide an exterior view in the area.
11. Provide as much natural lighting as possible in the water play area.
12. Provide for adult supervision in the area.
13. Provide adequate heating in the area.
14. Provide protection from circulation and other activities.

Objectives:
concept formation
sensory and perceptual acuity
eye-hand coordination
small muscle development

Participants:
children
teacher
teacher assistant

Molecular Activities:
pouring
floating/sinking
blowing bubbles
splashing
washing
measuring
beating
coloring
standing/sitting in water

cooking

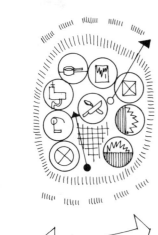

Cooking can be a valuable experience for children. Not only does this useful production give children satisfaction and a sense of responsibility, but also the activity is important for learning. For example, concepts about shapes and other properties of food can be formed as a result of involvement in cooking activities. Scraping and slicing vegetables require children to manipulate them with some degree of skill thus developing eye-hand coordination. Cooking also is a natural socializing activity that encourages the individual to participate in groups. An area for this activity must have enough space to accomodate several children simultaneously.

Design Requirements:
1. Provide both hot and cold food preparation equipment that is easy for children to handle in the cooking area.
2. Provide facilities for dish washing in the area.
3. Provide facilities for waste disposal.
4. Provide waterproof and easily cleanable working surfaces in the area.
5. Provide for storage and display of cooking utensils.
6. Provide protection from circulation and other activities.
7. Provide ventilation for the cooking area.
8. Provide visual access to the outside in the area.

Objectives:
eye-hand coordination   problem solving
concept formation
small muscle development
socializing   language development

Participants:
children
teacher
teacher assistant

Molecular Activities:
pouring
stirring
tasting
mixing
cooking
eating
measuring

Figure 108
Activity Centers.

art

The art work of children is a visual expression of their feelings about experiences which are personally significant to them. These feelings they choose to express can result from direct involvement in home or school activities or from vicarious experiences in listening to stories and reading. In order to express their thoughts visually, children must think about themselves and their physical and social environment. For this reason, art activities are valuable for intellectual development and for self image formation. Art can mean invention to children, and thus it becomes important for self expression, communication, and problem solving. Working individually and controlling their own actions, children learn technical skills and gain self reliance and positive self images. Variety in art activities is limited only by the teacher's choice of materials to make available for the children's use. Among many common art medias are painting with brushes and fingers, paper cutting and pasting, and clay modelling. An art area must be usable both by individuals and by groups without significant interference.

Design Requirements:
1. Provide for both individual and group activities in the art area.
2. Provide both vertical and horizontal work surfaces with ample space around them for activity.
3. Provide storage for these materials that is easily accessible to children.
4. Provide storage that is inaccessible to children.
5. Provide storage for incomplete art projects.
6. Provide a space for drying art work.
7. Provide for separation of incompatible art activities.
8. Provide in the area a washing facility, preferably a sink with a drainboard, that is easily accessible to children.
9. Provide flooring in the area that is easily cleanable and impervious to art materials such as paint and clay.
10. Provide visual access to the outside in
11. Provide protection from circulation and other activities.

Objectives:
positive self image
sensory and perceptual acuity
eye-hand coordination
small muscle development
self expression
visual discrimination

Participants:
children, teacher, teacher assistant

Molecular Activities:
finger painting, brush/easel painting, collage, paper mache, cutting, pasting, drawing/coloring, clay modeling, mural making, cleaning up, washing, mixing

eating

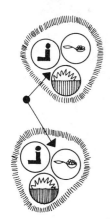

Occasionally children come to the child development center without having eaten earlier at home. Also, they usually develop healthy appetites as a result of active play. For these reasons, it is necessary that a time for eating be included in the center's schedule each day. Food gives children extra energy and frees them to become fully involved in learning activities. Moreover, eating itself can be a significant learning experience. It offers many opportunities for children to explore concepts such as color and texture in the foods they eat. Equally important is the chance it provides for children to learn about unfamiliar foods. Socialization in acceptable eating habits comes as a result of observing teachers and other children while they eat. Children also learn to take responsibility when they serve food and clean up. Children enjoy eating in small groups throughout the center, so that a specific eating place perhaps is unnecessary.

Design Requirements:
1. Provide a variety of settings in the child development center where small groups of children and adults can eat.
2. Provide an area where food can be distributed.
3. Provide comfortable, child sized tables and seating that can be cleaned easily.
4. Provide for family style serving in large bowls.
5. Provide utensils that can be used easily by children.
6. Provide storage that is easily accessible to children for food they bring from home.
7. Provide easily accessible facilities for hand washing.
8. Provide waste receptacles for excess food and disposable utensils.

Objectives:
concept formation
sensory and perceptual acuity
eye-hand coordination
socialization   language development

Participants:
children
teacher
teacher assistants
visitors

Molecular Activities:
serving food
drinking
eating
cleaning up

indoor active play

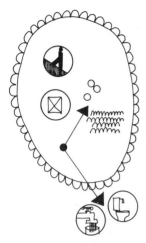

Children tend to become excessively active and excited. Under usual circumstances they are able to exercise and reduce their excitement during active outdoor play. However, problems arise when weather conditions such as cold and dampness prevent normal outdoor activities. Children still must have some means of releasing energy. The solution to problems of limited outdoor play is a provision for active play inside the child development center. An indoor area can provide children with a variety of activities for energy release and large muscle development. Climbing and active games are two types of play that can be facilitated in the area. An important environmental requirement of the area is that it be acoustically isolated from the rest of the center. The area must also accomodate a large number of children simultaneously.

Design Requirements:
1. Provide for a variety of activities in the indoor active play area.
2. Provide an open space in the area for active games.
3. Provide a facility for climbing in the area.
4. Provide equipment for active games.
5. Provide easily accessible storage in the area for equipment.
6. Provide flooring in the indoor active play area that reduces noise and

prevents falling accidents.
7. Provide acoustic separation between the active play area and other areas in the child development center.
8. Provide for adult supervision of the area.

Objectives:
large muscle development
eye-hand coordination
positive self-image
problem solving
concept formation
sensory development

Participants:
children
teacher
teacher assistant

Molecular Activities:
bending
squatting
crawling
climbing
stretching
balancing
falling
jumping
cooperating
running

dramatic play

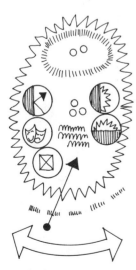

Fascinated by the experiences of everyday life, children enjoy interpreting these experiences and re-enacting them. For example, children assume adult roles in dramatic play and recreate a wide variety of behavioral situations involving role relationships. Among many common dramatic activities are housekeeping, shop keeping, and transportation play. The importance of dramatic play lies in children's development in understanding themselves and others and in their gaining confidence that they can be whatever they wish to be. Experiences are widened when children are allowed to act out new roles and situations they encounter. Also, dramatic play encourages development toward sophistication in oral expression. This activity usually is group oriented. However, it is necessary that a space for dramatic play provide some degree of privacy.

Design Requirements:
1. Provide for a wide range of dramatic activities by keeping a large variety of props and toys available to children.
2. Provide materials to allow children to create their own props for special activities.
3. Provide an area that can function as a stage for dramatic presentations.
4. Provide a full length mirror so that children can see themselves in role oriented costumes.
5. Provide storage for dramatic equipment that is easily accessible to children.

6. Provide a ceiling system that permits the hanging of lightweight props.
7. Provide lighting that can be directed toward the area specifically for dramatic presentations.
8. Provide flooring that reduces noise in the dramatic area.
9. Provide protection from circulation and other activities.

Objectives:
positive self image   social development
language development
role enactments
orientation in fantasy and reality

Participants:
children
teacher
teacher assistant

Molecular Activities:
dress up
puppetry
household
fire station
grocery store
hospital
special activities
setting up props
making special props
dramatic presentation

Figure 109
Activity centers.

music

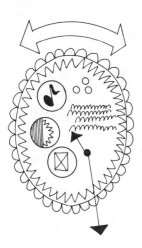

Musical interest is quite evident in the activities of children. It is desirable for a child development center to nurture this interest by emphasizing music as a daily activity. Making music and responding to it enhance intellectual, emotional, and social development in children. For example, singing is an important aid to the growth of language abilities. Also, it can be used to introduce and reinforce concepts. Singing, playing instruments, and dancing--natural group activities--teach children to cooperate with others in their social environment. Equally important is the pleasure children experience in making sounds and expressing their own musical ideas. Since musical play usually involves groups, it is essential that a music area accomodate varying numbers of children.

Design Requirements:
1. Provide for group activities in the music area.
2. Provide ample space for body movement.
3. Provide for informal singing in the area.
4. Provide for experimentation with instrumental noises.
5. Provide musical equipment that is easy for children to operate.
6. Provide for display of various musical instruments.

7. Provide storage for records and instruments that is easily accessible to children.
8. Provide flooring in the area that encourages lounging and reduces noise.
9. Provide for adult supervision of the music area.
10. Provide separation between the music area and other areas to prevent mutual interference.

Objectives:
concept formation
sensory and perceptual acuity
language development
rhythm and balance development
emotional development
social development

Participants:
children
teacher
teacher assistant

Molecular Activities:
listening
relaxing
composing
singing
dancing
operating equipment
handling instruments
manipulation

construction

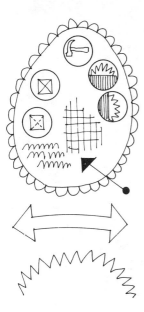

Children delight in building activities in a construction area. Hammering, sawing, and drilling allow them to release energy and hostility constructively. Moreover, such physical activity develops large and small muscles, eye-hand coordination, and visual acuity. Just as important to children is a development of confidence in their improving tool handling skills and pride in the objects they create. Construction activities are very active and noisy, and for this reason it is necessary that a construction area be separated acoustically from other activities in the child development center. Space in the area must be adequate for the simultaneous use of numbers of children.

Design Requirements:
1. Provide a variety of tools that are safe for children to use in the construction area.
2. Provide wood, nails, and other materials for building.
3. Provide horizontal work surfaces in the area with ample space for activity around them.
4. Provide storage that displays tools and building materials and that is easily accessible to children.
5. Provide ample space for displaying completed projects.

6. Provide flooring and work surfaces that reduce impact noise and that are easily cleanable of splinters and nails.
7. Provide for constant adult supervision of the area.
8. Provide easy access to first aide in the area.
9. Provide an acoustical separation between noisy construction activities and other quieter activities in the center.
10. Provide protection from circulation and other activities.

Objectives:
concept formation
large/small muscle development
self-expression
eye-hand coordination
visual discrimination
positive self-image
problem solving

Participants:
children
teacher
teacher assistant

Molecular Activities:
hammering
sawing
drilling
taking out/putting away equipment

cubby

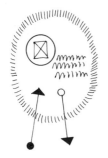

When a child has a private space to store personal items — a cubby — and when he sees his name labelling that space, he gains a feeling of self importance. It is therefore apparent that storage of this nature serves a mental function as well as the utilitarian function of housing a child's private possessions. A cubby area differs from a locker wrapping area in that storage here is for smaller items not necessarily associated with outdoor activities. For example, items may be art work or lunches brought from home. The cubby area must accomodate a number of children. However, activity in the area is individually oriented and private.

Design Requirements:
1. Provide independent storage spaces for each child's personal possessions that are easily accessible to children.
2. Provide for name labelling of each storage space.
3. Provide easy access to the cubby area from other activity areas in the center.

Objectives:
positive self image
personal storage

Participants:
children

Molecular Activities:
dressing/undressing
taking out/putting away items
storing personal possessions

locker wrapping

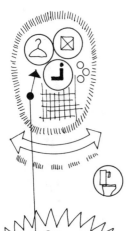

A locker-wrapping area functions specifically for the storage of extra clothing such as coats and boots that children do not wear inside the child development center. However, it is necessary that this clothing remain available to children during the day for outdoor play. Numbers of children dress and undress in the area simultaneously, so that it must be large enough to accomodate them.

Design Requirements:
1. Provide storage for wraps, boots, etc. that is easily accessible to children.
2. Provide for ventilation of wet clothing.
3. Provide storage for clean clothing.
4. Provide some child sized seating in the locker-wrapping area.
5. Provide waterproof, slip-proof, and easily cleanable flooring in the area.
6. Provide for adult supervision of the area.
7. Provide easy access to toilets and to the outdoor play area.
8. Provide separation between activities in the locker-wrapping area and other activities to prevent interference.

Participants:
children
teacher
teacher assistant
mothers

Molecular Activities:
taking off/putting on wraps
carrying personal items
storing personal items
handling parcels
talking
waiting
helping

**Figure 110
Activity centers.**

napping

Provisions for sleeping vary among child development centers due mainly to the length of time the children stay at the centers. Relatively long sleeping periods or short napping periods may be included, or it may be that no specific periods for rest are scheduled at all. However, provisions are necessary if only to give children an opportunity to rest from active play and to freshen themselves for more activity later in the day. Due to the variations in children's resting habits, it is necessary that the activity be an opportunity and not a requirement. Sleeping usually does not require a special space, but it is very individually oriented and private.

Design Requirements:
1. Provide for quiet, individual passivity in sleeping.
2. Provide pads or cots for sleeping.
3. Provide storage for sleeping equipment that is easily accessible to children.
4. Provide for warm flooring if pads are used.
5. Provide for darkening in sleeping areas.
6. Provide space for adult supervision of sleeping and circulation among children.
7. Provide protection from the noise of circulation and other activities.

Participants:
children
teacher
teacher assistant

Molecular Activities:
sleeping
resting
quiet play
whispering
reading
setting up cots or pads
getting cots or pads
storing linens

classroom wash

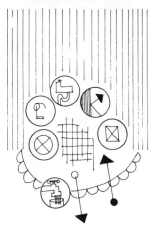

Several washing functions are served by a classroom wash area. Perhaps most important is hand cleaning associated with active play. Children get dirty during play and also have accidents such as spills that require washing. Also, children usually wash after toileting and before eating. It is not necessary for this activity to be limited to one particular area. Washing can be decentralized in order to be more closely related to active play areas in the child development center.

Design Requirements:
1. Provide sinks both for adults and for children in the wash area.
2. Provide towels at a location that is easily accessible to children.
3. Provide a child sized drinking fountain in the area.
4. Provide mirrors above the sinks so that children can see themsleves.
5. Provide water temperature controls in order to avoid scalding.
6. Provide storage and facilities for cleaning muddy boots, umbrellas, etc.
7. Provide surfaces in the area that are waterproof and easily cleanable.
8. Provide for adult supervision of the area.
9. Provide for draft minimization in the wash area.
10. Provide easy accessibility to the wash area from other activity areas both inside the center and outdoors.

Participants:
children
teacher
teacher assistant

Molecular Activities:
drinking
washing hands
cleaning objects
looking in mirrors

visual aids

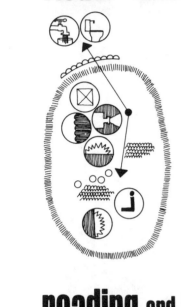

Viewing slides and films can add depth and scope to children's learning experiences. For example, this activity can be an important supplement to field trips or group listening and story telling. It can also introduce to children experiences that may not be accessible through reading or instruction. Consequently, it can give children valuable information and stimulate their intellectual development. The advantages of learning from visual aids warrant the inclusion of this activity in the child development center. Film viewing is usually a group activity, and therefore it requires a space large enough for a number of children. However, this activity does not require a special area in the center. Perhaps the large group area is best suited for learning from visual aids.

Design Requirements:
1. Provide space for a large group of participants.
2. Provide for darkening in the area.
3. Provide for quietness in the area.
4. Provide a large, light colored, vertical surface for showing slides and films.
5. Provide equipment for projecting slides and films.
6. Provide lockable storage for projection equipment.
7. Provide flooring in the area that encourages lounging.

Objectives:
intellectual development
language development
concept formation

Participants:
children
teacher
teacher assistant

Molecular Activities:
listening
questioning
viewing slides and films

reading and writing

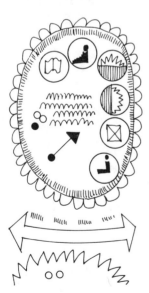

Language is the externalization of thought. Each word symbolizes a discreet concept. If specific language symbols, words in spoken or written form, are widely understood to be representative of concepts, then these symbols become a medium for thought exchange. During the socialization process, children are introduced to verbal communication when their parents use spoken words to teach them about their environment. Eventually, children acquire the ability to use speech in expressing their own thoughts. A very important task of the child development center is not only to nuture children's speaking skills but also to introduce language in its written form to them. Sophistication in reading and writing is a prerequisite for adequate performance in the social environment. In order to insure children's development of these cognitive skills, an area especially for reading and writing must be included in the center. Development in reading and writing is enhanced when these activities occur in other areas in the center. For example, written labels on items in the environment expand children's vocabularies.

Design Requirements:
1. Provide for quiet individual and group reading in the area.
2. Provide for shared experiences of informal story telling.
3. Provide for written expressions by individuals or small groups.
4. Provide type writers in the area near a sound absorbing surface.
5. Provide storage in the area that is easily accessible to children and that allows entire book covers to be visible.
6. Provide ample vertical surfaces for display.
7. Provide comfortable, movable seating for children and teachers.
8. Provide a floor surface in the area that encourages lounging.
9. Provide horizontal surfaces for large book reading and display.
10. Provide protection from circulation and other activities.

Objectives:
intellectual stimulation
acquisition of information
emotional development
interplay between reading and experience
skill development

Participants:
children
teacher
teacher assistant

Molecular Activities:
reading, browsing, relaxing, individual, isolation, story telling, typing, looking at displays, noting, relating, writing, dictating

Figure 111
Activity centers.

large group

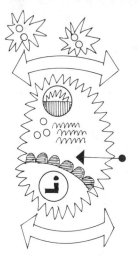

An area where all the children can come together at one time for large group activities such as dancing, watching films, or talking with their teachers as a group is essential to the child development center. When all the children can be together, they develop a strong sense of group solidarity. Flexibility is an important characteristic in this area. It must be adaptable to a wide variety of activities and also must accommodate activities that occasionally expand into it from the smaller learning centers. Openness and a very social atmosphere are desirable qualities in a large group area.

Design Requirements:
1. Provide easy access to the large group area from the smaller learning centers.
2. Provide a focal point in the area in order to control the children's attention.
3. Provide flooring in the area that encourages lounging and reduces noise.
4. Provide for darkening in the large group area.
5. Provide for adult supervision of the area.
6. Provide for circulation flow around the edges of the large group area in order to prevent activity fragmentation.
7. Provide visual access to the outside from the area.

Objectives:
individual functioning as a group member
group solidarity
language development

Participants:
children
teacher
teacher assistant
visitors
parents

Molecular Activities:
playing alone
playing in groups
reading
listening
dramatization
special group activities

block play

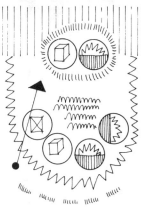

Block play serves various functions in the development of children. Building structures from blocks is one way in which children express themselves. Their expressions may be either abstract or representational. When children explore their personal ideas structurally, they observe physical principles and form concepts of size, weight, shape, and fit. Moreover, they must use their newly formed concepts in making decisions about what to build and how to proceed in building it. Interest, then, is in the process of building rather than in the final product. Children gain confidence and sense of achievement when they become skilled enough to build large, complex structures. Block play typically assumes two somewhat incompatible forms, active and passive in character. Often associated with the use of large blocks, active block play involves an aggressive use of power by children in testing themselves against their environment. However, children also like to retreat from their environment, and the use of small blocks is individually oriented to an extent that it is suitable activity for children seeking refuge.

Design Requirements:
1. Provide blocks that encourage balancing and climbing.
2. Provide ample and flexible space for large scale, active block play.

3. Provide protected spaces for passive, individual block play.
4. Provide storage for blocks that presents their building potential and that is easily accessible to children.
5. Provide display space for completed structures in the area.
6. Provide vertical display surfaces in the area.
7. Provide flooring and work surfaces in the area that reduce impact noise.
8. Provide separation between block play and other quieter activities.
9. Provide protection from circulation.

Objectives:
concept formation   problem solving
large/small muscle development
self expression   positive self-image
eye-hand coordination
visual discrimination

Participants:
children
teacher
teacher assistant

Molecular Activities:
building, stocking, arranging, destroying structures, balancing, climbing, taking out/ putting away equipment

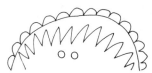

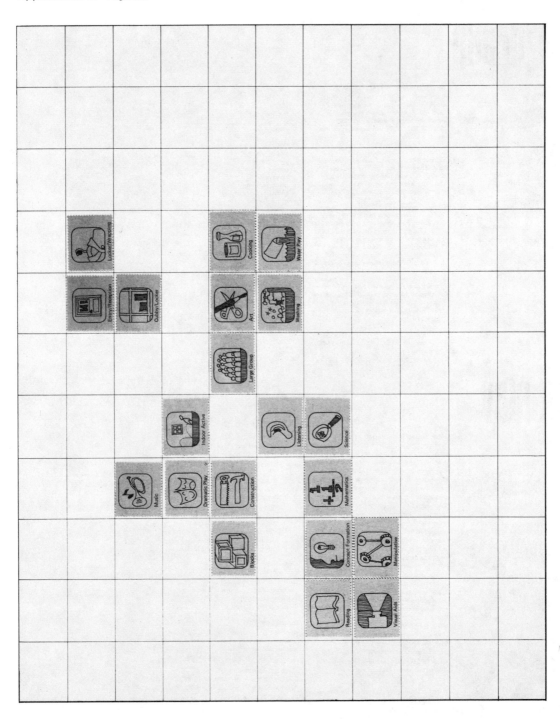

Figure 112
Interior spatial layout diagram.

activities, and by the participants and purposes of the activity center. The spatial needs that are not amenable to verbal description are noted in each of the adjacent diagrams.

Teacher's Planning Aid

Planning the children's center is a task requiring the knowledge of the architect as well as that of the teacher. The problem is similar to that of a puzzle. There are a number of pieces that must fit together in some logical manner. Unlike a puzzle, however, there is not one correct solution or one fit of pieces. The differences stem from the needs, values, and goals of teachers, parents, and communities. Yet the common aspect to all groups is the kind of activities children are engaged in, what they enjoy doing, and how they learn. The parts of this game represent what is common to all centers. How the parts go together or what pieces are included may vary from player to player. This planning game can provide the preliminary step in planning for physical changes.

Each of the diagrams in Figure 112 represents an activity in a children's center. From the set of diagrams, it is possible to plan a children's center or a classroom, as well as to remodel an existing building. The activity diagrams should include the administrative services of a center (entry, director, staff), the children's indoor activities (block, art, manipulative), and the children's outdoor activities (climbing, swinging). Through the use of diagrams, it is possible to plan relationships between activities and establish which activities should be close to one another and which require some separation.

The gameboard has a grid that corresponds to the size of each diagram. There are three rules for the diagrams and the grid board:

1. Each activity diagram should be placed on a vacant grid.
2. No two diagrams should overlap or occupy more than one grid cell.

3. Activities should be placed next to each other in terms of their requirements for privacy, accessibility, or relationship to each other.

While many of the activities seem to be related, each activity can have direct contact with a maximum of four other activities. This means that the placement of activities on the grid will require a decision on which are the most important relationships.

An architect, teacher, administrator or student who goes through this planning process will better understand the problems of planning as well as programming for physical changes.

PARTICIPATORY GAMES

The concept of a game is exceedingly general and includes any situation in which something is gained as a result of a proper choice of strategy. Simulation involves the imitation or conceptualization of some system wherein there is a conflict and a distribution of outcomes associated with the resolution of the conflicts. Thus the term *simulation games* corresponds to the early theoretical efforts from World War II when major breakthroughs occurred in applying theory to practical solutions to problems sometimes referred to as "war games." More recently, it was felt that the general values of a democracy imply that people should participate in those decisions that affect their environment. The emerging assumption is that expertise does not reside entirely in the designer but rather in all those whose interests are affected by a design problem.

Although participatory approaches run counter to two influential maxims—"Too many cooks spoil the broth" and "Who ever heard of design by committee?"—it is felt that increased participation can lead to increased efficiency and creativity in design outcomes. The key factor is the interaction between the user/client who furnishes the behavioral information and the designer as change agent who provides alternative options.

A participatory game is an approach that designers or programmers can employ to actively involve users in the process of designing where the users narrow the information gap in the program. Games can be designed to simulate a particular situation involving all participants in the process of negotiations and trade-offs. This interaction process must actively seek to make the participants aware of their own beliefs, goals, and ideals so that the choices and decisions they make are conscious and deliberate and are based on their own value system. Not unlike parlor games, the basic components to participatory games are a game situation, roles, rules, payoffs, and some type of evaluation. The effective organization of a game seeking collaboration includes the salient principles from group discussions and role playing together with a situational construct that simulates the stages of design. Although this design approach is in its infancy, the following discussion illustrates an early attempt at organizing an interactive process.

Relating Objectives for Learning to Eduction (Role)

In response to the shifting orientation from teacher-oriented to child-oriented educational facilities, traditional processes generating new concepts in school building are no longer satisfactory. Notwithstanding technological advances, curriculum changes, and the like, any facility is appropriate as it responds to the goals and objectives from which it grew.

In educational programming, particularly in decentralizing communities where the variation in ethnic and community background are the stimulus for change, strategies for citizen involvement facilitate the designer's decision-making process, as well as constructively provide for the opportunity to negotiate. Since the participation of citizens suggests involvement of nondesign groups, it is important that participants are contributing from their expertise and that the designer not abrogate his responsibility. Citizens' groups can respond effectively when the types of decisions required of them are carefully delineated and circumscribed. There also needs to be closure on the participatory experience with a cumulative effect such that there is a continuous development toward a clear direction.

In order to clarify this relationship and define a method in which these relationships might occur, a negotiation strategy—ROLE (Relating Objectives for Learning to Education)—was developed to support the notion that there are many areas of expertise required in the programming of the built environment.[6] ROLE is an abstraction of a complex decision-making process designed to integrate the knowledge of the players (architects, teachers, administrators) into a sequential set of activities. The negotiation stages encourage all the participants to share in the decision-making process, while the primary goal of this interaction process is to increase the level of awareness to a set of programming concepts as well as to clarify the value differences of the participants. In the process of programming facilities for educational purposes, it is necessary that those purposes or objectives are clearly specified in order that the designed environment can be supportive.

The game is organized into three basic components: objectives, learning methods and environmental settings. Each of the components were developed as a result of an intensive search to identify the most commonly stated objectives and learning methods from the educational literature. The accompanying settings were selected from periodicals to insure a wide array of pictorial alternatives.

The sequence of play begins with clarification of objectives, selection of appropriate learning methods to accomplish the objectives, desired role relationships between student and teacher, and the identification of environmental settings that facilitate the learning methods.

The game is played by groups of three to five people. To begin, each player selects from a listing sheet (Figure 113) no more than four objectives that seem to be most important. Aftter each player has made the necessary choices, the individual lists are pooled. Through negotiation, the group must choose

Figure 113

Objectives	Methods	Objectives	Methods
Developing Language Fluency	Competition	Developing Introspective Skills	Peer Counseling
Encouraging Student's Sense of Community Identity	Parent-Teacher-Student Integration	Developing Social Competence	Contract Teaching
Reinforcing Sense of Effectiveness of the Individual	Group Problem-Solving	Developing a Tolerance of Differences	Team Teaching
Developing Cognitive Skills	Student Participation	Developing a Sense of Responsibility	Audio-Visual Aids
Developing Motivation for Learning	Self-Presentation	Learning by Conditioning	
Encouraging Self-Expression	Field Trips	Encouraging Group Interaction	
Reinforcing Positive Self-Image	Small Group Discussion	Learning through Execution	
Developing a Sense of Confidence	Voucher System	Stimulating Curiosity and Imagination	
Developing Persistence Toward a Goal	Direct Experience	Developing a Sense of Reality	
	Role Play or Simulation	Achieving Intra-Sensory Integration	
Developing Concentration	Non-Graded Classes	Developing Motor Skills	
Developing Self-Regulation	Parent Participation	Learning by Example	
Learning by Discrimination	Lecture or Demonstration	Developing Memory Skills	
Developing Communication Skills	Graded Grouping	Developing Self-Actualization	
	Remedial Workshops	Encouraging a Sense of Trust	
Developing Concept Formation	Self-Directed Activities	Constructive Use of Fantasy	
Channeling Basic Biological Drives Constructively	Independent Study	Developing Perceptual Acuity	
	Evaluation and Testing of Students	Involving Parents in the Educational Experience	
Developing and Encouraging Resourcefulness	Open Classroom	Developing Social Awareness	
	Programmed Instruction		
Developing Initiative and Spontaneity	Individualized Instruction		
	Paraprofessionals		
	Community Resources		
	Community Involvement		

from these no more than four objectives, with the additional constraint that the selections should be incorporated into a unified educational program. Players are urged to forcefully support their individual choices, even if other members did not make the same choice, until they persuade or are pursuaded by others that an objective should be included in the final set. When consensus is reached, the group records its choice.

Next, the group examines each objective individually and selects learning methods (Figure 113) that identify strategies for accomplishing each one; the group then works through each objective completely before starting the next one. Some may relate to more than one objective. Having chosen at least one but not more than four learning methods for each objective, the group next qualifies whether each of the methods

is teacher or child directed. When a step is completed, the group's decisions should be entered on the ROLE record sheet (Figure 114).

Combining these two elements—objectives and learning methods—the group then selects appropriate environmental settings (Figure 116) conducive to fulfilling the requirements for each objective. The completed sets of decisions describe the process and mode of evaluation for planning an educational facilities program.

Inventory of Activity Data

The results of the ROLE game can be effectively utilized in the development of a program through the use of an inventory of activity data. The goals gener-

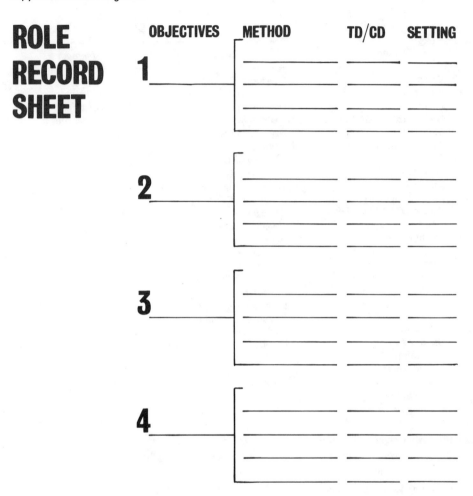

Figure 114
ROLE record sheet.

ated from the negotiation stages can help to focus the development for each primary activity. Primary activities are those for which the facility is to be designed. It is recognized that there are secondary activities as well that are necessary to support the fulfillment of the primary activities.

The data sheet (Figure 115) is a permanent record of the primary activities since they are to be described in relationship to the goals they must satisfy. Data sheets can be prepared by individuals or groups and can include spatial and material requirements as well as activity participants.

ACTIVITY DATA SHEET

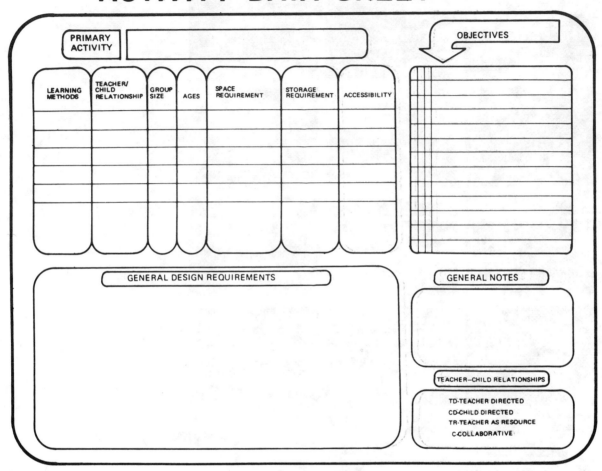

Figure 115
Activity data sheet.

Figure 116
Environmental settings.

The data sheet shown in Figure 116 was initially developed for an educational facility with the following goals:

Goal:	Developing a sense of responsibility.
Learning method:	Independent study.
	Nongraded classes.
	Field trips.
	Competition.

Goal:	Developing motivation for learning.
Learning method:	Lecture, demonstration.
	One-to-one student/teacher.
	Accessibility of resource.
	Student planning.

Goal:	Developing communication skills.
Learning method:	One-to-one student/teacher.
	Peer counseling.
	Accessibility to resources.
	Self-presentation.

Goal:	Developing self-actualization.
Learning method:	Nongraded classes.
	Independent study.
	Student planning.
	One-to-one student/teacher.

| Goal: | Developing resourcefulness. |

Learning method:	Accessibility of resources.
	Lecture/demonstration.
	Competition.
	Student planning.

As each primary activity is identified, the appropriate connections can then be made between the goal and learning method.

REFERENCES

1. M. Brill, "PAK: Planning Aid Kit" (Paper presented at the 123d meeting of the American Psychiatric Association, San Francisco, 1970).
2. C. Stewart and K. Lee, "Troika for Architectural Planning," in Association for Computing Machinery, *Annual Conference Proceedings* (1971), pp. 112–126.
3. C. Cave, "Layout in Open Spaces," *The Architect's Journal* 17 (October 1973).
4. H. Sanoff, J. Sanoff, and A. Hensley, *Learning Environments for Children* (Raleigh, N.C.: Learning Environments, 1971), pp. 19–77.
5. W. Moleski, "Behavioral Analysis and Environmental Programming for Offices," in *Designing for Human Behavior*, ed. J. Lang, C. Burnette, W. Moleski, and D. Vachon (Stroudsburg: Dowden, Hutchinson & Ross, 1974), pp. 303–314.
6. H. Sanoff, "ROLE: Relating Objective for Learning to Education," in *Designing the Method*, ed. D. Tester (Raleigh, N. C.: Student Publication of the School of Design, North Carolina State University, 1974), p. 231.

Conclusion

In this book design has been defined quite broadly to imply any human modification of the environment; this definition thus entails a process in which choices are made.

Traditional design consists of a process of people making decisions on the behalf of other people—decisions that affect yet another set of people.

In response to these views, programming has been described as a process for gathering information to define the problem and evaluate possible solutions. This process normally includes decision-making tools for determining the relative importance of information for discovering relationships and for resolving conflicts.

The issue of process is central to the theme of programming and was clearly the focus of attention of design theorists during the late 1960s and early 1970s. The process structure usually began by identifying user goals; then it defined relationships to these goals to activity or behavior requirements, and as a final step it attempted to correlate behavior requirements with physical systems that would satisfy them.

Today, the questions of content, in terms of information sources, organization, evaluation, and participation, become a critical set of issues. The factors contingent upon successful programming are the systematic and communicable nature of the programming process, which stimulates a dialogue between the client and community participants so that opportunities are created for mutual learning. The quality of decision making, then, is more a function of the negotiation process between the designer, the client, and the user than on the information-gathering processes per se.

The degree of subjectivity does not significantly vary between conscious, deliberate programming methods and traditional issue-based arguments between designer and client unless there is consensus about the need to learn about the problem. Tomorrow's designer will be responsible for facilitating that process of selecting appropriate methods and strategies and subsequently facilitating the process of mutual learning. This new role for the designer is one where there is a need to establish a social rather than personal validity to the process of choice.

It may be apparent that the programming methods reviewed did not consider such factors as symbolic or image value of a physical place, which are important information requirements for which designers are accountable. This is more a function of the state of the art of available information than a shortcoming of any programming process discussed.

Designers should not consider programming a replacement for the previous commitment to those principles of conservation, quality, and a myriad of other tenets subscribed to by the design world. In fact, it is of increasing importance that those traditional concerns of designers be made explicit and included in the programming process.

Bibliography

Agostini, Edward J. "The Value of Facilities Programming to the Client." *Building Research* (April 1969): 28–32.

Alexander, Christopher. *Notes on the Synthesis of Form*. Cambridge: Harvard University Press, 1971.

Alexander, Christopher; Ishikawa Sara; and Silverstein Murray. *A Pattern Language Which Generates Multi-Service Centers*. Berkeley: California Center for Environmental Structure.

Alexander, Christopher; Silverstein Murray; Angel Shlomo; Ishikawa Sara; and Abrams Denney. *The Oregon Experiment*. New York: Oxford University Press, 1975.

Alger, John R. M., and Hays, Carl V. *Creative Synthesis in Design*. Englewood Cliffs, N.J.: Prentice Hall, 1964.

Asimow, Morris. *Introduction to Design*. Englewood Cliffs, N. J.: Prentice Hall, 1962.

Balchen, Bess. "Where Programming is the Design." *AIA Journal* (April 1973): 38–47.

Briggs, William A. "Pre-Programming and Programming for the Live Performing Arts." *AIA Journal* (December 1964).

Bross, Irving. *Design for Decision*. New York: Free Press, 1953.

Canter, D. V. "Office Size: An Example of Psychological Research in Architecture." *Architects Journal* (April 1968): 881–888.

Canter, D. V. "The Measurement of Appropriateness in Buildings." *Transactions of the Bartlett Society* 6 (1967–1968): 40–60.

Canter, D. V., and Woods, R. "A Technique for the Subjective Appraisal of Buildings." *Building Science* 5, (1970): 187–198.

Clark, Jeffrey E. "Office Space Programming." *The Office* (June 1971): 27–36, 125.

Cogswell, Arthur, R. "Programming and a Computer-Based Cost Analysis System." *Building Research* (April 1969): 33–35.

Davis, Gerald. "The Independent Building Program Consultant." *Building Research* (April 1969): 16–21.

Davis, Gerald. "Using Interviews of Present Office Workers in Planning New Offices." *Proceedings of the Environmental Design Research Association Conference*. Los Angeles: University of California, 1972.

Deasy, C. M. "When Architects Consult People." *Psychology Today* (March 1970): 54–57, 78–79.

Design Research Society. *Proceedings: Design Activity International Congress*. London: Design Research Society, 1973.

Evans, Benjamin H., and Wheeler, C. Herbert, Jr. *Emerging Techniques to Architectural Programming*. Washington, D.C.: The American Institute of Architects, 1969.

Gutman, Robert. "The Sociological Implications of Programming Practices." *Building Research* (April 1969): 26–27.

Horowitz, Harold. "The Programs The Thing." *American Institute of Architects Journal* (May 1967): 94–100.

Jones, J. Christopher, and Thornley, D. G., ed. *Conference on Design Methods: Papers presented at the Conference on Systematic and Intuitive Methods in Engineering, Industrial Design, Architecture and Communications.* London: Macmillan, 1962.

Newman, Oscar. *Design Guidelines for Creating Defensible Space.* National Institute of Law Enforcement and Criminal Justice, Law Enforcement Assistance Administration, Washington, D.C., 1976.

Pena, William, M., and Focke, John W. *Problem Seeking: New Directions in Architectural Programming.* Houston: Caudill, Rowlett, Scott, Architects, Planners, Engineers, 1969.

"Performance Design." *Progressive Architecture*, 48 (August 1967): 103–153.

Perin, C. *With Man in Mind: An Interdisciplinary Prospect for Environmental Design.* Cambride: MIT Press, 1970.

Research Center, College of Architecture and Environmental Design. *Environmental Criteria: MR Preschool Day Care Facilities.* College Station, Tex.: Texas A and M University, 1973.

Richardson, Stephen. "The Value of a Program to the Architect." *Building Research* (April 1969): 40–42.

Rittel, Horst. "Rittel Think." *DMG Newsletter* 5 (Jan 1971): 2–11.

Rittel, Horst. "Son of Rittel Think." *DMG 5th Anniversary Report.* Berkeley: University of California Press, **pp.** 5–12.

Rossetti, Louis. Building Programming." In *Comprehensive Architectural Service—General Principles and Practice,* edited by William Dudley Hunt, Jr. New York: McGraw-Hill, 1965.

Seaton, Richard. "Research for Building Programming." *Building Research* (April 1969): 36–39.

Sommer, Robert. *Personal Space: The Behavioral Basis of Design.* Englewood Cliffs, N. J.: Prentice-Hall, 1969.

Studer, R. G., and Stea, D. "Architectural Programming, Environmental Design and Human Behavior." *Journal of Social Issues* 22 (Oct. 1966): 127–36.

Walton, W. W., and Cadoff, B. C. "Performance of Buildings—Concept and Measurement," *Proceedings of the First Conference in a Series of "Man and His Shelter".* Washington, D.C.: Building Science Series, No. 1, U.S. Department of Commerce, 1968.

Ward, Anthony, and Broadbent, Geoffrey. *Design Methods in Architectural* Proceedings of the Portsmouth Symposium, 1967.

Wheeler, Lawrence, and Miller, Ewing H. "Human Factors Analysis." In *Comprehensive Architectural Service—General Principles and Practice*, edited by William Dudley Hunt, Jr. New York: McGraw-Hill, 1965.

White, Edward T. *Introduction to Architectural Programming.* Tucson, Ariz.: Architectural Media, 1972.

Index